Copyright, Creativity, Big Media and Cultural Value

As the publishing, film and music industries are dominated by Big Media conglomerates, there is often recourse to simplistic ideological and conspiratorial readings of industry dynamics. *Copyright, Creativity, Big Media and Cultural Value: Incorporating the Author* explains why copyright is much more than a creator's private property right or a mechanism through which corporations control cultural production and influence mass consumption choices.

The volume is grounded in extensive, painstakingly detailed and colourful original archival research into business histories of major successful artists including Conan Doyle, Hall Caine, Margaret Atwood, Dame Nellie Melba, Radiohead and Banksy, and the industries and genres that grew up around their activities. Chapters address big questions about how copyright generates income and how distributions of profits are allocated in the publishing, film and music industries. It includes discussion of the creation of new formats, the interplay between old media and new technologies, international copyright reform and cross-industry relations.

Copyright, Creativity, Big Media and Cultural Value is a wide-ranging and important resource for students and practitioners of law and policy, media studies, cultural studies and literary history.

Kathy Bowrey is Professor in the Faculty of Law, UNSW, Sydney. She is a legal historian and socio-legal researcher whose research explores laws and practices that inform knowledge creation and the production, distribution and reception of technology and culture.

Copyright, Creativity, Big Media and Cultural Value

Incorporating the Author

Kathy Bowrey

Routledge
Taylor & Francis Group
LONDON AND NEW YORK

First published 2021
by Routledge
2 Park Square, Milton Park, Abingdon, Oxon OX14 4RN

and by Routledge
605 Third Avenue, New York, NY 10017

First issued in paperback 2022

Routledge is an imprint of the Taylor & Francis Group, an informa business

British Library Cataloguing-in-Publication Data
A catalogue record for this book is available from the British Library

Library of Congress Cataloging-in-Publication Data
Names: Bowrey, Kathy, author.
Title: Copyright, creativity, big media & cultural value : incorporating the author / Kathy Bowrey.
Other titles: Copyright, creativity, big media, and cultural value
Description: Milton Park, Abingdon, Oxon ; New York, NY : Routledge Books, 2021. | Includes bibliographical references and index.
Identifiers: LCCN 2020025931 (print) | LCCN 2020025932 (ebook) | ISBN 9780367192068 (hardback) | ISBN 9780429201035 (ebook)
Subjects: LCSH: Copyright. | Authorship. | Creative ability.
Classification: LCC K1440 .B695 2021 (print) | LCC K1440 (ebook) | DDC 346.048/2—dc23
LC record available at https://lccn.loc.gov/2020025931
LC ebook record available at https://lccn.loc.gov/2020025932

ISBN: 978-0-367-63115-4 (pbk)
ISBN: 978-0-367-19206-8 (hbk)
ISBN: 978-0-429-20103-5 (ebk)

DOI: 10.4324/9780429201035

Typeset in Bembo
by Apex CoVantage, LLC

Contents

Illustrations

Tables

Acknowledgements

This book has been in progress for many years. I have a very big list of people to thank for their help and support, for reading many clumsy drafts and for their thoughtful conversations, friendship and comments. Thanks especially to Peter Jaszi, Lionel Bently, Jose Bellido, Sam Ricketson, Martha Woodmansee, Mark Aronson, Fiona Macmillan, Isabella Alexander, Jill McKeough, Brad Sherman, Alain Pottage, Tanya Aplin, Catherine Bond, Michael Handler, Brent Salter, Rebecca Giblin, Toni Lester, Henrique Carvalho, Hyo Yoon Kang, Nicole Graham, Nofar Sheffi and Marie Hadley. Analysis of the archival material greatly benefitted from advice and feedback from Australian film historians Graham Shirley, Andrew Pike and Tony Buckley; and encouragement from literary scholars Katherine Bode and Rachel Franks. Thanks especially to my partner Lloyd, who does not really share my enthusiasm for the subject matter but gives great feedback and supports my ambitions, regardless. Apologies to anyone I have momentarily forgotten.

This research was supported by Australian Research Council Discovery Grant DP140100172, Kathryn Bowrey and Catherine Bond, *Australian Made: A History of Australian Copyright Law and Creator Success 1868–1968*, the Law Faculty at the University of New South Wales, and the Herschel Smith Visiting Fellow program at the Centre for Intellectual Property and Information Law (CIPIL) Cambridge University. Thanks to Jennifer Kwong, Freya Mehta, Anna Holtby, Erin Butterworth and Andrew Robertson for research assistance, and to Colin Perrin at Routledge.

Chapter 2 draws upon unpublished research in *Don't Fence Me In. The Many Histories of Copyright* (SJD Thesis, University of Sydney, 1994). Part of Chapter 4 has previously been published as '"The Berne Convention Is Our Ideal" – Hall Caine, Canadian Copyright and the natural rights of authors after 1886' in (eds) G. Austin, A. Christie, A. Kenyon and M. Richardson, *Across Intellectual Property. Essays in Honour of Sam Ricketson* (CUP 2020).

The book draws upon resources held in numerous public, private and personal archives. I am particularly grateful to the National Library of Australia, Emile Sarlija, Albert Garriga and Max Lakeman for assistance and permission to reproduce illustrations. Many librarians and archivists assisted me along the way. Thanks especially to Wendy Thirkettle and Sarah Christian at Manx National Heritage, Jackie Bishop at EMI Trust Archive, and Random House for permission to access Chatto & Windus materials. Greater Union/Event Cinemas – I am still waiting.

Abbreviations

BL	British Library
BRO	Bristol Record Office
EMI	EMI Trust Archive
MNH	Manx National Heritage
NAA	National Archives of Australia
NFSA	National Film and Sound Archive (Australia)
NLA	National Library of Australia
NRO	Norwich Record Office
SLNSW	State Library of New South Wales
SLV	State Library of Victoria
SRO, Vic	State Record Office, Victoria
TNA	The National Archives (UK)
UoR	Archive of British Publishing and Printing, University of Reading
V&A Theatre & Performance Archive	Victoria and Albert Theatre & Performance Archive (Olympia)

1 What is the significance of authorship in copyright?

In popular imagination the author is the beating heart of copyright, but not the primary beneficiary of it. The corporation is far better placed to maximise profit. This disjunct encourages an enduring and wide-reaching interest in understanding how copyright interacts with creativity, free speech, national cultures and new technologies in an advanced global economy. As the publishing, film and music industries are dominated by Big Media conglomerates today, there is often recourse to simplistic ideological and conspiratorial readings of industry dynamics – corporate greed is presumed to rule decision-making, the creator is addressed as a noble but disempowered victim rather than an agent of their own destiny, and the public are characterised as chumps fed a homogenised diet dictated from London, New York and Hollywood. There are very few scholarly works that trace the incorporation of authorship into modern industry dynamics, directly addressing public concerns about cultural hegemony in light of the development of the actual business practices of the global book, music and film industries. This book embarks on that project, offering a history of the media industries in the 20th century, linking the relevance of that history to 21st-century grievances about copyright.

A primary objective is to trace how the "culture industries" came to be perceived as "copyright industries" connected through the idea of authorship. Original archival research shows how celebrity authors and artists worked alongside industrial actors to build the infrastructure for the global exploitation of copyright. Chapters explain why copyright came to be much more than a creator's private property right or a mechanism through which corporations control cultural production and influence mass consumption choices. Analysis includes discussion of the creation of new media formats, the interplay between old media and new technologies, international copyright reform and cross-industry relations. The aim is to critically examine the role of authorship and its connection to copyright in the emergence of concentrated corporate control and the consequences for national cultural industries and diverse creators.

Discussion centres upon a neglected period in intellectual property history – from the late Victorian era to the mid-20th century, the period in which the modern business and legal infrastructure supporting international trade was assembled and when many of the mass media forms of cultural consumption that came to dominate the 20th century were adopted. The methodology is interdisciplinary and socio-legal. There was significant law reform in this period, including the *Berne Convention for the Protection of Literary and Artistic Works (1886)*, a UK-US settlement over trans-Atlantic copyright piracy (1891), and reform to modernise British copyright legislation (1911), including responding to the emergence of film and sound recording. In discussing these developments, law and society are not approached as separate institutions or related domains that merely interact. The ambition is not to trace external dynamics – political, economic and cultural influences – on the expansion of intellectual property rights in the 20th century, plotting the role of key actors whose efforts are identified as influencing law reform. Rather, the book adopts a more nuanced historical materialist methodology. The most important foundational IP content is not considered to be the technically circumscribed, limited property rights that originate with legislative enactment. The foundational subject matter of intellectual property – the law's subjects and objects – are addressed in terms of their constitution through historicising material interactions in cultural, economic and political, as well as legal-technical contexts. Tracing the interplay of normative and practical considerations that characterise the relevant legal relations and marginalise other factors is a priority.

Authorship is evaluated as the key normative consideration, but chapters do not assume a timeless, ontological security to the persona of the author. Authorship is identified in terms of both ideational and contractual expressions. This allows the reader to better understand how philosophy and the lived experience of the law interact, where the normative dimensions of authorship are inflected with the relevant actors' ideas about their entitlement to profit from creative labour and innovation, as well as acknowledging abilities and difficulties faced in constructing commercial opportunities to facilitate profitable exploitation of perceived legal rights. The notion of authorship draws support from related ideas about the political importance of private property rights, freedom of contract, freedom of expression, and innovation economics (where state-sanctioned monopoly rights are required to reward inventors).

Chapters trace how a universal idea of authorship transcended the earlier 18th and 19th centuries' Romantic confinement of the status of author to creators of particular literary genres and artistic forms – poets and expressive artists. Mid-late 19th-century copyright spokespersons were very successful in advocating the importance of the author's property right to civilisation. The most effective advocates were often popular writers and the very idea of copyright came to be idealised with reference to the imagined experience of the novelist, often positioned as an acute observer of society possessing special diagnostic insights into social and political ills. As a consequence of successful cultural and political interventions, far more limited and technically inscribed literary and artistic property rights were generalised. A new British copyright law emerged in 1911, encompassing broader classes of creators and beneficiaries. What has been neglected in copyright histories to date is the connection between this development and related restructuring of business affairs. Authorship was, in practice, reinscribed with very different qualities through the intersection of cultural, political, legislative *and* business activity.

Through a closer consideration of the connection between the politics of copyright law reform *and* transactional aspects of rights exploitation in practice, the broader significance of the transformation in the idea of authorship comes to light. The continuing resonance of the appeal of a universal idea of authorship has helped mask critical consideration of what went on in practice. It has always been difficult to trace political and industry machinations surrounding copyright policy and contractual terms, and especially to identify the distribution of benefits that followed from reforms. Such details have not been well scrutinised because of the secrecy that generally protects private business communications and contracts. Political conventions and practices also obscure the activities of diplomats, trade negotiators and industry lobbyists. Though difficult to research because these activities are conducted in private and if documented at all, correspondence is often protected by confidentiality for decades, these are incredibly important, under-utilised sources of information about corporate power and influence that need to be better incorporated into copyright historiography. Where relevant, the significance of new primary sources is explored in conversation with existing histories by business, humanities and legal scholars about the industries, companies and individuals concerned. Relevant intellectual property actors considered include authors, industrialists, entrepreneurs, corporate managers, agents, consumers, advocacy bodies such as author and publisher societies and other political lobbies, public servants and politicians. More details are provided in chapter descriptions that follow.

In evaluating the business affairs of authors it is important to acknowledge that despite the image projected in advocacy that highlighted the benefits of copyright to all in the abstract, not all writers exploited copyright in the same manner or had access to the same social privileges, though standard forms of exploitation did emerge. The relevance of writers' different personalities, personal objectives, knowledge, experience, social networks and fortunes is taken into account through a comparative evaluation of copyright exploitation by authors working in the same sub-genre – crime fiction – at roughly the same time. Analysis is then extended across later chapters to consider how other actors were impacted by particular reforms. This allows for a closer consideration of how copyright affects the commercial opportunities of different categories of writers and markets, including in education, theatre, film and music, as well as performers.

Insights into shifts in the practical significance of authorship are drawn from more than analysis of folders of surviving contracts and business correspondence, preserved and made accessible in public and private archives. A business history of copyright also requires consideration of the origins of particular media formats and the dominant commodity forms through which the public find a connection with the personalities attributed as authors of the works. This means there is more attention to the emergence of genres, media formats, entertainment technologies, marketing and advertising than is usually found in legal writing about copyright history and authorship.

Accessing this material helps avoid a major problem that arises in teaching copyright law. In explaining the subsistence or origination of an author's right there is recourse to a circularity. Copyright is explained as originating with the fixing of an original expression in material form by an author. The material forms recognised in legislation generally correlate to those efforts that emanate from the subjectivity of a creator who is designated as author-like, regardless of the medium. In copyright parlance, the playwright, librettist or lyricist, composer and the artist are all referred to as "authors" and first owners of copyright in their creations. This book unpacks this circularity, showing how the concept of authorship was stretched to permit an expansion in copyright subject matter. This entails decentring the idea of a stable or fixed author subject and legal object (the copyright work) "protected" by copyright. This is necessary not only to better understand the history of copyright. It is essential to scrutinising the value of copyright in a realistic way.

In reality it is the protection of the commodity form that matters most to those who seek to profit from the copyright. However, the relationship between copyright and the commodity form is not a simple relationship. Chapters assess the way an understanding of commodification impacts the crafting of the original work, the value of the copyright over its lifetime to the author and others, and the politics behind extending protection to new material forms, facilitated by the reimagining of the scope of authorship. The transition from original work to commodity form, and the way commodity forms influence creative and financial objectives, involves looking at much more than author contracts, especially as commodity forms were not stable in this period. Technological developments as well as social changes created new and unforeseen opportunities and obstacles for authors in exploiting copyright. Company, corporate and industry decision-making impacted upon decision-making about production and distribution of cultural commodities. The company and corporate realms of decision-making need to be included and evaluated as part of the legal domain of copyright to help us move beyond reproducing stories about the value of abstract assertions of rights and consider how financial outcomes for different kinds of creators and societies are generated.

Recently, copyright histories have begun to address what was distinctive about the inclusion of new subject matter in copyright, in particular, drama, music and art.[1] This is important work that helps rebalance a historical preoccupation with book publishing as the exemplar of all copyright. This book shares a similar commitment to exposing the importance of understanding the industrial specificity of copyright. Media-specific subject matter is also often considered in business, humanities and mass communications histories, but this literature usually has a lighter touch when it comes to factoring in the role and impact of copyright law reform. However, there is a difference in scope to previous works because contracts and other business correspondence are investigated as sources of core legal information about the significance of rights.

Second, copyright is not constructed as a taxonomic creation, disconnected from the law's operation alongside patent, trademark, corporation, competition and taxation laws, and trade policy. These other categories of law significantly affect the exercise of market power and intersect with copyright decision-making. Third, the book also moves beyond a restricted focus on a singular (celebrity) author, company, industry or media format. There is an interest in drawing out awareness of the shared agendas between print, film and music industrialists when it comes to copyright advocacy, as well as in controlling the exploitation of rights, and management of talent. Discussion of copyright closely engages with histories of new technologies, changes in business structures and also the development of international business networks and associations to show the advance of mutual interests through law reform and changes to business practice. These factors have materially impacted on the terms of author and artist contracts and the management of legal rights and restrictions.

In the period concerned, copyright law became international. However, the history of authorship is confined to analysis of English language markets, highlighting the relevance of place to appreciation of cultural and business opportunities created by copyright. Cultural, national and legal identities intersect through copyright practice and where one resides, or travels to, also affects the ability to act and fulfil ambitions. But is not assumed that jurisdiction, a nationally bounded idea of positive rights conferred on individuals, has the high degree of relevance generally afforded to it in traditional intellectual property scholarship. The late 19th and early 20th century was a time of cultural and industrial mobility for authors and entrepreneurs. Understanding the operation of copyright law beyond one's home mattered. Markets were becoming international to a far greater degree than at any other time. While the book's focus is oriented toward explaining the rise of large British and American multinational companies and the importance of London, New York and Hollywood to cultural production, the impact of political, legal and business dynamics on former British colonies such as Australia and Canada, is also brought to light. International copyright was conceived of by Western empires as a mechanism to support and extend political influence, economic power and share ideas on the progress of civilisation with the rest of the world, regardless of nationality. How this agenda was received in different markets and impacted on creative industries in places other than metropolitan centres warrants inclusion in any critical history of modern copyright. This theme engages a critique of a common presumption implicit in copyright scholarship – that international copyright mainly facilitated one-way trade from centre to periphery because of deficits in the colonial imagination and the relative absence of civilisation in those places.

To shift the reader's horizons, while still appealing to an existing knowledge base and engaging developed intuitions about copyright and corporate control, chapters introduce key literature and then problematise what we think we know about copyright with reference to a discussion of key moments affecting the development of the global book publishing, film and music trade. Where possible, by primarily centring the creator's agency and the consequences of their legal and business decision-making, chapters bring to light the dynamic and complex layers of negotiation that affect the cultural economy to disrupt existing simplistic ideas about what copyright law is and how it works.

Chapter overview

To help readers more clearly appreciate the content of the volume, a description of the particular chapters, including identifying key actors and scholarly work that is drawn into discussion, follows.

Chapter 2, 'Revisiting author theory in the domain of law' situates my interest in authorship alongside postmodern critiques of the author-function, in particular copyright scholarship inspired by Michel Foucault and Roland Barthes in the 1980s and 1990s. This literature was highly influential in stimulating research into the history of literary property and copyright. Drawing upon the work of literary theorist and copyright historian Martha Woodmansee, I remind readers of some of the cultural specificity of the Romantic idea of authorship that is often glossed over in legal histories today. The most important aspect relevant to the broader ambition of the book is consideration of the historic tension between the value of a work of art and a commodity. The significance of this tension is explored with reference to the Renaissance poet John Milton (1608–1674) and the Romantic poets William Wordsworth (1770–1850) and Samuel Taylor Coleridge (1772–1834). Literary theory is connected to publishing history through a discussion of the cultural status of different genres of literature and the qualities of fame. This background is then used to contextualise the rise of the novel as the exemplar form of writing in the 1880s that warrants copyright protection, under conditions where there were concerns expressed by the Society of Authors about the economic and legal literacy of writers and about the standard forms of publishing agreement in circulation at this time.

Chapter 3, 'A tale of three literary copyrights' explains how value is generated over the life of a copyright. In discussing the crime stories of Hugh Conway, Fergus Hume and Sir Arthur Conan Doyle, there is an engagement with publishing histories by NN Feltes, Alexis Weedon, Graham Law and Peter McDonald. Their work is linked to the significance of changes in publishing formats and construction of readerships to decisions each of these authors made about copyright exploitation. This includes a discussion of the Victorian genre of "sensation literature". It is argued that the rise in availability and popularity of crime, mystery and detective stories was sponsored by changes to copyright commercialisation practice, where the full potential of modern copyright law could be exploited internationally.

Discussion of the commercial options and copyright assignments attached to two early blockbuster detective novels, Hugh Conway's *Called Back* (1884) Fergus Hume's *The Mystery of a Hansom Cab* (1886), shows that literary historians have been mistaken in assuming a premature assignment of copyright meant that neither author received further royalties for their blockbuster stories. The business records of Conway's publisher, Arrowsmith (Bristol), and Hume's publisher, Jarrold & Sons (Norwich), reveal a far more positive outcome for both of these authors than previously appreciated. Nonetheless, because of limitations in the way both these authors perceived their copyright and transacted with the publishing industry, they limited the possibility of a far greater financial return. This matter is made clear by a comparison with the commercial decision-making surrounding Arthur Conan Doyle's *Sherlock Holmes* (1888) which found success following these earlier works.

How copyright came to be exploited internationally, leading to the division of publishing markets into two spheres ruled from London and New York is the focus of Chapter 4, 'Imperial copyright and its costs'. Following the copyright settlement between Britain and the United States over American piracy of British works, leading to the passing of the *Chace Act* (1891), Canada threatened to withdraw from the Berne Convention. This exercise of political sovereignty was curtailed through a combination of cultural, legal and political campaigns. A very prominent personality involved in this activity was the "English Tolstoy", romance writer Sir Thomas Henry Hall Caine (1853–1931). The celebrity author embarked on a tour of Canada and America, advocating the idea of universal copyright and against Canadian copyright supremacy. His tour was made at the request of writer and founder of the Society of Authors, Walter Besant; Caine's American publisher, William Appleton; and Joseph Chamberlain, former President of the British Board of Trade and head of the Colonial Office. The intervention ultimately produced a reliance on British and American book imports across the British Empire, throttling independent publishing in British dominions with long-term and significant implications for their authors and reading publics.

The chapter draws extensively on Caine's personal papers held on the Isle of Man, including official communications, published and unpublished thoughts, correspondence with publishers, and journal and newspaper clippings on copyright. It shows why international copyright remains imperial by design, exploring the implications for the Australian publishing industry today. This entails a discussion of the educational market, which encompasses two sectors, resources for school students and academic and professional publishing, where prominent Australian novelists have carried on the tradition of actively engaging with copyright law reform on behalf of publishers, helping sustain ongoing imperial power asymmetries into the 21st century.

Analysis of how cultural markets are controlled from afar through copyright is extended in Chapter 5, 'Print capitalism meets Hollywood. The work of industrial authorship'. This involves exploring how the interests of authors, playwrights and publishers were disrupted by the emergence of film, connecting British laws that protected literary property and performance rights to the international exploitation of these rights in the Victorian era. Market disruption is evidenced by reference to an original rights analysis of Denis Gifford's catalogue of 2,774 silent film adaptations (1896–1915). Though law reform soon followed, the chapter explores a fundamental shift in the industrial significance of authorship, as individual and family firms gave way to multi-national enterprises, contractual terms become standardised and the negotiating power of any individual actor was substantially diminished. It was the new multinational companies and cross-industry alliances that were empowered while the natural rights of the author were de-natured, diluted, and copyright's ideologically celebrated characteristic property – primarily rewarding creative, as opposed to commercial, endeavour – was fundamentally disrupted.

The research of US film historian Janet Staiger is drawn upon to explain the rise of American film combines. Confidential business communications, contracts and in-camera evidence given to Australian Royal Commissions into the film industry in the 1920s and '30s fleshes out further detail. This includes revealing for the first time the real extent of local collusion with the Motion Picture Producers and Distributors Association of America over setting standard terms of trade. It was not necessary that Hollywood own or directly interfere in the running of domestic firms to control international silent and talkie film distribution and exhibition markets from an American base – a situation that radically disadvantaged independent and local productions.

Though, from an economic perspective, copyright appears to serve as a tool of cultural imperialism here, it was not copyright, nor the director, producer or studio's vision that exclusively determined Hollywood content for overseas audiences. In Australia, while Hollywood provided around 90% of silent films, over half of these were censored, and not only by the state. The largest Australian film distributor renamed, re-edited and reshot films to remove excessive references to American values and patriotism, anticipating that such content would not find a receptive audience. These re-edited films then travelled the globe. This chapter reminds us how and why cultural markets require a sensitive touch, where copyright is merely one of a number of complex factors that impact on the audience's cinematic experience.

Chapter 6, 'Why does a gramophone maker deserve a copyright? The role of celebrity, women and consumer markets in the recording industry' looks at the role of intellectual property in the rise of a "technology company", the British Gramophone Company (1897), which was linked to the large US firm, His Master's Voice (HMV) that became EMI (1931–2012). Based upon company records, it advances an original feminist reading of industry dynamics focussing on explaining the commercial strategy behind their efforts to obtain a celebrity endorsement from Nellie Melba (1861–1931), darling of the opera season at Covent Garden and the New York Metropolitan Theatre, and a role model for the modern woman. She represented a glamorous lifestyle, evoked establishment values, yet being colonial born, her success was attributable not only to her own talent, but also to the virtue of her personal endeavour reaping rewards. Based upon a reading of Cambridge historian Peter Martland's *Recording History. The British Record Industry 1888–1931*[2] and a study of gramophone patent and trademark registrations in the UK, it is argued that it was more the management of cultural agendas and the ideology of intellectual property rights that propelled the firm to success than the strategic management of any portfolio of legal rights.

In advancing a feminist reading of the industry, the chapter exposes the invasions of privacy and other abuses involved in the effort to recruit Melba, and what she personally got out of this arrangement. It shows how this relationship with Melba and the celebrity of other recording artists was leveraged against music publishers to establish a novel kind of copyright for recording companies – an exclusive right to their sound recordings. The chapter concludes that the fixation on the deal as the heart of the music business – the contractual negotiations and the protection of defined intellectual property rights attached – comes from a gendered understanding of law and business. It allows the role of law to be scrutinised in an insular and self-protective context. This problem is discussed in terms of its relevance to recent studies of the lack of gender diversity in popular music. It is argued that addressing institutional discrimination is not about changing attitudes alone, but more critically considering the history of the legal objects and subjects that are produced in the music industry.

The concluding chapter, 'Why Margaret Atwood, Radiohead and Banksy are not anti-copyright' explores responses to the corporatisation of creativity by three extremely well-known creators and cultural commentators. It links their distinctive personal critiques of commodification and concerns about conventional copyright practice, and platform capitalism, to many of the historical developments explored in this book. These three creators work in different mediums and draw upon very diverse experiences as professional authors and artists; however, they all raise the question whether it is possible to resist commodification and retain a space for art. In addressing the similarities and dissonances between their positions the discussion explores how and why the traditional idea of copyright continues to resonate, but it is also being transformed as contemporary artists, lawyers and entrepreneurs exercise more direct control over business and legal relations.

Change in the significance of copyright and better outcomes for creators can come about when the value of authorship is reconsidered in light of a deeper understanding of how law functions in the cultural marketplace. It is hoped that this volume will support this endeavour by drawing upon a more critical understanding of copyright's history in the 20th century and, in helping shift how relationships between art, law and society are perceived, deliver more control over creative lives than was evident in the previous century.

Notes

1 Isabella Alexander, *Copyright Law and the Public Interest in the Nineteenth Century* (Hart Publishing 2010); Derek Miller, *Copyright and the Value of Performance 1770–1911* (CUP 2018); Elena Cooper, *Art and Modern Copyright: The Contested Image* (CUP, 2018)

2 Peter Martland, *Recording History: The British Record Industry 1888–1931* (Scarecrow Press, 2013)

2 Revisiting author theory in the domain of law

Over 50 years ago Michel Foucault observed that "the coming into being of the notion of the author constitutes the privileged moment of individualization in the history of ideas, knowledge, literature, philosophy, and the sciences".[1] While Foucault, Barthes and other postmodern literary scholars have had a considerable impact upon copyright historiography, the conventional approach has been to highlight the influence of the idea of the "author as owner" in civil society, Parliament and case law reasoning. Legal writers puzzle over the significance of the first literary property law, the *Statute of Anne* 1709,[2] and its subsequent interpretation in *Millar v Taylor* (1768) and *Donaldson v Beckett* (1774).[3] There are quibbles about the extent of the legal embodiment of the idea of authorial property compared with public good arguments, with all sides ultimately highlighting a lack of clarity in settling the philosophical foundations and jurisprudential limits to the author's right.[4] Much of this conventional legal historiography alienates creative writers. It can appear insensitive to concerns about the fragility of economic life within the literary profession and a rebuttal of authorial self-identification as the rightful, natural owner of property in literary creations. There is a need to begin bridge-building between copyright historiography and author-centric perspectives of copyright. This requires an historical recontextualisation of author theory, addressing its socio-legal and economic implications.

The chapter begins with a brief discussion of some of the philosophical foundations of authorial property claims that have come to influence perceptions of the economic reward due to writers. This includes highlighting the origin of persistent cultural discriminations that elevate some kinds of writers and creators over others. I start with a brief discussion of the distinction in status between the writer, the artist and the poet in the Renaissance, to help identify the distinctive properties of the Romantic poet and artist. I then explain the novelist's ambivalent cultural status in the 19th century due to the intrusion of more developed commodity relations affecting evaluation of these literary efforts. In line with the analysis of Martha Woodmansee's seminal work, *The Author, Art, and the Market*,[5] I explore how the tension between art and commodity came to be negotiated within the idea of copyright. The notion of copyright comes to encapsulate an imagined dichotomy that distinguishes aesthetic from commercial value incorporated within the very idea of the right. The artist as an expressive individual is imagined as owning an aesthetic property that inhabits a different realm to the author as a man (or woman) of business who negotiates with the publisher over the right to mass produce copies of the "original". This distinction between copyright's aesthetic and economic properties also encapsulates a public/private distinction. Aesthetic merit is often assumed to be a matter that should be evaluated in public. However, the economic details of authorial property are largely negotiated in private, defined by the terms of author contracts that, in an age of liberalism and freedom of contract, are appreciably under-studied. The Romantic, liberal construction of what copyright entails was capitalised upon by celebrity authors and their publishers in the late 19th and early 20th century. It led to the incorporation of the author into an infrastructure for the global exploitation of creative works, where the creator had little power to negotiate terms. The industry mechanisms, political strategies and legal reforms that facilitated this occurrence form the basis of the analysis in subsequent chapters of this book.

The printing press as an agent of change?[6]

Many copyright histories imply a natural association between the origin of a reproductive right and the press. Copyright is treated as a form of literary property that developed from the regulation of the press, leading most legal historians to quickly turn to a discussion of the significance of the *Statute of Anne* 1709.[7] However, it is difficult to generalise about the economic significance of writing in the Renaissance and Enlightenment periods. An enormous range of literature was published during the Renaissance. Apart from a wide variety of religious literature, there were books aimed at the "professions" such as law and medicine, calendars and almanacs with information about the weather, gardening, farming, veterinary and other useful information, astrological predictions, poetry, romance novels, prose, plays, ballads, folk tales, news broadsides, caricatures and political pamphlets. Such material was produced under varying circumstances, with all sorts of motivations. This makes it difficult to make generalisations about the writer, publisher and reader, and in particular about what respective parties' "rights" to a text may have been. There is a further complication – as licensing and censorship operated across the centuries, there were strong motivations for all those involved in the production and consumption of printed material to keep the nature of their involvement with some of this literature hidden. We know most about writings in the periods where such regulation was comparatively lax. However, there has been far more interest in analysing the property claims attached to works of genius, than to "hack" and "scribal" works. This high/low distinction itself requires further explanation.

In the Renaissance, works of genius were visionary works. A vision was produced by a solitary human creator (even though God or Nature may have so inspired him or possessed her). Technical mastery of the craft was also essential so that the genius could execute his or her work in a way that it inspired others.

But technical proficiency alone would not give rise to any lasting ownership in a work, deserving an attribution of it as his or her progeny. By point of comparison, all the artisan had was a technical competency, a practical rather than intellectual skill and for this reason the artisan had no enduring relationship with what he or she produced.[8]

The lowly status attributed to one who partakes of the "mechanical arts" derived in part from the classical belief that a man's experience and moral virtue was limited by the nature of the task – to produce as directed by one's employer and in accordance with tradition,

> A man who follows such a trade . . . will be following one determinate occupation, and will discover an interest in promoting the interests of that occupation, and his own success in it; and his concern with what is good for himself, or for one interest group, will prevent him from arriving at an understanding of what is good for man in general, for the public interest, for human nature. Second, the experience that falls in the way of such a man will be too narrow to serve as the basis of ideas general enough to be represented as true for all mankind, or for the interests, even of his own country. Third, because mechanical arts are concerned with *things*, with material objects, they do not offer the opportunity for exercising a generalising rationality: the successful practice of the mechanical arts requires the material objects be regarded as concrete particulars, and not in terms of abstract and formal relations among them.[9]

In the medieval and Renaissance period it was thought that the artisan had a "practical intellect". The artisan's lodge or guild contributed to a culture of anonymity. The guild was a powerful organisation when Church and town corporations were practically the only purchasers of works of art. These co-operative organisations facilitated the engagement of free labour for large projects. Large projects required a variety of labourers, many of whom would come from out of the town. These workers had to be able to work together efficiently and be able to withstand interruptions and changes in tempo as work timetables fluctuated according to the funds available. What the guild did was provide the worker with a level of security in this environment, by developing precise rules regarding the taking on, payment and training of workers; the hierarchy within the workplace; and special restrictions on the intellectual property rights of members in their own work. Hauser argues that the aim of this was to ensure the "unconditional subordination of the individual to the artistic requirements of the common task".[10]

Poetry however, was never considered a mechanical art, and it permitted personal recognition,

> The mechanical arts have bequeathed to us the names of only the most famous architects, but every poem has a definite author, who is aware of his own originality in style and thought. . . . From the eleventh century

> onwards, poets were quite aware that their work was a means of immortality . . . the new generation of poets were always court poets, immersed in the life of the Aristocracy and honoured in the households where they lived. The poet did not work for God, nor for a community; he did not work at projects which would be completed by others after him; he did not try for the approval of the erudite. What he wanted was the glory of quick success and personal fame.[11]

In the Renaissance, the poet achieved a status quite different from the artisan who, even if aware of his importance, was encouraged to cultivate attitudes of humility and a desire for anonymity.

We have ended up with far more detailed consideration of the labour of the poets than, for example, that of the broadsheet writer, because poetry has long been considered a superior art. It transcends daily political turmoil and, "above" history itself, is therefore ironically worth preserving for posterity. The poet has also been considered an "intellectual" subject worthy of the attention of educated gentlemen, in a way that the writer of popular fiction or journalism has not.

A further reason we know of particular poets is because they were later claimed as the forebears to the Romantics. In the 19th-century copyright debates, they were held up as examples of the exploited, who suffered at the hands of avaricious booksellers. This has also enhanced perception of their historical significance. There is also the matter that we know of the famous poets because, at least occasionally, they took recourse to formal legal mechanisms in order to protect their "rights". Poets, such as John Milton and Alexander Pope, asserted a property right in their creations.

The property of the poets – John Milton (1608–1674)

Some accounts of Milton's property interest in his works hold him up as an example of the Renaissance scribe to whom copyright was not available. For example, Saunders suggests,

> The positive right – the right to publish copies – . . . was simply not available as a right that the author could hold or contract to accord to another. Milton's 1667 conveyance of Paradise Lost to the stationer Samuel Simmons is usually cited as an instance of the conveyancing procedure:
>
> "And the said John Milton . . . doth covenant with the said Samll. Symons . . . that hee shall at all tymes hereafter have, hold, and enjoy the same [All that Booke, Copy or Manuscript of a Poem intituled Paradise lost], and all Impressions thereof accordingly, without lett or hinderance of him. . . . And that the said John Milton, . . . shall not print or cause to be printed, or sell, dispose, or publish, the said Booke or Manuscript, or any other Booke or Manuscript of the same tenor, or subject, without the consent of the said Samll. Symons."

> The capacity to enter into a negative covenant of this sort is not the stuff of which the Romantic notion of the author is made.[12]

However, as has been pointed out,[13] this interpretation of the agreement is misleading. Whilst Milton "lost" his interest in the poem to the stationer by the conveyance, the conveyance was not for scribal labour alone. The terms of the conveyance clearly show Milton is significant as an author because, unlike many of his contemporaries, he assigned interests in *editions*.[14] He understood the value of his creation as an intangible property related to the worth of his particular composition or expression.

To suggest that Milton's copyright precedes from a "negative covenant" misconstrues the nature and properties of legally enforceable agreements at this time. A positive public authority was not required to create private property-like rights. The fact that Milton bothered to formalise his assignment, and the publisher accepted these terms, suggests that citizens did feel competent to arrange their own legal affairs and adapt existing legal procedures as suited. There had been little attempt to systematise English law at this time and it was not conceived of as an orderly body of rules. Different jurisdictions, rules and procedures could be utilised to achieve various results, hence the practice of law was in a sense "creative", even though "adapting" procedures to fit the occasion was not necessarily understood as actively shaping the future direction of the law.[15] Tomás Gómez-Arostegui's painstaking research into copyright enforcement from 1557 to 1800 has revealed a significant volume of litigation in different tribunals enforcing different kinds of property rights: printing patents; the copyright obtained by guild registration at the Stationer's Company of London before[16] and after the *Statute of Anne*; and to a lesser degree, enforcement of "common-law" copyright and natural law claims to own literary property. Sadly, there is no comprehensive record of what was argued by parties in court.[17]

The property of the Romantic author

Woodmansee notes that well into the 18th century there was an unstable notion of authorship,

> He was first and foremost a craftsman; that is, he was a master of a body of rules and techniques, preserved and handed down in rhetoric and poetics. . . . However there were those rare moments in literature to which this concept did not seem to do justice. . . . To explain such moments a new concept was introduced: the writer was said to be inspired, by some muse, or even by God.[18]

The Romantic poets were attracted to the Renaissance poets, claiming Milton in particular as a worthy forebear. Milton was especially well known, his triple function as politician, scholar and poet having led to innumerable works about him, both commentaries and biographies. Further, his writing style, so full of personal utterances, lent itself to biographical interpretation.[19] Wordsworth had no doubts about Milton's authority and public importance, as one of his sonnets indicated,

> Milton! thou shouldst be living at this hour:
> England hath need of thee: she is a fen
> Of stagnant waters: altar, sword and pen,
> Fireside, the heroic wealth of hall and bower,
> Have forfeited their ancient English dower
> Of inward happiness. We are selfish men;
> Oh! raise us up, return to us again;
> And give us manners, virtue, freedom, power.
> Thy soul was like a Star, and dwelt apart;
> Thou hadst a voice whose sound was like the sea:
> Pure as the naked heavens, majestic, free,
> So didst thou travel on life's common way,
> In cheerful godliness; and yet thy heart
> The lowliest duties on herself did lay.[20]

But what qualities was it that the Romantics recognised in the Renaissance writers?

It is clear that the Romantics admired the "moral leadership" of the Renaissance poets, however the Romantics transformed the significance of this role. Coleridge admired Milton, "himself is in every line of *Paradise Lost*".[21] But whilst Milton might have agreed that he was present in the work, he would have distanced himself from any excessive identification of the work with his personal life; for example, Coleridge's explanation of his description of the Garden of Eden with reference to Milton's personal sympathies and wants aroused by an "apparently unhappy choice in marriage".[22] The Romantics transformed the nature and function of poetry into something intensely more private and personal than before. Whilst works were still seen to address the general condition of humanity, they were more often discussed as reflections of the individual and his or her concerns and nature. In the 19th century, it was the novel rather than the poem that served a diagnostic, public, moral function.[23]

The Romantics returned to the organic as the model of artistic production, a model that had been abandoned for the machine view of progress in the early Renaissance,

> By the end of the eighteenth century, under the influence of, most notably Rousseau, the metaphor of organic growth had replaced more mechanical, rational images of the processes governing art: ignorant of, or indifferent to, rules and reasons, the artist creates by blind necessity, like Nature itself. Such a view was given added intellectual authority by Kant; against

> the then prevailing Enlightenment view (derived from Locke) that true knowledge is only gained empirically, via the senses, Kant asserted that knowledge is essentially innate – arising from within the individual, rather than derived from without; for Kant, *Genius* is the name given to the "innate, productive capacity", a gift of nature, which produces art "from within". In a well known statement of 1800, Wordsworth writes: "all good poetry is the spontaneous overflow of powerful feelings".[24]

The Romantics adopted a distinction between organic and mechanical production,

> An Original may be said to be of a *vegetable* nature; it rises spontaneously from the vital root of genius; it *grows*, it is not *made*; imitations are often a sort of *manufacture*, wrought up by those *mechanics, art* and *labour*, out of pre-existent materials not their own. . . .
>
> . . . Modern writers have a *choice* to make . . . they may soar in the regions of *liberty*, or move in the soft fetters of easy *imitation.*[25]

Even though Pope himself had also ascribed to the idea of Nature as the inspirational force that guided his work, the Romantics distanced themselves from his example. Pope's preoccupation with bringing forth well-worn themes marked him as an imitator, rather than as a truly inspired genius. However, Romantic poetry was not just the spontaneous outpouring of feeling. Rather feeling was to be recreated imaginatively, reflected upon and qualified by the constraints and pleasure of poetic form,

> While the poet's feelings animate the poetic utterance, "the music of harmonious metrical language" helps create a distinctively poetic feeling of delight that tempers the powerful emotions associated with expressions of the deeper passions. Wordsworth thus says that the end of poetry is "to produce excitement in co-existence with an overbalance of pleasure".[26]

The poem was not designed to meet with conventional tastes – it was to be judged by its sincerity in reflecting "the actual state of mind of the poet while composing".[27]

This placed the Romantic poet in conflict with the traditional expectations that marked literary production under a system of patronage. By the 19th century, patronage as a source of income was on the decline. However, it was still significant enough for William Blake to complain,

> The Enquiry in England is not whether a Man has Talents & Genius, But whether he is Passive & Polite & a Virtuous Ass & obedient to Noblemen's Opinions in Art & Science. If he is, he is a Good Man. If not, he must be Starved.[28]

The marketplace was not seen as much of an "alternative". To the extent that the Romantic poet created a truly original work, the work would have limited prospect for immediate market success. This is reflected in Coleridge's lament that,

> the most prudent mode is to sell the copy-right, at least of one or more editions, for the most that the trade will offer. By few only can a large remuneration be expected; but fifty pounds and ease of mind are of more real advantage to a literary man than the chance of five hundred with the certainty of insult and degrading anxieties.[29]

A similar sentiment is captured in Wordsworth's complaint,

> Away then with the senseless iteration of the word *popular* applied to new works in poetry, as if there were no test of excellence in this first of the fine arts but that all men should run after its productions, as if urged by an appetite, or constrained by a spell.[30]

Another writer of the time complained,

> It has of late become so much the fashion . . . to view every thing through commercial medium, and calculate the claims of utility by the scale of *The Wealth of Nations*, that it is to be feared, the Muses and Graces will shortly be put down as unproductive labourers, and the price current of the day considered as the only criterion of merit.[31]

The Romantic author shared the Renaissance ideal of an "Art" that united by transcending daily mundanity, whimsy and antagonisms. However, he or she was also moved by fear of the social fragmentation and alienation inherent in the adoption of a rational, atomistic perspective of the world. Accordingly, artistic vision was explained as a form of "natural" opposition to the "mechanical" world. And unlike the Renaissance genius who created alone but was trained and inspired by city life, he or she identified with country, and produced "innately". The appeal of the Romantic position was that in locating the work in the natural self, meaning could be kept safe from "worldly" contamination.

By the late 18th century the classical association of art with history and tradition had lost its appeal. In the first place "authentic art" had come to include "traditions" and "virtues" that in previous times would have been considered irrelevant to public life and the ethical ideals of the aristocracy. The soft and hitherto private virtues of amiability, kindness and compassion were elevated to the dignity of public virtues. In 1786 one writer observed that "by far the greater share of glory attends upon what are called great actions" – which are in fact "glorious to the individual alone".[32] Second, and particularly in association with historical painting, images of the present had come to be presented *in terms of* the classical past,

> This relationship was expressed not only superficially, in details of costume and physiognomy, but also structurally, through a radical condensation of narrative into a single, emblematic instant – significantly, Barthes calls it a hieroglyph – in which the past, present, and future, that is, the *historical* meaning, of the depicted action might be read.[33]

Events were being lifted out of time and place,

> Thus to Robespierre ancient Rome was a past charged with the time of the now which he blasted out of the continuum of history. The French Revolution viewed itself as Rome reincarnate. It evoked ancient Rome the way fashion evokes costumes of the past. Fashion has a flair for the topical, no matter where it stirs in the thickets of long ago; it is tiger's leap into the past.[34]

The Romantics broke with the notion of a cultural unity represented by an appeal to tradition and popular iconography.

As a "public" reading of the work was to be distrusted, the virtue of art came to rest in its ideological purity, or as Coleridge put it, in its symbolic rather than its allegorical meaning. Coleridge suggested that,

> The Symbolical cannot, perhaps be better defined in distinction from the Allegorical, than that it is always itself a part of that, of the whole of which it is the representative.[35]
>
> . . . the latter (allegory) cannot be other than spoken consciously; whereas in the former (symbolism) it is very possible that the general truth represented may be working unconsciously in the writer's own mind during the construction of the symbol.[36]

The shift to symbolic meaning entailed the interpretation of the work in isolation from society and the fragmentation of meaning therein. The art work no longer had to be decoded.[37] The art work embodied a pure essence. It embodied,

> the ideal of a formally unified, centred, *concentrated* composition whose meaning could be communicated at a glance.[38]

In Coleridge's terms a "public" reading of a work was actually redundant. If "the symbol is precisely that part of the whole to which it may be reduced. . . (t)he symbol does not represent essence, it *is* essence".[39] A "public" reading that seeks to find instances of a universal truth in a particular work is not required.

The judgement would be nonsensical. In grasping the particular, the universal is implicitly understood along with it.[40] Further if the symbolic is constructed intuitively, "rational" deliberation would simply risk the truth of the work. As Frederic Jameson notes,

> Modernism's formulation of the problem of representation. . . [was] borrowed from a religious terminology which defines representation as "figuration", a dialectic of letter and the spirit, a "picture language" (Vorstellung) that embodies, expresses and transmits otherwise inexpressible truths.[41]

The rejection of allegory involved the advocacy of a mode of representation derived from within its own pure space, and a mode of understanding radically distinct from verbalisation.[42] The attraction of the "self as origin" of the meaning of art made sense because it housed the potential for continual acts of regeneration,

> The self as origin is safe from contamination by tradition because it possesses a kind of original naiveté.[43]

However, although Romanticism suggested a creative personality in isolation from society, the reality was that it proposed a hierarchy within society: one group, that Modernism later branded as the "avant garde", of artists and their critics, and the other, the mass of producers and consumers. The avant garde continued the tradition of constituting a public space for "art". They presented a "superior consciousness" that "ke(pt) culture *moving* in the midst of ideological confusion and violence" through the pursuit of original, authentic or non-derivative works.[44] And this community existed in contradistinction to the mass who spent their leisure time in consumption. Mass market products were seen to have a parasitic relationship with "genuine culture" – feeding off and appropriating it, transforming the "original work" into "kitsch".[45]

This rationale is reflected in Wordsworth's need to create "tastes",

> "if there be one conclusion" that is "forcibly pressed upon us" by their disappointing reception, it is "that every Author, as far as he is great and at the same time *original*, has had the task of *creating* the taste by which he is to be enjoyed".[46]

It is also apparent in his appeal to a distinction between the "public" and the "people",

> Towards the Public, the Writer hopes that he feels as much deference as it is entitled to; but to the People, philosophically characterized, and to the embodied spirit of their knowledge . . . his devout respect, his reverence is due.[47]

The distinction here relates to a distinction between society as a collective of disparate individuals, and society as a collective in the true sense, as people sharing a common humanity. To the Romantics, genius incorporated not only authorial self-validation, but a wider affirmation of shared human values,

> a conclusion about personal feeling became a conclusion about society and an observation of natural beauty carried a necessary moral reference to the whole and unified life of man.[48]

Though poetry generally focussed on the subjective experience of the individual, this did not mean that the individual was naturally isolated from others. The Romantic poet appealed to an essential harmony between man and nature, individual and society, a harmony that had been sabotaged by industrialisation.

The Victorian novelist in a commodity market

Renaissance and Romantic sculptors, painters and poets all successfully advocated for an enhancement of their standing in society. A consequence of their efforts was the lodging in the collective psyche, pride in, and respect for, a class of workers who hitherto had been considered as craftsmen. But it is problematic to include Victorian fiction writers or novelists as an entire class alongside this elite group. Literary studies scholar Richard Altick notes that, "religious magazines echoed with denunciations of the novel, which was believed to stimulate the imagination to a false perception of reality".[49]

The more popularist genres, including realist, historical and sensation novels, engaged major debates about literary value and their effects on readers,

> Rhetoric about how novels corrupt readers' morals and corrode their cognitive capacities – especially when the vulnerable reader referred to is a young woman – intensified as the novel famously rose to power as a literary genre in the 18th century. By the latter 19th century, essays debating (and, more often than not, debasing) the value of reading fiction had become a staple of the periodicals in which much of the period's fiction was first published.[50]

Production factors affected some assessments,

> The saga of the three-volume novel and the circulating libraries is a case in point. From the middle of the 19th century, the Victorian reader's association of the high-priced three volume novel with circulating library control of the market for fiction, and her knowledge of the fact that to be successful, novelists had to produce work of a suitable length for circulation in that form, meant that the format itself was read by many as a concession to the economic over the literary; the 'three-decker' had become a cultural symbol of mechanistic causality and commodified fiction.[51]

Cyclical forms of reading, such as subscription libraries and serialisation that made works very widely accessible to middle- and working-class readers, was similarly criticised.

The novel's rising cultural presence was marked by shifts in understanding relations between author and reader. Barbara Hochman writes,

> After Romanticism . . . the act of writing for the public was imagined with decreasing anonymity and increasing relish. On the face of it, the rhetoric of self-disclosure and the image of reader as personal friend became less loaded, more acceptable.[52]

She notes that magazines and periodicals increasingly included articles about the lives of authors that purported to disclose the face behind the "writer's mask" and the "inside story". By the late 19th century the personality of the author came to be recognised as a potential marketing asset, a position not all authors were comfortable with. Josephine Guy notes that Oscar Wilde complained that the advertising of *The Ballad of Reading Gaol* made him feel like "Lipton's tea".[53] "Actual" and commercially motivated biographies and personas capitalised upon a Romantic emphasis on the expressive authenticity of the author. Many authors cultivated their public profiles, while complaining about the commodification of their identity.

Fiction writers, alongside poets and artists, lobbied Parliament to reform literary property law in the 19th century and achieved some success.[54] Advocacy drew upon the history of aesthetics, focussing on a particular claim – that the author possessed a natural right to their original expressions. Yet the growing commercial culture that made writing more attractive as a profession also generated tensions amongst authors,

> as literary agents, editors, and other middlemen made the route from manuscript to publication ever more cumbersome, the idea of a book as a ground of felt contact between writer and reader was progressively destabilized.[55]

While the author's name might signify ownership of the text, the author's imagined location in the text became harder to identify.

In discussing the origins of the Society of Authors (1884), historian and novelist Walter Besant wrote,

> During the last few years, there has been a constant stream of abuse, detraction, and wilful misrepresentation of our work poured upon us continually. Chiefly we have been reviled for daring to ask what our own property means. . . .
>
> For the moment any author begins to make practical investigation into the value – the monetary value – of the work which he puts upon the market – a hundred voices which cry out upon the sordidness, the meanness, the

> degradation of turning literature into a trade. We hear, I say, this kind of talk from our own ranks.[56]

Advocacy drew upon an 18th-century German philosophical distinction between two kinds of property to try to distance concern about trade considerations debasing intellectual achievement.[57] Besant told potential recruits to the society,

> There are two values of literary work – distinct, separate; not commensurable – they cannot be measured – they cannot be considered together. The one is the literary value of a work – its artistic, poetic, dramatic value; its value of accuracy, of construction, of presentation, of novelty, of style, of magnetism. . . .
>
> But once finished and ready for production, then comes in the other value – the commercial value – which is a distinct thing. Here the artist ceases and the man of business begins.[58]

Copyright was justified in the name of the former – the need to protect a unique, original expression. Author advocacy deflected questions about how the property right serves commodity production by prioritising valorisation of the persona of the author as artist and the sanctity of the authorial creation.[59] These special, cultural works could be distinguished from ordinary commodities and "domestic" works lacking an assertion of ingenious activity. That the author's work can be multiplied and sold without endangering its claim to be an original work of art became one of the paradoxes of the legal formulation.

The author as businessman

In his 1950s sociological survey of authorship between 1800–1935, Altick explored the social origins and gender of 1,100 British and Irish writers listed in the *Cambridge Bibliography of English Literature*. Class was indicated by considering the occupation of the father. Across the entire time span, 10.6% of authors were born into the nobility and gentry; 86.3% into the middle class; 3.1% into the working class. The proportion of women writers to men remained fairly constant, ranging from 16–22%.[60] Altick drily notes, "The woman's place in the home was not at the writing desk". The middle class was significantly over-represented, constituting only 25% of the total population, yet half of all writers listed were the children of physicians, teachers, lawyers, government officials and, especially, persons associated with the arts, formerly artisan classes.[61] However, the commercial portion of the middle class was poorly represented.

In a period where upward mobility was a matter of intense discussion, a gentleman may aspire to be both an artist and a man of business. However, retiring from active commercial life remained the most reliable indicator that one had joined the upper class. It was inappropriate for a gentleman to "talk shop" in public, although the private gentleman's club, that "distinctly male space existing somewhere between the public and private spheres", could prove useful in cementing social standing and enhancing business connections.[62] Of course, there were also other venues that were useful meeting places for particular artisan trades and occupations. Nonetheless, given the commonality in social standing amongst authors and their writing peers indicated by Altick's demographics, there is a serious question about the depth of business knowledge and skill set of "self-educated" writers who sought to conduct their own affairs in an increasingly complex publishing landscape.

The Society of Authors identified a number of practical impediments that frustrated negotiation of a fair return. Where the author had sufficient capital upfront and leisure time to manage publication decisions, this was considered a method by which the author could gain a fair return, as the author would normally retain the copyright.[63] Through this means the author could also seek to influence the presentation of the commodity and the distribution – choosing the paper, binding, inclusion of colour and so on, and determine whether, when and with whom cheaper reprints should be printed.[64] Nonetheless, these contracts were criticised because the author had no means to verify the costs, sales or return figures reported. It was dependent upon maintaining good personal relations with the publisher, at a time when the ambitions and pressures facing the family firm and new classes of middlemen, including literary agents, were transforming the conception and scope of the publishing enterprise.[65]

Publishing on commission, where an author paid the whole expense of printing a work, was estimated as the most common method of publishing in Britain for approximately three-quarters of modern fiction until 1890 and described as "the only method for publishing philosophical, scientific, and technical works; it is nearly always the only method of publishing poetry".[66] Marketing costs, including the cost of review copies, would be deducted from author royalties. That the author should bear the main financial risk of publication was seen by some as appropriate given the uncertainty that came with estimating in advance of publication the degree of public appetite for the title.

An ambition of the Society of Authors was to educate authors about equitable contractual terms, alerting members to the going rates for different kinds of exploitation that, with foresight, might be achieved in publishing agreements. Suggested value hierarchies reflected cultural discriminations about the significance of particular literary markets in the late 19th century. Higher royalties could be secured for a London or New York publication with value diminishing for secondary rights in England; secondary rights in America; and rights in the colonies and dependencies of Great Britain. The recommendation was that authors and publishers receive a 50/50 split in all cases, which was rarely achievable in practice.[67] The Society also promoted authors' syndicates, where experts could offer a fair opinion on the market prospects for a work. The early editions of the Society of Authors' publication, *The Author*, contained full-page advertisements of these new services with the 'The Authors' Syndicate' operating out of the Society offices.[68]

A degree of shopping one's work around was entirely normal but very commonly led to a disappointing return. As will be seen in the following chapter, a writer might aspire to attract a reputable and experienced publisher, but without personal contacts and recommendations by literary elites it could be a struggle just to have one's manuscript read. Rejection was a common experience. Whether or not judged prudent by the author, selling the entire copyright outright was often demanded, the alternative being remaining unpublished. The ability of publishers to accumulate en masse copyrights relatively free of idiosyncratic authorial decisions influencing production schedules and the presentation of commodities, was a precursor to industrial standardisation of terms.

Once a bad bargain had been struck, if a "reputable publisher" was involved, it may have been possible to appeal to honour and a sense of justice shared by gentlemen of character and have it set aside. Whether "character" was most corroded by individualism or socialism was a topic of political debate, but all gentlemen would feel the sting of an accusation that they were of bad character.[69] However, it was hard to dispute a signed contact in court. By the late Victorian period, contract law itself had become more abstract and formalistic to better suit perceived needs of commerce: "entrepreneurs demanded above all else . . . advance and certain notice of the legal climate in which they hazard their capital".[70] There was a diminishing scope for moral and economic arguments to influence judicial enforcement of contracts. In any case, one would need an established legal principle, such as actual proof of fraud, for the courts to set an agreement aside – not simply evidence that a bad bargain had been made. Lay appeals to unconscionability and unreasonableness were not sufficient legal grounds to interfere with freedom of contract.[71]

The economic literacy of authors and lawyers

There are a number of intersecting factors that stifled development of a sophisticated understanding of copyright's economic function into the 20th century. Philosophically, the public benefit in respecting authorial property was advocated. Quality literature could instruct and delight the public, create a shared sense of belonging in an often harsh commercial world and help intellectualise class struggle. But it was, at best, questionable to descend to exposing the particulars of ones' business affairs to debate in public discussion. Further, the Society of Authors sought to work in harmony with established, reputable publishers, not alienate them. Their educational mandate appealed to the intellect of liberal individuals, especially those who sought the rewards of a comfortable life and upward mobility through pursuit of writing as a profession. Authorial success was credited in critical acclaim for one's works and public recognition of one's name, not the size of royalties per se. Social criteria undercut the development of any comparable degree of solidarity that could be found amongst an artisan class, where, through conflict with capital, efforts might help advance wages and conditions of labour.

The legal formulation of copyright helped a Romantic sensibility to endure into the 20th century. There was no particular legal barrier to Romantic philosophy informing judicial interpretation of copyright or being deployed to support the valorisation of other creators seeking the advantages imagined attached to these rights – with national and international law aspiring to conformity in "standard" minimum requirements.[72] Other justificatory theories of property could be substituted to justify rights in non-expressive works.[73] Case law method, focussing on the individual facts and taxonomy, helped obscure anomalies that might emerge across the treatment of different classes of copyright works.[74] And legal positivism, a style of logical reasoning that focussed on doctrinal precision in interpreting the technical words in the statute, would further assist in closing down inquiries into the coherence and implications of particular cases for the whole domain. There was nothing within copyright jurisprudence or in contract law of the late 19th century to encourage detailed scrutiny of the terms executed in publishing agreements and the implications for professional authors. Further, conventional legal historiography, including many works informed by a Foucauldian sensibility, have remained tethered to analysis of a Romantic Victorian characterisation of the significance of copyright, focussing predominantly on the origins of copyright, rather than inquiring into the value of copyright in practice. This has further retarded a critical consideration of how the author came to be incorporated into commercial empires in the 20th century.

The next chapter focusses on the commercial decision-making of three late Victorian novelists as a stepping off point in beginning a more detailed investigation into the economic conditions of authorship and the modern industrialisation of author-publisher relations.

Notes

1 Michel Foucault, 'What Is an Author?' in Josué V Harari (ed), *Textual Strategies* (Cornell UP 1979)

2 An Act for the Encouragement of Learning, by Vesting the Copies of Printed Books in the Authors or Purchasers of Such Copies, during the Times Therein Mentioned (*Statute of Anne*) 1709, 8 Anne, c19

3 *Millar v Taylor* (1768) 4 Burr 2303, 98 Eng Rep 201; *Donaldson v Beckett* (1774) 4 Burr 2408, 98 Eng Rep 257

4 See for example, Ronan Deazley, *On the Origin of the Right to Copy: Charting the Movement of Copyright Law in Eighteenth Century Britain (1695–1775)* (Hart Publishing 2004); Jane C Ginsburg, '"Une Chose Publique"? The Author's Domain and the Public Domain in Early British, French and US Copyright Law' (2006) 65 Cambridge LJ 636; Tomás Gómez-Arostegui, 'Copyright at Common Law in 1774' (2014) 47(1) Connecticut L Rev 1; Kathy Bowrey, 'Law, Aesthetics and Copyright Historiography: A Critical Reading of the Genealogies of Martha Woodmansee and Mark Rose' in Isabella Alexander and Tomás Gómez-Arostegui (eds), *Research Handbook on the History of Copyright Law* (Edward Elgar 2016)

5 Martha Woodmansee, *The Author, Art, and the Market* (Columbia UP 1994)

6 The title and discussion is influenced by Elizabeth Eisenstein, *The Printing Press as an Agent of Change: Communications and Cultural Transformations in Early Modern Europe* (CUP 1979)
7 See Raymond Astbury, 'The Renewal of the Licensing Act in 1693 and Its Lapse in 1695' (1978) 33 Library 296; Peter Prescott, 'The Origins of Copyright: A Debunking View' (1989) 12 EIPR 453
8 Arnold Hauser, *The Social History of Art* (Routledge & Kegan Paul 1951) 179
9 John Barrell, *The Political Theory of Painting from Reynolds to Hazlitt* (Yale UP 1986) 7
10 Hauser (n 8) 256
11 Umberto Eco, *Art and Beauty in the Middle Ages* (H Bredin tr, Yale UP 1986) 115
12 David Saunders, *Authorship and Copyright* (Routledge 1992) 49
13 Peter Lindebaum, 'Milton's Contract' (1992) 10 Cardozo Arts & Entertainment LJ 439. See also Mark Rose, 'The Author in Court: Pope v Curll (1741)' (1992) 21 Cultural Critique 197
14 Lindebaum, ibid 441
15 For a discussion of the order of the law and the attitudes of the profession see Stephen White, *Sir Edward Coke and the Grievances of the Commonwealth* (Manchester UP 1979) 46–51, 76–85; CW Brooks, *Pettyfoggers and Vipers of the Commonwealth* (CUP 1986) 217–226; Wilfred Prest, *The Inns of Court under Elizabeth I and the Early Stuarts 1590–1640* (Longman Group, 1972) 137–173
16 See Ian Gadd, 'The Stationers' Company in England before 1710' Alexander and Gómez-Arostegui (n 4) 81
17 H Tomás Gómez-Arostegui, 'What History Teaches Us about Copyright Injunctions and the Inadequate-Remedy-at-Law Requirement' (2008) 81 S Cal L Rev 1197; H Tomás Gómez-Arostegui, 'Equitable Infringement Remedies before 1800' in Alexander and Gómez-Arostegui (n 4) 195
18 Woodmansee (n 5) 36
19 MH Abrams, *The Mirror and the Lamp: Romantic Theory and the Critical Tradition* (WW Norton & Co 1953) 250
20 As quoted in CWRD Moseley, *The Poetic Birth: Milton's Poems of 1645* (Scholar Press 1991) 5
21 Abrams (n 19). Abrams goes on to note the dearth of Romantic literature devoted to explaining Milton's identification with the Devil in *Paradise Lost*
22 Abrams notes that Coleridge felt burdened with a similar marital problem. Ibid 253
23 Moseley (n 20) 6
24 Victor Burgin, *The End of Art Theory* (Palgrave Macmillan 1986) 150
25 Edward Young, *Conjectures on Original Composition* (1759) as cited in Raymond Williams, *Culture and Society 1780–1950* (Penguin Books 1971) 54. Abrams notes the similarity between this and Coleridge's formulation (n 19) 199
26 Dugald Williamson, *Authorship and Criticism* (Local Consumption Publications, U of Sydney P 1989) 5
27 Abrams as quoted in Williamson, ibid 7
28 William Blake, *Annotations to Reynold's Discourses* as cited in M Foss, *The Age of Patronage* (Hamilton 1971) 110
29 As cited in Richard Patten, *Charles Dickens and His Publishers* (Clarendon Press 1978) 22
30 As quoted in Williams (n 25) 51
31 Martin Archer Shee cited in Barrell (n 9) 50
32 *The Microcosm* No 4 (27 Nov 1786) as quoted in Barrell (n 9) 55
33 Craig Owens, 'The Allegorical Impulse: Toward a Theory of Postmodernism' in C Owens, S Bryson, B Kruger, L Tillman and J Weinstock (eds), *Beyond Recognition: Representation, Power and Culture* (U of California P 1992) 58
34 Walter Benjamin as quoted in Owens, ibid 59
35 Coleridge as quoted in Owens (n 33) 62–63

36 Ibid
37 Burgin notes that such was the complexity and obscurity of allegorism by the Rococo period that it was often felt necessary to produce extensive explanatory pamphlets along with the paintings. Burgin (n 24) 115
38 Ibid
39 Owens (n 33) 62
40 Ibid 68
41 As quoted in Craig Owens, 'Representation, Appropriation, and Power' in Owens et al (n 33) 110
42 Victor Burgin, 'The Absence of Presence' in C Harrison and P Wood (eds), *Art in Theory 1900–1990* (Blackwell 1992) 1098. It is interesting to consider how such a view can be accommodated in a legal domain, historically a space for verbalisation
43 Rosalind Krauss, *The Originality of the Avant Garde and Other Modernist Myths* (MIT Press 1986) 157
44 Clement Greenberg, 'Avant-Garde and Kitsch' in Harrison and Wood (n 42) 531
45 Ibid 534
46 As quoted in Martha Woodmansee, 'The Genius and the Copyright: Economic and Legal Conditions of the Emergence of the "Author"' (1984) 17 Eighteenth Century Studies 425, 429
47 Ibid
48 Williams (n 25) 48
49 Richard Altick, *Victorian People and Ideas* (Dent & Co 1974) 190
50 Debra Gettelman, 'The Victorian Novel and Its Readers' in Lisa Rodensky (ed), *The Oxford Handbook of the Victorian Novel* (OUP 2013)
51 Rachel Sagner Buurma, 'Publishing the Victorian Novel' in Rodensky, ibid 90–91
52 Barbara Hochman, 'Disappearing Authors and Resentful Readers in Late-Nineteenth Century American Fiction: The Case of Henry James' (1996) 63(1) ELH, 177–201, 178, n8
53 Josephine Guy, 'Authors and Authorship' in Joanne Shattock (ed), *English Literature 1830–1914* (CUP 2010) 18. This is also discussed in Ch. 4
54 Catherine Seville, *Literary Copyright Reform in Early Victorian England* (CUP 1999)
55 Hochman (n 52) 178
56 Walter Besant, *The Society of Authors: A Record of Its Action from Its Foundation* (Incorporated Society of Authors 1893) 13–15
57 Woodmansee (n 5) 50–52
58 Besant (n 56) 15–16
59 Woodmansee (n 46) 425–448
60 Richard Altick, *Writers, Readers and Occasions* (Ohio State UP 1989) 97–98, 100
61 Ibid 101
62 Amy Milne-Smith, *London Clubland: A Cultural History of Gender and Class in Late Victorian Britain* (Palgrave Macmillan 2011) 9
63 S Squire Sprigge, *The Methods of Publishing* (Harrison & Sons, Incorporated Society of Authors 1890) 71
64 Alexis Weedon discusses Wilkie Collins's and Ouida's successful exploitation of copyright in *Victorian Publishing, the Economics of Book Production for a Mass Market, 1836–1916* (Ashgate 2003) 141–143. For a discussion of Charles Dodgson, Robert Louis Stevenson and Walter de la Mare's negotiations of production details, see Jose Bellido and Kathy Bowrey, *Adventures in Childhood: Intellectual Property, Imagination and Exploitation*, (CUP forthcoming)
65 This is primarily taken up in the following two chapters
66 Sprigge (n 63) 71
67 (1897) 6 The Author 34
68 'The Authors' Syndicate' (1891) 1(2) The Author 341
69 Stefan Collini, 'The Idea of Character in Victorian Political Thought' (1985) 35 Transactions of the Royal Historical Society 29

70 Chambliss and Seidman, quoted in RB Ferguson, 'The Horwitz Thesis and Common Law Discourse in England' (1983) 3 OJLS 34–35. The class view remains that of PS Atiyah, *The Rise and Fall of Freedom of Contract* (OUP 1979)

71 SM Waddans, 'Unconscionability in Contracts' (1976) 39(4) MLR 369

72 This was a matter discussed in the Royal Com. on Laws and Regulations relating to Home, Colonial and Foreign Copyrights Report (C 2036, 1878) and at the *Berne Convention for the Protection of Literary and Artistic Works 1886*

73 Ronan Deazley, *Rethinking Copyright: History, Theory, Language* (Edward Elgar 2006); Isabella Alexander, *Copyright Law and the Public Interest in the Nineteenth Century* (Hart Publishing 2010)

74 For a discussion of the anomaly of photography see Kathy Bowrey, 'Copyright, Photography and Computer Works – the Fiction of an Original Expression' (1995) 18(2) UNSWLJ 278

3 A tale of three literary copyrights

Like other property rights, copyright is not a thing owned by the author. It is a legal relation with many moving parts, linking the author directly to the producer and, indirectly, to distributors and consumers. It is easy to forget that our understanding of the author and the significance of their work is affected by the contractual agreements that shape the commodity forms through which we experience the author's creation. Despite our daily experience of familiar kinds of commodities – novels, magazines, plays and films – there is nothing immutable about the content of author agreements that determine the kinds of commodities produced or how and where these products are distributed. This is especially the case when new literary genres are being defined.

This chapter looks at three authors credited as contributors to the development of the detective story. The first two wrote blockbuster sensations: Fred Fargus (1847–1888) published *Called Back* (Arrowsmith, Bristol, 1884) under the name of "Hugh Conway"; New Zealand-born colonial Victorian Fergus Hume (1859–1932) wrote *The Mystery of a Hansom Cab* (Kemp & Sons, Melbourne, 1886). Both stories sold thousands of copies in multiple countries, were republished in many book formats, serialisations and retold on stage and film. Both authors went on to publish further works but could not repeat the phenomenal initial success. The conventional wisdom is that neither did well from copyright due to a premature assignment of rights. Arthur Conan Doyle's (1859–1930) first publication that featured Sherlock Holmes, *A Study in Scarlet* (Ward Lock & Co, London 1887) soon followed their success, failing to arouse anywhere near the same level of popular interest as Conway's or Hume's stories. Doyle also prematurely assigned rights to *A Study in Scarlet* for £25, far less than the £80 received by Conway or Hume's £50. Yet, Doyle went on to become famous to such an exceedingly rare degree that his signature characters continue to flourish even after the expiration of copyright over 130 years later. The chapter seeks to explain the authorial decision-making that contributed to different professional trajectories and outcomes. In comparing three stories of copyright exploitation I link the understandings of their cultural and economic significance and value of their productions to decisions they made about copyright. I also consider how each responded to the challenge of financial disappointment, and how the authors' self-perception and understanding of the market possibilities for a new genre directly affected the return on their copyright.

Copyright and commodity culture

Some literary historians imply that Conway and Hume are under-appreciated contributors to the rise of the detective novel. They lost their fortunes, and perhaps also their place in literary history, due to professional inexperience and copyright illiteracy. This is not an unreasonable theory taking into account the clumsy, limited patchwork of Victorian-era copyright legislation, the lack of an American copyright and these authors seeking to publish at a time when the few legal treatises on the subject were hardly amenable to skim reading.[1] However, in publisher archives I was soon confronted by a surprising coincidence. Both Conway and Hume successfully negotiated further payments from publishers for their big stories *after* they had signed away their entire copyright. This was disconcerting. The copyright transactions Conway and Hume entered into did not provide a full or accurate picture of their most important financial dealings with publishers. This was also confounding because my research did not gel with Hume's much-cited Preface,[2] first published in a Jarrold & Sons edition (1896), in which he informs readers he only received "£50 for the entire copyright" to *The Cab*. What an audacious claim! Hume received further royalties for the very edition in which he published this. Did Hume surmise that sad stories about authors and the loss of his copyright would intrinsically appeal to the public and help push further sales? Was he such a whimsical character that he actually misunderstood his own situation, even at that point in time? Looking in the archives brought into question the reliability of the sources from which literary history is reconstructed. To some degree this is a problem all historians have to manage. But in this scenario, it also forced a confrontation with a more foundational issue of copyright history. What sources are needed to understand what copyright is, once you begin to question the reliability of the legislative framework and the contracts based upon it, as is usually trusted by legal and literary historians to give this legal subject matter purpose and definition?

Liberal political theory, as well as the modern idea of the rule of law, presses for certainty in the definition of legal rights. This entices the legal scholar to find logic, limits and hard lines around legal subject matter and, especially, private property. Lawyers who share the British tradition of literary property are trained to understand that, after *Donaldson v Beckett* (1869),[3] copyright is not a natural right; the court failed to endorse any particular philosophical foundation of literary property which left copyright primarily defined with reference to the acts of Parliament. As defined in positive law, modern copyright is in fact an aggregation of limited exclusive rights as recognised by the legislature. The author is granted a time limited right to publish, reproduce, adapt, translate, perform and communicate the work to the public. The royalties that attach to these acts are determined by the publishing contract.

Nonetheless, lawyers, as well as non-lawyers, often fall into the trap of talking about copyright as if it were a thing, even if, through further delving into the contract it can be disaggregated into smaller discrete transactions – bounded rights that all flow from the author's expression in a manuscript. Tracing copyright assignments from this point of origin to the first publisher, and tracing the chain of title thereafter across subsequent assignments or licenses of particular rights, is a conventional way of describing the life of a copyright. In this chapter I will show why focussing on the legal origin of copyright ownership and thereafter tracing assignment and licensing of exclusive rights fails to portray how copyright circulates and generates value as a form of property in a modern economy. Copyright generates significance and value through a process of commodification. How the publisher and author approach commodity relations changes the very identity of the copyright and in turn, the financial outcomes for all parties.

Literary history identifies the late Victorian era as a time of significant change. The rise of the mass market for literature is connected with an increase in literacy and in popular reading of all sorts, the introduction of new formats, marketing and pricing models, and the entry of new entrepreneurs. Feltes[4] and McDonald[5] analyse refinements in the content and ideology of literary culture, particularly genres of popular reading, that supported the mass commodification of literature. Weedon[6] traces transformations in book production, distribution and consumption practices, including noting the changing relationship between libraries and publishers that signalled the decline of the three-decker novel. Law[7] plots the profitableness of serialisation rights in this era. Copyright – *conceived as an exclusive monopoly right that originates with the author* – is identified as the foundation of this blossoming trade, with rights transferred between author and publisher, and publisher and publisher. In histories of the British publishing industry, estimation of the value of copyright routinely references the number of copies printed and sold. Copyright territories may expand with new treaties and domestic law reforms; however the character and function of copyright is treated as relatively immutable and stable throughout the late 19th and into the 20th century. This is even the case with Peter McDonald's very insightful chapter, 'Light reading and the dignity of letters. George Newnes Ltd and the making of Arthur Conan Doyle'.[8] Though McDonald explains in compelling detail that "the success, and so the status, of the detective genre was largely an effect of its modes of publication and distribution",[9] there is no significant analysis of the copyright transacted by Doyle and his agent AP Watt.

This chapter seeks to address this oversight. Changes in literary, cultural and economic relations are explicitly linked to transformations in the legal form and circulation of copyright as an economic right. The three authors discussed help highlight differences in the way the properties of copyright were conceived and transacted as the publishing industry expanded in the late 19th century. Conway and his publisher Arrowsmith thought of copyright in the same manner that many legal and literary historians do – in terms of the exchange value of the rights to the story consumed as *a petty commodity* (even though it may be circulated in various formats).[10] A fair measure of the market price for the copyright for the author is imagined with reference to receipt of a proportionate share of royalties on each and every copy of the story published. For the publisher, there is an expectation of profit commensurate to expenditure on production and marketing costs, as well as a healthy margin for bearing the investment risk. However, Hume's first publisher, Trischler, understood the market opportunity in a more aggressively entrepreneurial light. He approached copyright as an investment opportunity and shifted commercial risk to his investors. He structured his business to facilitate intense, *short-term exploitation of potential demand for petty commodities*, and then hyped sales potential until the possibility of a short- or medium-term market return was exhausted. Trischler operated a number of publishing companies in this manner, extracting profits along the way, leaving his investors and debtors to carry their losses. By way of contrast, Doyle developed a far more stable, predictable model of copyright exploitation, and one that facilitated the multiplication of returns over the long term. A shift away from conceiving the value of his copyright in terms of sales of the novel to producing original stories published in serialised magazine format was central to this success. While he was far from the first to understand the value of serialisation and syndication, Holmes, Watson and other recurring characters invented by Doyle provided a hook that could sustain a multi-vocal and inter-generational conversation between Doyle, his publishers and multitudes of readers, theatre goers, film and television audiences across the globe. The form and content of his stories produced a copyright value that exceeded confinement to any particular material form or cultural product. *The potential readership became the commodity*. Conventionally readers are regarded as rational individuals, consuming literature-as-commodity, according to personal whims and information needs. But a closer analysis of the property relation being constructed through this author's contract with his publisher reveals that readers were being assembled as readerships or audiences, whose predictable, collective consumptive behaviours rendered them commodities that could be captured and exchanged on the market. The property defined in Doyle's contract for future Sherlock Holmes stories was very abstract – rights to a series of stories yet to be written, based upon a particular or "signature" story-telling formula and fictional characters that the public associated with the author's name. This reconceptualisation of the value of Doyle's copyright was more amenable to profitable sub-divisions across mediums, time and place. His characters inhabited an imaginary realm that could be endlessly recreated, so long as the author (and his successors) cared to reinvest in it. This new model of exploitation was co-developed with a new kind of professional who was more than a mere "literary agent" or middleman between writer and publisher. With regard to Doyle's interests, Watt generated ongoing business for himself and returns for his client by tightly calibrating the content of the exclusive rights, with risk limited and profit maximised by the tight structure of these commercial transactions.

The chapter begins with a brief discussion of sensation novels – the genre linked by literary historians to crime, mystery and detective fiction. The changing commercial prospects for this kind of literature in the 1880s is then outlined. Cultural, business and legal affairs are closely related. Deciding what to write is not immune from considerations of who the reader might be and how the work might be sold. This has particular relevance for Conway, Hume and Doyle, as all three set out to write commercially successful stories for wide distribution, consciously drawing upon features they admired in successful works by other authors. The business relations of Conway, Hume and Doyle are then discussed in detail. With each author I plot the deals done with reference to the author's professional aspirations, including considering how these changed over their lifetime, alongside their understanding of the significance of their creations, associated economic value, decisions made about copyright and consequently how the value of literary property was understood. In conclusion I return to a discussion of the legal preconditions for the rise of the detective novel. Economic and legal factors influenced the crafting of the commodity form that undergirds this kind of story. The rise in availability and popularity of crime, mystery and detective stories was sponsored by changes to copyright commercialisation practice, where the full potential of modern copyright law could be exploited internationally. The political machinations that allowed for publishers to aggregate rights and expand the infrastructure of exploitation across the oceans is taken up in Chapter 4. The extension of these new economic relations – from book to drama to film – is the focus of Chapter 5.

A new variety of the sensation novel: the proto-detective story

Sensation novels include works disparate in terms of style and content yet identified at the time by reviewers as united in the promise that they would physically and psychically stimulate the body. It is a very porous Victorian literary genre. Writers grouped together under the term include Wilkie Collins, Charles Dickens, Charles Reade, Edward Bulwer-Lytton, Caroline Norton, Catherine Crowe and Ouida.[11] Sensation works drew upon and in turn stimulated further current thinking about psychology, transgressive morality, crime, domesticity, women's sexuality, visual perception, science, invention and travel.[12] Dramatic themes include impersonation, insanity, scheming, jealousy, blackmail, inheritance, conspiracy, deceit, forgery and abduction. Despite regular protests at its vulgarity and complaints that it fostered an appetite for moral degeneracy, many writers, including many women, found success writing sensation stories.

In 1861 one reviewer for the *Spectator* observed,

> We are threatened with a new variety of the sensation novel, a host of cleverly complicated stories, the whole interest of which consists in the gradual unravelling of some carefully prepared enigma.[13]

From here a link between sensation novels, and detective, mystery and crime literature emerges.[14] However, there are a range of other influences that impacted upon the growing popularity of these stories.

Commercialising stories

Literary historians identify the mid-late Victorian era as a time of strong demand for books. The materiality of mass market literature was also changing. In addition to serialisation in monthly or weekly magazines and newspapers, Eliot and Nash note,

> By the 1870s a fiction publisher had at his disposal a range of formats which would allow him, in a matter of a few years, to explore a range of readers and markets with the same product: from a three decker at 31s 6d, to a single volume cheap reprint (3s 6d–6s), to a yellowback (1s–2s), to a paperback (at sixpence or under). In other words, in a matter of a few years a reader could buy a novel, that had originally appeared at 31s 6d, at 1/63rd or less of its original price. . . . Publishers could also sell unbound stock to jobbing printers who would bind and sell the books under their own imprints at even lower prices.[15]

The three-decker novel, the staple of circulating libraries and once the most lucrative form of publication for authors,[16] struggled to make a profit in a market dominated by reprints. The single volume first edition novel, priced at 6 shillings, took its place. Then publishers, including Conway's publisher, Arrowsmith, experimented with publishing popular novels priced at 3s 6d. Shilling shockers, one-sixth the price of the first cheap reprint of the three-volume novel, but twice the cost of a sixpence paperback reprint, also emerged.[17]

The timing of releases also changed in the second half of the mid-19th century. The October–December window for release of books grew in significance. Alongside this, there were shifts in book subject matter made available for sale. In the first half of the 19th century, religious books comprised approximately 20%, whereas fiction and juvenile literature combined made up 16% of titles. By the first decade of the 20th century, religious books made up only 9%, whereas fiction and juvenile literature now comprised 30% of all titles.[18] By the close of the century it was the most important season for the release of new titles, with publishers eventually targeting October as the most important month. Closer attention to the timing of releases allowed for more efficient stock management and advertising impact.[19]

A particular format, Victorian festive reading – the Christmas Annual – was also transformed. Conway's *Called Back* was first published in this format, priced at sixpence. In the 1860s these gift editions were lavish, deluxe editions. By the 1880s,

> [These] had been superseded by a more ephemeral kind of object. Their descendants were decidedly cheaper publications that one could purchase

> for the modest price of one shilling; consequently, simpler production values were the norm with these late nineteenth-century festive titles. The paper covers, binding, dual column page layout, and lengthy bound-in advertising that bookended the literary pages of the sixpenny 1883 number in which *Called Back* was published would likely have led consumers to view the Arrowsmith title as a publication of the periodical class. The lower production values of these second-wave festive annuals were not encoded to inspire the same impulse to cherish and retain such artefacts for their aesthetic attractiveness, even if one had received the object as a gift from a dear friend or close relative.[20]

While not quite a form of disposable literature, the multiplicity of available formats encouraged a new way of thinking about the value of a good story.

A longstanding source of supplementing income also came from dramatisation. It was difficult to protect books and plays against unauthorised dramatisation throughout the 19th century. There were different sources of rights – a performance right under the *Dramatic Literary Copyright Act* 1833 (3 & 4 Will c.15) and a literary copyright under the *Copyright Act* 1842 (5 & 6 Vict c45). What rights existed, and the respective term of protection, depended upon whether a work was unpublished, printed or performed, and in which order the publication or performance occurred. An author could achieve a dramatisation right with careful co-ordination of special performances "for copyright purposes", that coincided with the date of first publication.[21] However, even with registration of the performance right and of a publication, due to a very narrow, literalist test for copyright infringement being applied it often proved difficult to protect the author's interest.

The 1878 Royal Commission on Copyright acknowledged that British copyright legislation was piecemeal and overall, "wholly destitute of any sort of arrangement, incomplete, often obscure and . . . ill-expressed".[22] Reform was delayed due to questions raised by Ireland and Canada and also the negotiation of a multi-lateral international copyright treaty, the *Berne Convention for the Protection of Literary and Artistic Works (1886)*. Great Britain was an original signatory. A first step in implementing the Berne Convention was to pass the *International Copyright Act 1886* (49 & 50 Vict c33).[23] This was a significant step for colonial authors like Hume. It meant that literary works (excluding newspapers) first published in the Australian colonies would also obtain a British copyright, rather than first publication outside the UK precluding this. Securing an American copyright was far more difficult in this period, but not impossible. If the British publisher could arrange for simultaneous publication and copyright registration in the US, it was possible for British authors to obtain an informal American copyright, by way of "trade courtesy", where the rights of established American publishers were generally respected. As is explained in the following chapter, the legal situation was significantly improved after 1891.[24]

Overall, the cultural, economic and legal landscape was highly dynamic at this time. The capacity for inexperienced authors to understand and navigate their legal rights or economic opportunities would clearly have been very difficult, especially for British subjects who resided in British dominions. However, robust negotiation with publishers was supported by broad appeals to the cultural and economic importance of the creative author's labour,[25] at the same time as the means by which copyright generated value was being re-engineered.

Hugh Conway's *Called Back*

Called Back is a story of romantic infatuation with a mysterious woman, Pauline March – "that pale, pure face, those dark, dreamy, far-away eyes, are out of the common run of womanhood".[26] The first crime involves the narrator, Gilbert Vaughan, blinded by cataracts "witnessing" a murder, only to be disbelieved by police. His eyes are successfully treated after the incident. He marries the beauty only to discover on the honeymoon that there are obstacles to sex and companionship – Pauline has "a child's mind in a woman body" and no memories of her past.[27] She must be a victim of some horrendous trauma. Vaughan investigates this second crime, only to uncover that they are related. Pauline's relatives are exposed as Italian revolutionaries who have swindled her trust fund and murdered her brother, Anthony, to cover up their illicit activities – the very crime Vaughan inadvertently stumbled into. Pauline was present at the murder and has suffered mental distress and amnesia ever since. Her brother's identity was then assumed by Macari, a "Blackguard communist". A recurrent theme in the story involves personal struggles with trust in the modern city – of one's senses and civil society – in particular, the institutions of family, marriage and police. Vaughan is not really a detective, at least compared to later iterations that solve mysteries by applying logical deduction. Vaughan solves the crimes with supernatural guidance. Through the mystical touch of Pauline's hand, Vaughan was "called back" to the scene of the original crime seeing events through Pauline's eyes. She follows his journeys to locate the culprits through dreams. As a consequence of their radical political affiliations, the villains all meet with unpleasant deaths.

Commercialising the story

Conway initially struggled to find a place for his tale anywhere. He then sold the entire literary copyright to the Bristol publisher, JW Arrowsmith, in 1883 for £80,[28] soon coming to regret it.

The initial run for *Called Back* was 6,000 copies, but after positive reviews of the Christmas Annual were published by newspaper proprietor, Henri Labouchère, 350,000 copies went on to sell in the first three months.[29] There was no significant advertising expenditure on *Called Back*. It was not judged as needed. The story was quickly pirated as serialised versions of the stories appeared in the colonies, before Arrowsmith could avail himself of the opportunity to publish there. In a letter about these piracies Conway wrote to Arrowsmith, "I don't know what to say about those Australian devils. By the time we could do anything the tale would be finished so we could only sue for damages".[30] It was clearly copyright infringement that could have been pursued through the courts, but compensation was only available for the lost license fee for serialisation. Damages were calculated in terms of a simplistic idea of the market value of the subsidiary right. There was no compensation available for spoiling any potential colonial market for a book edition itself. In this context, Arrowsmith thought the trouble and expense of taking legal action in the colony was not worth pursuing. However, Arrowsmith still soon arranged for international publication during 1884, recouping his original investment by this alone. The Royalty book shows entries for continental rights (£30); translations into German (£21) and French (£20); America (£10); Australia (£10).[31] As will be seen, in addition to the upfront fee, the publisher probably also received a small royalty per copy on these editions.

To capitalise on the public interest in the title, Conway, with art critic and playwright Joseph William Comys Carr, produced a play which was very successful. He assigned the performance right to a highly successful actor/manager Edgar Bruce and it ran for 219 days at the newly built Prince's Theatre, London.[32] It ran for eight weeks at New York's 5th Avenue theatre, before touring the American provinces.[33]

Arrowsmith was publisher for Bristol University and the publication of *Called Back* was sufficient to retrieve the Arrowsmith Annual from financial disaster. Conway soon put pressure on Arrowsmith to set aside the entire agreement, arguing that the "phenomenal success" was a "fluke". He also confided that he had only accepted the original £80 because he had lost badly the previous night at the card table and had needed to settle the debt. He argued that the publisher should give him a further £100 and publish future editions on a half-profit arrangement.[34] Signalling the legal distinction between publication and performance rights, Arrowsmith replied that he would have felt a compulsion to do more but for the fact that Conway, owning the performance right, did very well out of the play.

This only infuriated Conway further. He berated Arrowsmith over ethics noting that the original agreement was entered into after being advised of a likely sale of only 14,000 copies.[35] He threatened to criticise Arrowsmith in public and in private,

> I am anxious to avoid saying a word which will cause you any pain . . .
> In reply to your question what do you expect me to do:
> Macmillan's who paid Anstey £25 for *Vice Versa* sent him £500 after its success. Enoch and Sons music publishers have torn up in the last three years three contracts under which Milton Wellings bound himself to them for a term of years. [Conway wrote some of the lyrics]. Rockel sent Weatherly £100 to acknowledge his . . . success of a couple of songs. I could multiply instances and I am sure you cannot blame me if I asked and expected to receive from you what I should speak of hereafter as really generous treatment in acknowledgement of having placed in your hands

> what I firmly believe will at least be talked about and written about as the literary success of the century.[36]

At this time Arrowsmith and Conway were directly negotiating over his follow up thriller *Dark Days*, which was to be released as the 1885 Christmas Annual. Conway cheekily suggested he could publish with the most respected publishing house, Macmillan, naming the publication, "Hugh Conway's Christmas Annual".[37] His quip signals an understanding that his name now had a market value, over and above the value of any particular text to which the copyright attached.

In the surviving correspondence neither party referred to the law as a relevant authority that should resolve their disagreement. This may be due to a shared disregard for it, given political recognition that it was a hopeless statute. However, this was also the age of "gentlemanly capitalism" where businessmen raised finance and realised opportunities leveraged through their private networks. As Richard Altick notes,

> The essence of morality is summed up in the single word, 'respectability'. . . . Here, of course, individualism ceased. Respectability was not subject to private definition; its attributes represented a consensus. They include sobriety, thrift, cleanliness of person and tidiness of home, good manners, respect for the law, honesty in business affairs, and, it need hardly be added, chastity.[38]

Even though the transaction concerned a lower class of literature, Arrowsmith's reputation and to some degree, his business credit, was linked through assessments of character, in particular as vouched for by fellow members of private clubs.[39] Eventually, Conway's reference to current notions of propriety and fairness being observed by reputable book and music publishers, his reminder that both parties moved in the same social circles, and the pressure to conclude business over *Dark Days*, was sufficient. In June, Arrowsmith agreed to pay to Conway 1 penny per copy for the next 50,000 to 100,000 copies of *Called Back*, and £8 per thousand till the end of the year of 1886, "after that time to stop".[40] This was in addition to another £210 that had already been forwarded by Arrowsmith in attempts to placate the author at some unknown time.[41] Giving some indication of the huge sales achieved, royalties paid to Conway's estate for just six months, Jan–Jun 1886, were £8.8s.

In August 1884 Conway assigned his British copyright to Arrowsmith for *Dark Days* for £80 *plus* 2 pence royalty per copy. The addition of a per copy royalty shows he had learnt from experience. With significant commercial foresight, Arrowsmith also arranged for simultaneous publication by Henry Holt & Co to secure an American copyright for the title. Arrowsmith and the author shared a royalty of 10% of the retail price for this edition.[42] Even though the anger expressed across numerous letters suggest they had been engaged in a very heated dispute over *Called Back*, again Conway and Arrowsmith did not care to draft any formal written agreement.

Graham Law notes that after the popularity of *Called Back* Conway soon found success placing a number of stories[43] until his premature death from typhoid in 1888. *Called Back* remained sufficiently popular in the following decades and was retold on film more than once; however neither Conway nor his estate appear to have received royalties.[44]

How did Conway understand the value of his copyright?

Conway had a traditional Victorian business relationship with his publisher where copyright value was primarily attributed to a notion of a fair return related to the number of copies of the story sold. The author was no victim of circumstance. He was not passive with regard to asserting his interests. He recognised new commercial opportunities and he learnt from mistakes. For example, in addition to arranging for dramatisation that would be licensed in different jurisdictions, he sought the services of literary agent AP Watt to negotiate serialisation rights. Law notes that his "best" story, *A Family Affair*, was serialised in Carr's monthly *English Illustrated Magazine* from October 1884, then published as a triple-decker from Macmillan the following year.[45] Conway and Watt were inventive in pushing the boundaries of existing rights, seeking to outwit pirates by publishing the title *Dark Days* accompanied by a bogus story of half a dozen pages or so, in an attempt to indirectly obtain copyright protection for the title itself and confuse those that might want to publish an unauthorised serialisation.[46] Conway used the idea of law strategically – relying upon creative ideas of legal protection and ignoring legal limitations as his conscience dictated. However, throughout Conway's negotiation of financial opportunities he was limited by his understanding of the market. His idea of entitlement was assessed in terms of the exchange value of the story as a simple commodity, primarily as a novel published in the English language and secondarily as a play. The way Conway approached copyright constrained and limited its value. He entered into agreements with publishers when the market prospects and potential value of the copyright was most uncertain – before first publication. Though commercial risk was borne by both parties, the publisher could limit their financial risk by limiting the print run. The author was far more vulnerable and unable to judge if any of the "subsidiary rights" had any commercial value at this time. As we will see, there were other ways to manage the commercial risk associated with publication.

Fergus Hume's *The Mystery of a Hansom Cab*

The Mystery of a Hansom Cab is also a story of a murder, marriage and inheritance. The crime is a murder that takes place when a hansom cab is hailed for a drunken man by a bystander, and the two then leave together. After the bystander alights, the body of the victim is found. Police Detective Grub says early in the story, "Who is the dead man? Second, What was he killed for? And Third, Who did it?". The dead man turns out to be Oliver Whyte, who was "promised" the hand of Madge by her father, Mark Frettlby. An unsuccessful Irish suitor, Brian Fitzgerald, is charged with the crime but his motive evaporates once it is revealed the marriage between Madge and Whyte had already been called off. In the absence of another suspect, the prosecution proceeds. The real mystery is why Fitzgerald will not testify to clear his name or explain the outcome of his own investigation of the crime. It is another team of investigators, Fitzgerald's lawyer Carlton and a sympathetic Detective Kilsip, who trace the accused's movements to an inner Melbourne slum where Fitzgerald interviewed some hard-living inhabitants. They discover Fitzgerald is selflessly protecting Madge. Years ago, her father had become enamoured with a show girl, Rosanna Moore and married her, fleeing to England. Madge's legitimate step-sister, Sol Rawlins, is now living in a Melbourne slum. The killer of Whyte is his friend, Moreland, who had wanted to blackmail Mark Frettlby and ruin Madge's reputation. At the conclusion of the mystery Fitzgerald and Madge marry and leave for London.

The story is an exploration of Victorian patriarchy, infidelity, blackmail and "ruined" women. Of particular interest is the rich description of "Marvellous Melbourne" and the seedy underside of urban life. There is also discussion of the machinations of a jury trial – providing readers with a rare snapshot of contemporary life in the modern colony. Emotional connections are forged by the sympathetic portrayal of downsider Rawlins and her loyalty to disreputable members of her slum community, the higher morality of Fitzgerald and the pure and innocent Madge. The virtue of Carlton and Kilsip going to great lengths to ensure an innocent man not be hung adds a reassuring counterbalance to the harsh portrayal of city life in the bustling colony.

Hume's misleading account of commercialising the story

In his new Preface to the Jarrold & Sons 1896 edition of *The Cab* Hume told readers it was the first book he had written, the work coming about from trying his hand as a novelist after failing to secure any interest in his plays in 1880s Melbourne. He had consciously sought to imitate the style of the French writer, Emile Gaboriau, after being advised by a bookseller that this kind of mystery novel "had a large sale". He claimed he drew upon personal experience of high and low Melbourne society, "All the scenes in the book, especially the slums, are described from personal observation; and I passed a great many nights in Little Bourke Street, gathering material".[47] *The Cab* was passed on by a major colonial publisher, most likely George Robertson of Melbourne,[48] so he struck out on his own and self-published. Public demand was so great that the first edition of 5,000 published by Kemp & Boyce sold out in Melbourne within a month, as did a further two editions. As the work was originally written by Hume "to attract local attention", perhaps with a view to generating some interest in his plays, he then sold the entire copyright, including international rights, for £50.[49]

The Cab was taken up by a consortium of businessmen, the Hansom Cab Publishing Company, who published the work in the United Kingdom.

"Phenomenal sales" followed, especially Hume tells us, after his talent was vouched for by "a very kind and generous criticism" by the leading theatre critic for the *Daily Telegraph*, Mr Clement Scott. The book went on to become a best seller in Britain and America. Yet despite achieving a most remarkable popular reception selling over 375,000 copies by 1896, Hume noted that, "far from making a fortune out of the book, all I received for the English and American rights, previous to the issue of this Revised Edition by my present publishers, was the sum of fifty pounds".[50] Adding to his sense of grievance he says he was bedevilled by imitators and fraudsters who tried to appropriate his identity claiming themselves to be the true author of *The Cab*.

Hume was a man who was ill-suited to his original profession, the law. He escaped from the cultural constraints of living in the South Island of New Zealand, where his father was a well-known doctor and proprietor of a mental asylum. His move to Melbourne was motivated by an interest in advancing his theatrical ambitions. In his last days, Hume believed himself a tragic reincarnation of a guillotined French aristocrat, his live-in "companion" John Melville, a reincarnation of medieval philosopher and Franciscan friar, Francis Bacon.[51] With a love of drama and gift for melodrama Hume could provide an entertaining account of his life. But it was a misleading one.

Correcting the record

Hume did experience difficulties in attracting a publisher for his manuscript in 1885. In the 1860s and '70s there were significant debates about how colonials could learn to recognise and to produce worthy literature and art. Hume suggests in his 1896 Preface that he thought his work had been rejected due to an anti-colonial prejudice, given the diminished educational and social opportunities that was assumed to mark a colonial upbringing.[52] If George Robertson had passed on the opportunity to print and sell *The Cab* he may have also objected to the coarse language and the representation of Melbourne low-life. Unlike his Sydney-based namesake, (George Robertson of Angus & Robertson), though he had published works by Australian writers, Robertson of Melbourne had not acquired much of a taste for "an Australian outlook".[53] Hume deliberately sought to produce a popular "social realist" work and he chose a French writer as his inspiration because "the detective stories of Gaboriau had a large sale".[54] He was not seeking to mimic British or Continental works of high distinction.

An earlier interview with Hume's business partner, Frederick Trischler, points to the prejudices of colonial readers as also being a source of the problem,

> [T]he managing director of the biggest publishing company in the Australian colonies, . . . told him that even if he took the financial risk and published the work himself, his firm would not put their name to it; that *it was no use offering a book to the Australian public that had not previously been submitted to the judgment of the English trade*; that it was a colonial work written by

> a colonial and therefore was not worth putting a penny into. *Hume offered to pay the whole cost if they would undertake the publishing*, but they refused to have anything to do with it, and he had to take his MSS. home with him and bear his disappointment as best he could.[55]

It was common for colonial authors to test themselves abroad in the mid-late Victorian era. Bode's quantitative study of Australian colonial publishing suggests "in the 1870s and 1880s, one in every three book editions of Australian novels were first, and in most cases only, published in the colonies".[56] Thus roughly two-thirds were first published in Great Britain, where the work would have a full British copyright instead of a limited colonial one, and potentially reach a vastly larger market than that which could be reached within the colony. It made cultural and economic sense to publish in Britain. Census data for 1891 reports a total population for Greater London, 5,633,332; England and Wales, 29,001,008, while the colony of Victoria (exclusive of Chinese, Aborigines and "Half-castes") was only 711,973.[57]

Hume himself was doubtful his work would find much success. He originally sought to negotiate a print run of a mere 500 copies.[58] Given he was contemplating paying for publication this could also be a reflection of his available finances, although he later says he did carry the whole cost for the first print run of 5,000.[59] It took him six months before he connected with Trischler, who claimed to have had a prior connection with the printers, Kemp & Boyce. When he revised the work across editions he did tone down some of the coarse language; however, this aspect was still criticised as a corrupting force on young women.[60]

The Cab was printed by Kemp & Boyce on 23 October 1886. When the first edition sold out by November 1886, a further three runs were arranged. Approximately 25,000 copies sold within a few months.[61] It is probable that at least the first, and possibly all four editions, were published subject to a profit-sharing agreement between Hume and Trischler. The work had a blue card cover. Though it was very similar in format to Arrowsmith's Christmas Annual 1883, priced at 1 shilling (12 pence), *The Cab* was twice as costly. It carried advertising that appeared on the inside of the front cover, the outside and inside of the back cover, with an additional two pages of advertising at the back. Given the subject matter of the book – the mystery of a murder that takes place in the back of a cab – it is quite amusing that there are cab-themed advertisements; one suggesting readers take a hansom cab to the Chipperfield Ironmongers in Elizabeth St, Melbourne, another for the American Carriage Company in Brunswick.[62]

"Australia Felix": the cab becomes "speculative property"

Hume saw *The Cab* in simple commercial terms similar to Conway, where the object of consumption was entirely his creation. However, as has been foreshadowed, there were some unique features about the exploitation of *The Cab*. Trischler differed from Arrowsmith in terms of class and education. A more aggressive approach to capitalism was one consequence of his experience in San Francisco and colonial Victoria. Parallels in exploitation of *The Cab* can be drawn with earlier speculation in gold mining leases and, in particular, his personal experience of the Melbourne 1880s land boom where,

> Clergymen, labourers, widows, schoolmasters – all grasped at the chance of quick wealth and invested their savings. Many borrowed widely to invest more than their assets were worth, and the later formed a pitiful kite-tail to the catalogue of insolvencies.[63]

Trischler's association with Melbourne bankers may have encouraged him to devise a high-risk strategy for generating profits from a boom copyright where the greatest risk was borne by his investors.

Until the 1890s, in Britain and especially in the colonies, there were difficulties regulating companies and banking arrangements. Registered companies with limited liability were difficult to set up. Many businesses operated as a partnership or unincorporated company. These structures presented significant problems in holding the promoters who issued the prospectus and directors of the company who managed the business to account: amongst each other, to creditors, debtors and investors.[64] In 1862 the British Treasury ceased interference in the colonial banking system, leading to divergence from British banking rules. Colonial Victoria had a largely unregulated "free banking" system. Throughout the 1870s and 1880s, due to demographic changes and immigration, the population of Melbourne swelled. In the city centre simpler wooden buildings were replaced by sandstone, granite and shopping arcades. On the city outskirts new residential suburbs sprang up. A plethora of new building societies and land banks were established. The absence of banking regulation encouraged a mania of speculative land and stock market investment.[65] Though most institutions were underpinned by British funds, colonial banks had a much higher reliance on deposits as a percentage of assets than their British counterparts.[66] Building societies were also permitted to buy and sell or mortgage freehold estate. Land banks could use saving deposits, issue shares, float loans, discount promissory notes and perform all the functions of an established bank. Building societies and land banks drew lines of credit from the more established colonial banks, as well as raised capital from British banks. Bank, building society and land bank directors used deposits (largely from wage earning classes) to compete for the best real estate, driving up property prices well beyond the value of the return achievable from sales and rents. The greedier directors drew upon depositors' money as if it was their own to support property speculation.[67] As inflationary pressures grew, British banks sought to limit further exposure. This, and a period of industrial unrest, led to the land boom petering out and a major banking crisis. All bar one bank with a head office in Melbourne collapsed in 1893, with ramifications for many other banking institutions and businesses across all the Australian colonies.[68] A major period of depression followed. Investigations revealed common banking practices had included "falsifying of balance sheets, the payment of dividends from non-existent profits, and the publication of misleadingly optimistic forecasts. . . [by] Men who were widely known and trusted".[69]

It appears that there were insufficient funds for reprinting *The Cab* throughout 1887. A loan was arranged from the Land Credit Bank. Hume's registration of his Victorian copyright on 20 April 1887,[70] six months after the work had gone on sale, was possibly prompted by the need to use the copyright registration as a security for the loan.[71] In this period there were two distinct sources of copyright, the common law right to the unpublished work that originated when the author penned the work and a statutory copyright that originated when the author published the work. Registration was not essential but it was required if the owner was to enforce their interest in the published work in court.[72] It would not be prudent for any investor to lend funds for a publication venture where the copyright in the work was unregistered, and as such, was unenforceable. Registration could serve as security for the loan, especially where, as in this case, Trischler and Hume probably had no significant real estate or chattel property.

Four months later copyright was assigned in full to Mrs Jessie Pearson Dove Taylor for £50.[73] Jessie Taylor is noted on the registration form as the wife of Land Credit Bank manager George Nicholson Taylor. Both George and Jessie were investigated for financial fraud in 1891 which was discovered after the Melbourne Commercial Bank sought to call in overdrafts. This led to an inspection of the books. The Taylors had used investors' deposits as their own, mostly reinvested in land speculation, to the value of £100,000, a sum equal to the entire capital of the bank when it was incorporated in 1876. George was sentenced to eight years hard labour for fraud in 1892.[74]

The timing of the Victorian registration, the assignment of the copyright to Jessie Taylor soon after, and, in 1890, her gaining an injunction to prevent Kemp & Boyce printing more copies of *The Cab*[75] suggests Jessie, rather than the Bank, was personally involved in financing the publication.[76] However, her involvement in banking fraud involved her husband channelling money into his wife's account at the Land Credit Bank. Jessie's investment in *The Cab* may have been a form of money laundering. Windfall "royalties" from the book would have been useful for covering up income received from other sources. As will be discussed later, Trischler's creative puffery about *The Cab* sales would have only aided in any deception. At this point it is worth noting that the assignment was solely to Taylor. There was never a formal assignment of copyright to Hume's chum or self-described "literary agent", Trischler. His model of exploitation did not necessitate his owning copyright at all.

In interviews given in the UK, Trischler said it was his idea to bring the novel to London. He suggested he sent out a "few feelers" and received offers from two large British publishers, then decided to come over and publish the work himself.[77] However, a contrary explanation he gave to a New Zealand newspaper seems far more plausible,

> some copies appeared to have reached England. A London publishing house instructed their agent by cable to offer me certain terms for the international copyright. At this time I had no intention of publishing in England, but this offer opened my eyes. The agent receded somewhat in his terms, and I broke off negotiations and offered the copyright to another London publishing house of high repute, making the terms, as I thought prohibitory. Within four days of the receipt of my letter they wrote back offering me 75 per cent of what I asked. I refused it, got a few Melbourne capitalists to join me, brought the work over here to publish it, and in this little big-style of an offer we have been doing and are now doing a business such as astonishes the London publishing trade.[78]

The Cab was the first Australian colonial novel to significantly benefit from the *International Copyright Act* 1886 (UK) that protected literary works first published in the Australian colonies. Prior to this enactment, first publication in the colony had precluded obtaining a British copyright.[79] Trischler had relatively little publishing experience, especially with regard to international copyright and the situation in the Australian colonies.[80] It is far more probable that British publishers had alerted their agents to the changing market for colonial works and they made the first approach. In doing so Trischler was alerted to much wider commercial opportunities created by international copyright law.

It is unknown whether the international interest in *The Cab* precedes Hume's assignment of his copyright to Jessie Taylor.[81] Hume was a common-law trained barrister and it is not clear how much he knew of copyright law or of the negotiations conducted by Trischler. Prior to *The Cab* Hume had written short stories for newspapers in New Zealand, a number of plays and poetry. Though he notes in his 1896 Preface that his plays went unpublished, this is also misleading. Hume's works were being performed, arguably the most relevant indicator of a playwright's reception. Four of his plays were staged in the period he was writing and publishing *The Cab*, but none attracted much public interest.[82] In 1887 *The Bigamist* was produced in New Zealand. However, Hume's business partner from New Zealand, Mr Calthorpe-Mallaby, proved unreliable. He absconded to London and staged it without crediting Hume, renaming the play *The Mormon*. It was a flop and Hume complained that,

> It is not plagiarism he has been guilty of, but something worse, as he not only placed his name to the piece, but took it away from the Colonies without my permission. . . . He has spoilt any chance the comedy might have had in London of making a success.[83]

It may be that Hume was so concerned with pursuing the "theft" of *The Bigamist* and the implications for his career as a famous playwright abroad that he lost track of what was happening with *The Cab* in mid-late 1887. He did not initially consider the outright sale of copyright to be an unfair bargain. He told a reporter that, "I can't complain; they gave me a good sum down for the copyright; though had I known that the success was going to be so immense, I would never have parted with the book".[84] The reference here to "they" suggests he was aware that Trischler was in some kind of business partnership and that there were larger plans afoot.

The Hansom Cab Publishing Company was established in London by Trischler in late 1887 as an unincorporated company – either a partnership or joint stock company (with transferrable shares). *The Cab* was entered into the British copyright register as a literary work on 28 Oct 1887. To register the copyright, an applicant had to certify that they were the proprietor of the copyright of the book, and so, to correspond with the colonial register, the application form was filled out in the name of the current Victorian proprietor of the copyright, Jessie Taylor. Trischler signed as witness. There are some discrepancies in the writing on the form and there is no evidence Jessie went to London.[85] At this point in time, it is impossible to determine if her signature at the bottom was genuine. The suggestion is not that Trischler was defrauding Taylor, but it raises further questions about the character of the parties whom Hume trusted.

Taylor, if not also Trischler, was well aware of how to raise finance in a boom market. As the promoter of the company Trischler soon issued a prospectus seeking British investors,

> In a yellow envelope, illustrated by an allegorical engraving, and bearing the title of "A Message from Australia; a Literary Tribute to the Mother Country" we have the announcement (with specimen) of a work by Mr Fergus W. Hume, an Australian author. It is called "The Mystery of a Hansom Cab", and purports to be a sensational, startling, and realistic study of Melbourne social life: and, after announcing that *25,000 copies were sold in three days* comes the astounding information of the establishment of a "Hansom Cab" Publishing Company on Ludgate Hill. "Australia Felix" is the motto heading the prospectus. . . . This hold (sic) intrusion of a "Hansom Cab Company" has taken our English authors by surprise, all the more as coming from our adolescent colony.[86]

A degree of creative puffery by promoters of new business ventures was tolerated by the law. It was difficult to hold promoters, as well as the eventual company directors, to account for false misstatements and fraud.[87] Trischler's press release sensationalised the venture by changing the news of 25,000 copies sold in three months to the sale occurring *within three days*. In keeping the Australian theme uppermost in the public imagination he also ignored the reality that Hume self-identified as a New Zealander of Scottish parentage. It is not known precisely whom all his investors were but he referred to two Australians – one would be the registered copyright owner Jessie Taylor. In unrelated litigation between the Company and another author, Vere Shaw, one proprietor at that time was listed as a tailor from Conduit St, London. The release of the book was supported by a multitude of postcards and liberal offers to the trade of return sales.[88]

The Hansom Cab Company 1888 publication is based upon the Kemp & Boyce edition, though the advertisement for the Melbourne Ironmongers is replaced by one for the Orient Line fortnightly mail service via the Suez Canal.[89] Trischler continued the strategy of hyping *The Cab* by reporting "extraordinary figures of bona fide sales" that were reprinted in the newspapers. He now claimed a sale of 372,869 in five months.[90]

The sales phenomenon became an independent news story that served the ambitions of the Hansom Cab Publishing Company very well. Many in the British press thought it exceptional that,

> Moreover the novel is not a native product, but an importation from Australia – and so is the firm of publishers. So far these facts were unfavourable rather than otherwise. The insular taste and prejudice, which are distinguishing characteristics of the British public, have in this case been overcome by the remarkable skill and enterprise of this new Australian publishing company.[91]

Another newspaper reported,

> Further more (though we say so who should not) there is something in advertisements. The curiosity of the unsuspecting reader, on the look-out for a new "sensation", is first of all stirred by the title, then by the picture on the title [the actual cab whirling its murdered occupant through the lonely street], then by rumour that this "startling realistic" work has already been sold out in a score or so of editions, and that the "Hansom Cab Publishing Company" are printing more.[92]

The crass commercialisation was criticised in the press, especially in New Zealand, "A very large sum of money is being (most injudiciously, I think) expended on advertising the "Hansom Cab mystery".[93] One commentator expressed concern about the lack of credit being afforded to the birthright of the author,

> Advertising on the large scale is an excellent thing when you get it done cheap. What do you suppose, now, the popularity of the "Mystery of a Hansom Cab" is worth to New Zealand?
>
> Not a brass farthing. Nobody in England is aware that New Zealand has any share in paternity of the prosperous "Hansom". . . . Couldn't we admit his genius provisionally – till we see further, reserving the right to throw him overboard afterward if he fails to become rich and famous?[94]

There were numerous parodies.[95] One skit credited the book to the NZ parliamentarian, Robert Stout, with whom Hume had articled as a young Dunedin lawyer. The writer identifies numerous scholarly references and the writer's knowledge of Greek myth, Latin and Shakespeare, pointing out, tongue in cheek, that these would clearly be beyond what one could expect from Hume's provincial education in New Zealand. The proof includes a comparison between sentences from *The Cab* and Stout's speeches as recorded in Hansard.[96]

Every author shares pro rata?

So far as can be ascertained Hume never publicly criticised Trischler or the Hansom Cab Company over royalties, even when there was clear provocation. In 1889 Trischler told the British press that,

> Every author we [the Hansom Cab Publishing Company] publish shares in our success and is paid a royalty on every copy of the book that we sell. I learned my business in America, where we are not in the habit of grinding people down for the sake of making a lot of money out of their literary abilities. Every author shares pro rata in our success.[97]

In the same interview Trischler also claimed, "We make very few bad debts". His claim of paying royalties on every copy to authors was clearly untrue with respect to *The Cab*. It was also untrue with respect to *Jubilee Plunger. How I lost £250,000 in Two Years* (1889) where a copyright dispute with the ghost writer ended up in court over the payment due, which was tied to number of sales. It was claimed in the press as another "boom book". However, in litigation Trischler gave evidence that "it would be mathematically impossible for him to give any evidence of the number of sales".[98] It is not clear why this should be so. The situation would, of course, make determining whether any work was a financial success and calculating due royalties on every copy exceedingly difficult. His answer further points to Trischler's financial model as having little to do with selling petty commodities. Public belief in the value a boom copyright provided was a useful hook to convince punters to part with their savings. It was a means for establishing a more complex set of legal and economic relations, essentially allowing the "publisher" to commodify his investors.

There were press reports that the Hansom Cab Publishing Company had run into financial difficulties in the second year after its launch.[99] Given the company history and legal loopholes it may have been part of the original plan. The firm was soon succeeded by the incorporated company Trischler & Co Ltd. This company appears to have been assigned copyright in *The Cab*, but within three years this venture too had failed and the £10,000 capital was unable to be traced.[100]

From book to play

Hume followed Trischler to London in 1888 where he was to live in Britain for the rest of his life. As with Conway, to capitalise on public interest he sought assistance of a moderately successful English playwright, Arthur Law,[101] to co-author a dramatic work of *The Cab*. It ran for a creditable 100 performances in London.[102] It also toured British provinces and was also performed in the colonies and New Zealand.[103] The play did well enough to inspire the taking of the play to America. However, following poor reviews in New York, it closed within a week.[104]

To invigorate public appetite for the play and renew book sales, a highly amusing publicity campaign was launched in London.[105] It involved dressing up the Oxford Theatre frontage as a police station and whetting "public curiosity with the assertion that the production of the dramatic version was delayed only by the necessity of having built in Melbourne, and having sent from Melbourne a Hansom cab of the real Melbourne pattern".[106]

> Then it becomes known that this remarkable story is about to be dramatised, in token of whereof a procession of real hansom cabs, each with its ghastly effigy inside, parades the busy London streets, till they are stopped by the police and indulged with an injunction in the Law Courts. Then comes the play with its sensational placards and portrait-heads of all the characters. Then the run of the book revives, and periodical bulletins of the circulation appear, until at last the grand announcement is made that the record has been beaten. Nothing succeeds like success, as we have ourselves assisted to demonstrate by buying a copy and devoting a whole column of *The Mercury* to its consideration.[107]

Though he did not benefit from the new book sales, assuming he was entitled to a share of the royalties for the authorised dramatic adaptation, the performance right should have returned Hume a reasonable sum.

The Jarrold & Sons edition (1896)

In 1894 Jarrold & Sons purchased the rights to numerous works by Hume including *The Lone Inn. A Mystery* (1894), *The Expedition of Captain Flick* (1895), *The Mystery of Landy Court* (1896) and, for £50, from Trischler & Co's bankruptcy trustees, *The Cab*.[108] Both *The Cab* and *Landy Court* were released at the same time. *Landy Court* was prominently advertised as "by the author of *The Mystery of a Hansom Cab*". The Jarrold & Sons' press clipping file suggests *Landy Court* was well received, although one uncharitable review in the *Birmingham Post* described it as "a book which no novel reader of taste and experience will lay down without a heavy grudge against the author". It was considered to be "a degraded perversion" of Wilkie Collin's *The Moonstone*.[109]

This edition contained the misleading Preface penned by Hume. The Preface infringes the copyright in the original review of the book by Clement Scott in 1888, if the takings were without Scott's blessing. Interestingly, Hume omits reference to Scott's praising of Trischler as "a good angel of genius" and a favourable comparison of Trischler with the "enterprising Bristol Publisher" Arrowsmith. Though clearly not legally required to, Jarrold & Sons elected to pay Hume royalties for both their 3/6 cloth edition and the 1 shilling Empire edition of *The Cab*.[110] The publisher could have just paid Hume a modest fee outright for his plagiarised contribution. The firm's generosity was clearly tied up with the publisher's interest in branching out into publishing mysteries on the back of the name of an established writer.[111] But it may also have been felt as simply a gentlemanly thing for the established Norwich firm to do, in a similar vein to the generosity publishers had afforded to Conway and Anstey.

Hume avoids directly mentioning that Jarrold & Sons was paying him a new royalty for the new edition, carefully choosing his words so as not to lie to readers – "far from making a fortune out of the book, all I received for the English and American rights, *previous to the issue of this Revised Edition* by my present publishers, was the sum of fifty pounds". Why? Perhaps it was considered gauche to air such matters. Perhaps it was thought the sad "real life" story would motivate readers to buy another copy. The omission certainly helped the copyright narrative that he was a victim of a premature assignment to circulate unchallenged.

Jarrold & Sons clearly, though relatively modestly, profited from their relationship with Hume and the investment in *The Cab*, with money coming in from licensing various editions.[112] At some point Jarrold & Sons also entered into an agreement with Curtis Brown, a new international newspaper syndication agency,[113] which entitled Jarrold & Sons to a 10% royalty on any international sales of rights to *The Cab*. Twenty years after the story had first come to public attention, even during the war years, this arrangement still netted them modest sums ranging between £2–£11 a month.[114]

In 1896 when Hume was discussing the new edition of *The Cab* with Jarrold & Sons, moving picture rights were not a matter he and the publisher would have discussed: "the kinema was not in existence when I wrote the book".[115] There were three silent film productions of *The Cab*. Two were made in Australia, one directed by WJ Lincoln in 1911, who made a film of *Called Back* the same year.[116] The British version by Ideal Films was produced under license from Jarrold & Sons.[117] There was a clause in the contract that led to a reversion of all rights to Jarrold & Sons once royalties dipped below an average of £25 a year for five consecutive years. Ideal Films was not free to sell the rights to another film-maker without Jarrold & Son's agreement. When Australian actor Arthur Shirley sought to make another film of *The Cab* in the 1920s, it is probable that Jarrold & Sons was the relevant rights holder, but there were no negotiations between Shirley's company Pyramid Pictures and the publisher. The reason for this is explored in Chapter 5.

How did Hume understand his copyright and financial misfortune?

As a professional writer in London, Hume had far greater access to publishers than in the colonies and, due to his past success, new manuscripts would be read by publishers. However, over the course of his four decades as a professional writer he did not change his approach to copyright negotiation – he understood it as an exclusive right to a story that would be serialised is newspapers, syndicated by news publishers and, if it had attracted interest, published as a popular novel. Hume should, by no means, be considered as an unsuccessful writer. He published a very large number of novels and short stories in Britain and the US, numbering well over 150. Works by Hume continued to appear as serialisations in newspapers throughout his life. As he consented to these publications he was presumably paid. Many works were well reviewed. A large number ran to multiple editions and were translated into French and German.[118] Like his contemporary Conway, he appealed to the conscience of his publishers and the public, rather than to the law, for support. He never thought to re-evaluate how copyright could work to support writing as a profession.

Does Hume deserve his reputation as a victim of misfortune, a man "plagued by ill-luck?"[119] Assessments of Hume as a sad, impecunious writer read his actions as those of a hapless, unsophisticated dreamer and story-teller. They fail to consider that as a professional writer he also promoted an image of himself. Hume participated in writing his own biography for dramatic effect, containing significant omissions and, undoubtedly, playing with word choice for his own amusement. In addition to the wording of the Preface, he toyed with his publics when in 1925, Arthur Shirley's new film of *The Cab* was to be released in Australia. Arthur Shirley was Australian by birth, but after alienating local theatre proprietors, he went to Hollywood and found success. Shirley then returned home to try his hand as a film producer and director. Due to his international profile his activities were closely followed in the press. The release of his film of *The Cab* renewed interest in Hume and his personal story. Hume told the Australian public,

> I am unable to write owing to illness, and having passed through many years of trouble, I am in want of money to keep me going. I am much in need of rest and comfort.[120]

Shirley soon announced he was launching a public appeal for the writer to which his production company had contributed a substantial sum.[121] Yet, two months later Hume told his English *Daily Mail* readers that,

> I have neither need of, nor do I want, the subscriptions of any of the people who have read my books.
>
> I love *what might be imagined is my poverty*.[122]

Though he was not a wealthy man[123] he made a steady living from his writing. He told *Daily Mail* readers that, at age 65, he had just finished his 137th novel: "It is my ability to write a readable detective yarn in a month that has kept me hammering all my life". Yet, Hume's stories had no commonly recurring exotic locations, characters or detectives. This proved to be a problem, particularly as the eccentric detective soon became a recognisable feature of the genre: "After Poe, Dickens, Collins, Gaboriau, and Hume, readers expected detectives to be eccentric".[124] While Hume had paved the way for Doyle's Sherlock Holmes and Hal Meredeth's Sexton Blake (the "poor man's Sherlock"), he failed to grasp the significance of the new aspects of detective stories that were attracting return readers.

Arthur Doyle's *A Study in Scarlet*

A Study in Scarlet shares similar themes to that of Conway and Hume but Doyle's interest in crime entails a deeper exploration of violence and its ramifications. It begins with an introduction to the enigma that is "Mr. Sherlock Holmes". Watson is intrigued by the man and initially very sceptical of Holmes's self-proclaimed superior crime-solving abilities that set him apart from all others. He is annoyed by Holmes's derision that targeted fictional detectives Watson (and Doyle) was fond of, Edgar Allan Poe's Auguste Dupin and Gaboriau's Lecoq.[125] Part One of the story involves the exposure of two brutal crimes. The first is the murder of a well-dressed American, Enoch Drebber, found in an abandoned house, no sign of robbery, no visible injury, with someone else's blood splashed all around. Holmes finds various clues overlooked by police and begins various inquiries when a murder of another American, Joseph Stangerson, occurs. A complicated sequence of events is set in train by Holmes, who quickly apprehends a perpetrator. How the devil did Holmes deduce this and why did these two murders occur? Part Two explains the mysteries through a flashback that features romance, violence and revenge. It centres on the short, fraught life of Lucy, a young woman adopted by farmer John Ferrier. Having been rescued from the desert, the little family come to live in a Mormon farming community near Salt Lake City where control is exercised by the prophet Young and community Elders, Drebber and Stangerson. Suspicious of polygamy and fearful of the tyrants, tensions come to a head with Lucy's coming of age. It is made clear that Lucy is expected to choose a husband amongst the Elders or their sons so that they might obtain Ferrier's property, but she is attracted to another, the fatefully named Jefferson Hope. Because the comeuppance of the two monstrous men has been flagged in Part One, suspense pivots on a horrible sense of foreboding linked to anticipation of sexual violence against Lucy in her forced marriage, as the 29 days given to deliver up Lucy are counted down. Hope and Lucy's father plot an escape. After plans go awry, Ferrier is killed and Lucy is married to one of Drebber's sons. She dies within a month. "With indomitable patience and perseverance, Jefferson Hope possessed also a power of sustained vindictiveness".[126] The reader comes to understand, if not approve, his plotting of revenge. The journal of Dr Watson reveals Hope's confession to the murders and Holmes's explanation of the clues and events that led him to the arrest. When credit for solving the crime is attributed in the press to Detectives Lestrade and Gregson, Holmes declares "Populus me sibilat, at mihi plaudo. Ipse domi stimul ac nummos contemplar in arca" (The public hiss at me, but I cheer myself when in my own house I contemplate the coins in my strong-box).[127] Holmes is a professional private detective. His fee provides sufficient satisfaction.

Commercialising the story

Peter McDonald describes Sherlock Holmes's creator as "the embodiment, and indeed champion, of middle-class cultural values" – neither a purist nor a profiteer.[128] This cultural positioning was a consequence of Doyle's personal values, approach to aesthetic theory and idea of professionalism. In a speech to the Society of Authors later in his career, Doyle lectured,

> This art of ours, which has to appeal to the infinite variety of the human mind, should be treated in a very broad and catholic spirit. . . . There is nothing more absurd than the realist who denies merit to the romance writer, unless it be the romance writer who sneers at the realist. A healthy taste should respond to honest words of every kind.[129]

Though at one point Doyle suggested being chased by "a howling creditor" was a primary motivation to write early in his career,[130] he sought to distance himself from what he considered profiteering, which was linked to dishonourable self-publicity. Doyle singled out the romance writer Hall Caine for his "ludicrous and offensive" behaviour in self-promotion based upon "wire-pullings and personality",

> If those who are successful advertise their own wares, and use the machinery of the Press in order to whet curiosity about their own book before it has come into the hands of the critics, the young aspirant naturally comes to imagine that this is the cause of the success, and by imitating the same tactics the whole tone of the profession becomes lowered.[131]

The profession of writing had "unwritten laws" based on "honourable traditions" and "gentlemanly etiquette". "Tactics" designed to attract attention to oneself, rather than let the critic and the public judge literary worth, would degrade literature and its standing as a worthy pursuit. Ideas about the strictures of literary professionalism would lead him to reconsider how commercialisation should be approached. Doyle did not disregard the necessity of publicity for his name if he was do well as an author,

> I could go on doing short stories for ever and never make headway. What is necessary is that your name should be on the back of the volume. Only so do you assert your individuality, and get full credit and discredit of your achievement.[132]

However, he advocated for reputation based upon an assessment of one's literary efforts, not whinging about "the gigantic task and colossal work. . . (and) of the difficulties that have been overcome".[133] Honest criticism was essential to writing as a profession, and reviews "influenced (consciously or not) by commercial considerations" were a scandal.[134]

Although he had previously published several short stories for modest sums, including some published by James Payn in the literary magazine *The Cornhill*, in keeping with the magazine's tradition, Doyle's early contributions were anonymous.[135] He described *A Study in Scarlet* as "fresher, crisper and more workmanlike" than his earlier efforts, which recently had included a historical novel, *The Firm of Girdlestone*, which he had failed to place. *A Study in Scarlet* also initially faced rejection: by *The Cornhill*, Arrowsmith (unread) and Frederich Warne. It was finally accepted by Ward, Lock & Co, hardly Doyle's preferred publisher. He described the firm as specialists in "cheap and often sensational literature". The firm refused his request for royalties, requiring full assignment of the copyright for £25.[136] Publication was then delayed due to a perceived glut of cheap fiction. It was published as "Beeton's Xmas Annual" of 1887, printed in London, New York and Melbourne, in a volume including two drawing room plays (with engravings).[137] It was priced at 1 shilling and included advertisements on the inside of front and back covers. It also included illustrations of a "tubby decadent" Sherlock Holmes and "stocky" Watson by DH Friston. It sold out in 14 days and was republished as a single 1 shilling volume in June 1888, with six new line drawings by the author's father, Charles Doyle. It was reprinted in 1889.[138] At this time there was no thought of a follow-up Sherlock Holmes story.

Doyle's next work, *Micah Clarke* (Longmans, 1889), was another historical novel. Though not a "boom book", it was favourably reviewed. It led to a dinner meeting with an American agent of Lippincott, also attended by Oscar Wilde. The outcome was that both authors were commissioned to write for *Lippincott's Monthly Magazine*. For £100 Doyle penned a second story containing Sherlock Holmes and Watson, *The Sign of the Four*, published in February 1890.[139] Wilde contributed *The Picture of Dorian Grey*, published in July. The magazine also sold for 1 shilling in the UK, 25 cents in the US. In addition, *The Sign of the Four* was published as a book edition by Lippincott in the US and Spencer Blackett in Britain, and also serialised in three provincial British newspapers.[140] Doyle's story was then republished in *Six Complete Novels by Famous Authors: From Lippincott's Monthly Magazine* by Ward, Locke and Co, 1890. Doyle then returned again to writing historical fiction, the genre in which he believed he produced his "higher work". *The White Company*, set at the time of Edward III, was serialised in *The Cornhill* from January to December 1891 with the by-line noting the author as "A Conan Doyle. Author of 'Micah Clarke'". It was published as a three-decker novel in the same year.[141]

Commercialising Holmes and Watson

RL Stevenson's *New Arabian Nights* (1882) and *More New Arabian Nights* (1885) and Poe's Dupin stories, had used a "connected story" to good effect.[142] The idea of constructing a connecting narrative and the attraction of monthly serialisation appealed to Doyle. Though he had earned little from his past writing,[143] he appreciated that his reputation was growing. His confidence was sustained by seeing more of *The White Company* appearing each month. However,

> Considering these various journals with their disconnected stories it had struck me that a single character running through a series, if it only engaged the attention of the reader, would bind that reader to that particular magazine. On the other hand, it had long seemed to me that the ordinary serial might be an impediment rather than a help to a magazine, since, sooner or later, one missed one number and afterwards it lost all interest. Clearly the ideal compromise was a character which carried through, and yet instalments which were each complete in themselves, so that the purchaser was always sure that he could relish the whole contents of the magazine. I believe that I was the first to realise this and "The Strand Magazine" the first to put it into practice.[144]

Doyle was acquainted with the founder of the Society of Authors, Walter Besant, who "estimated that there were some 15,000 people in London who followed a literary career. No more than fifty writers in Britain and the United States made £1,000 or more a year by writing novels".[145] Doyle calculated that with series he could earn up to four times as much from a single-volume publication.[146] Further, so long as he retained the rights, if the series proved successful it was then possible to publish a single volume with his name prominently on the cover as well.

Doyle sought Watt's assistance to place a series of six stories. Because the stories had not yet been written, the literary property could only be defined with reference to the recurring fictional characters and the author's name, with Watt pressing Doyle for the "exact working" for the "collective title of the Sherlock Holmes series".[147] It was "in effect, treated as a single commercial transaction"[148] with the royalty calculated by the word, a necessary consequence of the unfinished nature of the manuscripts.

The *Strand Magazine* was first produced in 1891 by George Newnes who had found success with *Tit-bits*, a magazine established with £500 capital from his Manchester vegetarian restaurant. It was pushed through WH Smith's bookstalls, for lower-middle class readers.[149] With *Strand Magazine*, Newnes had higher aspirations. He included 'Portraits of Celebrities' "engraved from photographs" in an attempt to sell space for a higher class of advertiser.[150] The format included 45% adult genre fiction, with stories designed to appeal to men and women, and 10% to children.[151] It was one of a few outlets that would publish stories over 8,500 words. The publishing strategy was based on "readability", not "a fetish of 'big names'".[152] Watt licensed publication rights at £4 per 1000 words. This amounted to just over £200 for the six stories, less Watt's commission which varied from 15% to 6% depending upon the value of his services for each story. Doyle's name soon became very well-known with queues forming at news-stands on publication day.[153] Watt also licensed the series to the owner of a newspaper syndicate in New York, SS McClure, for £50 (or £1 per 1,000 words), pressing both outlets to agree not to publish until the *Chace Act* came into effect in July 1891, whereby a British author could obtain an American copyright.[154] By October 1891 *Strand Magazine*'s Greenhough Smith requested a further six more stories, with Doyle upping his fee to £50 a story.

With the foresight to back himself, Doyle invested £250 in the first stock issue by Newnes. George Newnes Ltd was capitalised at £1,000,000 with the prospectus noting that *The Strand Magazine* sells 450,000 copies per month and growing, with very large circulation in America.[155] Recognising that his writing was increasing the value of the company, Doyle's investment would rise to £5,291 by the end of the year.[156] Circulation grew from 200,000 in February 1891 to 275,000 in 1892.[157] Following further requests for more stories, in early 1892 the royalty requested was £1000 for 12, with Doyle mistakenly thinking it might deter *Strand Magazine*. These stories were then collated into book form, *The Adventures of Sherlock Holmes*, also published by Newnes in late 1892. It had a print run of 10,000 copies, priced at 6 shillings with gilt edges, a light-blue cloth cover. It is described by McDonald as a "deluxe book-version of the *Strand Magazine* itself".[158]

Doyle did not treat Holmes and Watson as his exclusive personal property. As has been commented on with surprise by some biographers, Doyle was not concerned with closely controlling how his characters were represented by illustrators or on the stage. He imagined his creation as "more beaky-nosed, hawkfaced" than Sidney Paget's depiction with deerstalker cap and cape. The first authorised play was by American playwright, director and actor William Gillette, who added a pipe,

> Since he used my characters and to some extent my plots, he naturally gave me a share in the undertaking, which proved to be very successful. "May I marry Holmes?" was one cable which I received from him when in the throes of composition. "You may marry or murder or do what you like with him", was my heartless reply.[159]

Doyle noted that Paget and Gillette's characterisations of Sherlock were "very largely" the reason for his longevity.[160] He was genuinely surprised at receiving letters addressed to Holmes and Watson as if they were real people and was not prepared for the insults when he had the temerity to kill off Holmes in 1893 so that he might be free to write other fiction. He returned to writing further Sherlock stories in 1901 due to "the temptation of high prices".[161]

Doyle described Holmes as a character that,

> admits of no light or shade. He is a calculating machine, and anything you add to that simply weakens the effect. Thus the variety of the stories must depend upon the romance and compact handling of the plot.[162]

The mystery element – inventing a crime, a solution and then plotting the course of detection and unique characters – though tedious to execute, was a relatively easy formula to repeat. The challenge, as he saw it, was,

> now that I had no longer the excuse of absolute pecuniary pressure, never again to write anything which was not as good as I could possibly make it, and therefore I would not write a Holmes story without a worthy plot and without a problem which interested my own mind.[163]

This included imaginings of Victorian masculinity, foreign and exotic places, contagion, spiritualism and Empire.[164]

Doyle had to tolerate countless authorised and unauthorised adaptations, in books,[165] plays[166] and films.[167] There were also many parodies and pastiches, including some by Doyle himself, his friend, *Peter Pan* author JM Barrie, and Mark Twain.[168] His irritation at American piracies was diffused pragmatically and philosophically. He wrote letters to American journals complaining about the belated republication of early stories that "were meant to have the ephemeral life that they deserve".[169] In his memoir he noted that a consequence of a lack of a US copyright prior to 1891 led to "early American editions which might have been printed on the paper that shopmen use for parcels". He saw the cheapness of the publications inevitable when any other publisher might undersell the edition, with both American authors and publishers harmed because "what belongs to everyone belongs to no-one".[170]

How did Doyle understand his copyright?

What set Doyle apart from Conway and Hume was his appreciation that if the mode of exploitation was taken into account alongside the crafting of the story, and the story-telling style was paired to the name of the author, this could greatly affect the value of the copyright. While serialisation had significant potential to produce regular income and popular stories could thereafter follow in other formats, readership might be maximised if the narrative structure rewarded faithful and faithless readers alike. It was not serialisation that accounted for his early success. It was his recognition of the commercial value of the ephemeral properties associated with the story – the author's name, story titles, characters, stock elements. Though not directly protected by copyright law, these characteristics were integral to the generation of a reliable, distinctive identity that enhanced recognition of the author's name and creations in a mass market flooded with cheap literature. It was not simply the merit of the stories themselves that drove financial reward, but their positioning as a distinctive series that could distinguish his writing from other stand-alone stories. And of course, as well as investing in his characters, Doyle invested in his UK publisher's company as well.

Doyle's innovative story-telling occurred at a time when there was considerable debate about what acts constituted copyright infringement, and in particular the divide between a new work and an infringing adaptation.[171] At the same time that Doyle innovated with the form of story-telling, technical legal descriptions of what copyright law actually protected started to change. For example, in 1902 eminent copyright lawyer, EJ MacGillivray wrote, "Whether if no actual sentences be taken it is an infringement of copyright to take the characters, the sequence of events, and scenes, in short, the plot, is doubtful".[172] By 1911 MacGillivray had changed his mind about the same body of law,

> It has never actually been decided that it would be an infringement of the copyright in a play to take the plot, characters and principal situations and write a novel based thereon. It has been said that so long as there is no copying of the words there is no infringement. Probably, however, it is an infringement under the existing law.[173]

British and American jurisdictions both rejected the idea of copyright protection for "stock characters". While British courts did not go so far as to afford protection to characters independently of their expression in a particular story, US courts would eventually do so.[174]

The role of literary agent, AP Watt

Graham Law notes that Watt was one of the most significant literary agents of his time in part because he acted like a syndicator. He competed head to head with them, "writing round to large numbers of newspaper proprietors in order to set up simultaneous serialisation of his authors' latest novels".[175] His agency had both publishers and authors as clients. He tailored royalty negotiations to an assessment of the commercial value of the literary content. He told one interviewer,

> for different books different agreements. You cannot lay down a fixed rule for the sale of all books, and the royalty system is by no means good unless you are getting the proper royalty, a point which, . . . is governed by the selling price of the book, the cost of production, the probable sale, and other considerations.[176]

McDonald notes,

> Though primarily concerned with commercial value, he [Watt] inevitably based his always fallible decisions on considerations about his author's cultural status, the cultural value of their texts, and their suitability for certain markets and readerships.[177]

Watt's interest in tailoring copyright transactions to the specific cultural content and calculating an appropriate royalty in view of the particular market and readership facilitated a most profitable exploitation of Doyle's copyright. While it was the author that provided the impetus to develop licensing to better support the writing of connected narratives, Watt had the established networks, sufficient experience and reputation to convince Greenhough Smith to take a risk. *The Strand* was still in its early days and experimentation with the format was acceptable to readers. It was a fortunate combination of timing. By retaining long-term control over the rights, staging delivery dates for the Sherlock series, limiting the number of stories included in transactions, licensing reproduction in various formats and places, it was possible to periodically recalibrate the value of the enterprise to different parties at different points in time, as popular demand shifted and grew.

In the licensing of Sherlock stories, Watt was more than a middleman negotiating rights to a story or acting like a syndicator of serialisation rights. In the 1890s there was great uncertainty surrounding the public appetite for any particular story in a market flooded with cheap literature. Both Conway and Hume assigned rights to a boom story at a time when it was difficult to assess the fair value of the copyright for it. The willingness of their publishers to offer additional payments over and above what the law demanded points to a wider recognition of the unfairness of this situation for writers. However, boom books were hardly the norm. Doyle did not anticipate his authorship of a boom book, or even a boom series: "the character [of Sherlock] had a consistently unplanned influence over the course of his author's career".[178] Doyle sought Watt's assistance in licensing copyright to create more reliable, predictable income streams. Negotiation of acceptable terms was not dependent upon anticipation of creating a boom book to generate predictable custom in the first place. It was also not dependent upon crass commercialisation and self-promotion.[179] Though not anticipated from the outset, the author, his agent and many publishers soon correctly identified that the Sherlock series was a vehicle for assembling and aggregating pools of readers for a new sub-genre – the primary commodity produced by Doyle and Watt. It was different to established forms of newspaper syndication of stories because this was an author-centric and sub-genre specific commercialisation strategy not tied to any extant creative work. It reduced the risk associated with problems of literary quality and unpredictable demand for any particular story, while increasing the market value of the publishing outlets where future stories might appear. After the success of the first experiment, expansion of the enterprise did not expose author, agent or publisher to significant new financial risk or require additional capital outlay. As Watt's initial fee structure indicated, his workload diminished after the publication of the first story while the readership continued to grow.

Though Doyle's personal ethics meant that he remained loyal to *Strand Magazine* he resisted the offer of a retainer or formalising the arrangement.[180] This situation helped maintain a climate in which Watt could engage in vigorous negotiation for particular readerships across the full range of formats and releases. While Doyle complained that he was soon bored by the tedium of writing to a formula, he informed his agent that it only took him about a week to get one done.[181] His frustration with this model for exploitation of literary property is well summed up in his banter with Greenhough Smith, "You will be amused to hear that I am at work upon a Sherlock Holmes story. So the old dog returns to his vomit".[182] Doyle's experiment in story-writing suited maximal copyright exploitation. It supported the commodification of Sherlock audiences into the future, where renewal was always possible so long as new credible stories could materialise and the public did not tire of the formula altogether.

What the detective story reveals about copyright in modernity

In his 'A defence of detective stories', the creator of the "Father Brown" stories, GK Chesterton described this genre as "the earliest and only form of popular literature in which is expressed some sense of the poetry of modern life".[183] He goes on to define the detective novel with reference to Sherlock's preoccupation with descriptive minutiae – the "romance of detail in civilisation", as well as noting the genre's connection with humanism, psychology, and Christian morality. It is these very characteristics that irked some highbrow critics.[184]

Chesterton's allusion to "the poetry of modernity" also signals other aesthetics and rhythms of the early 20th century – the commodification of everyday life. The modern detective novel is a genre that capitalises on a productive dialogue between the familiar and the unexpected. The modern detective story is capable of producing dedicated communities of readers – followers of the form and character of the story-telling and the distinctive characters that propel the story forward. This form of story-telling is designed to surprise *and* withstand sustained repetition, simulation, variation and reinvention. By the 1930s Dorothy L Sayers would note that mystery stories were no longer read in back-kitchens but in Downing Street, Bloomsbury studios, bishop's palaces and kept in the libraries of eminent sciences, in part due to "so great and good a *vulgarisateur* as Sir Arthur Conan Doyle".[185] The golden period of 20th-century crime writing follows after Doyle. Well-known authors include GK Chesterton, Agatha Christie, Dorothy L Sayers, Dashiell Hammett, Ngaio Marsh, Josephine Tey, Margery Allingham, Georges Simenon and Raymond Chandler. That this genre would emerge alongside the development of the copyright agent, syndication and international law reform is no accident. The detective story is a form of cultural production that can be licensed to exceed the confines of an original publication in order to animate a following – to produce a future audience – the most valuable form of literary property that can be constructed in modernity. This is the reason Doyle and his estate did so well for so long, while Conway and Hume were less handsomely rewarded. Respective financial outcomes had nothing to do with luck, misfortune or authorial inexperience with publishers, but how the authors understood their financial prospects and played the publishing game to benefit from the greatly expanding opportunities for exploitation of copyright. The international dimension of this form is the focus of the next chapter.

Notes

1 See Ronan Deazley, 'Commentary on Copinger's Law of Copyright (1870)' in L Bently & M Kretschmer (eds), *Primary Sources on Copyright (1450–1900)*. www.copyrighthistory.org
2 Iterations include: Pauline M Kirk, 'Hume, Fergusson Wright (Fergus) (1859–1932)' in *National Centre of Biography, Australian Dictionary of Biography* (21 Jan 2012). http://adb.anu.edu.au/biography/hume-fergusson-wright-fergus-3817/text6053; Hugh Greene (ed), *The Penguin Complete Rivals of Sherlock Holmes* (Penguin 1983) 715–716; Simon Caterson, 'Fergus Hume's Startling Story' Inside Story (8 May 2012). http://inside.org.au/fergus-hume-startling-story; Lucy Sussex, *Blockbuster!: Fergus Hume and the Mystery of a Hansom Cab* (Text Publishing 2015)
3 4 Burr 2408, 98 Eng. Rep. 257
4 NN Feltes, *Literary Capital and the Late Victorian Novel* (U of Wisconsin P 1993)
5 Peter McDonald, *British Literary Culture and Publishing Practice 1880–1914* (CUP 1997)
6 Alexis Weedon, *Victorian Publishing: The Economics of Book Production for a Mass Market, 1836–1916* (Ashgate 2003)
7 Graham Law, *Serialising Fiction in the Victorian Press* (Palgrave Macmillan 2000)
8 McDonald (n 5) 118–171
9 Ibid 132
10 This thinking accords with what Feltes describes as an early or immature form of capitalism. (n 4) 66
11 Laurie Garrison, 'Taxonomies of Stimulation: Science, Gender and Sexuality in the Sensation Novel Debate' in *Science, Sexuality and the Sensation Novels, Pleasures of the Senses* (Palgrave Macmillan 2011)
12 These are just some of the themes discussed in Lynne Pykett, *Nineteenth Century Sensation Novels* (2nd ed, Liverpool UP 2011); Andrew Maunder (ed), *Sensationalism and the Sensation Debate* (Routledge 2016)
13 'The Enigma Novel', quoted in Garrison (n 11) 24
14 For literary influences see Anne Humphreys, 'British Detective Fiction in the 19th and Early 20th Centuries' in *Oxford Research Encyclopedia of Literature* (published online, OUP June 2017)
15 Simon Eliot and Andrew Nash, 'Mass Markets: Literature' in David McKitterick (ed), *The Cambridge History of the Book* (CUP 2009) 423
16 First publication in a newspaper or magazine did not preclude the author pursuing publication of a novel. s43 *Copyright Act* 1840, 5 & 6 Vict c45 recognised the right of authors to reserve the right to publish in book format where a story had first been published in a magazine or newspaper. If the full copyright had been assigned to the magazine publisher, it reverted to the author after 28 years. Alexis Weedon notes that the author may receive as much as £100 for a three-decker novel. See (n 6) 97
17 Eliot and Nash (n 15) 424
18 One study compares titles listed in Bibliotheca Londinensis 1800–1850 and Publishers' Circular 1900–1909. Simon Eliot, 'Some Trends in British Book Production' in John O Jordan and Robert L Patten (eds), *Literature in the Marketplace* (CUP 1995) 34–38
19 Ibid
20 Paul R Rooney, 'Festive Reading and Seasonal Terrors: Hugh Conway's Called Back (1883), Late Nineteenth-Century Gothic, and "Arrowsmith's Christmas Annual"' (2018) 23(4) Journal of Victorian Culture 556, 558–559
21 See Derek Miller, *Copyright and the Value of Performance 1770–1911* (CUP 2018) 183–203

22 Copyright Commission, *Report of the Royal Commission on Copyright* (C 2036, 1878) vii–viii
23 See Deazley (n 1)
24 These legal dynamics and the benefits to authors and publishers is the focus of the next chapter
25 See Brad Sherman and Lionel Bently, *The Making of Modern Intellectual Property* (CUP 1999); Isabella Alexander, *Copyright Law and the Public Interest in the Nineteenth Century* (Hart Publishing 2010)
26 Hugh Conway, *Called Back* (Collins Crime Club ed, JW Arrowsmith 1883/2015) 39
27 Ibid 54, 59
28 Royalty book, Records of JW Arrowsmith Ltd. BRO: 40145/P/1a
29 Graham Law, 'On Wilkie Collins and Hugh Conway "Poor Fargus"' (2000) 3 *The Wilkie Collins Journal*; Clement Scott, 'Echoes of the Week' 3 Dec 1887, republished as 'The Mystery of a Hansom Cab' *The Evening Star* (Otago), 21 Jan 1888, 2
30 Fred Fargus to JW Arrowsmith, 29 Oct 1884, Records of JW Arrowsmith Ltd. BRO: 40145/P/61
31 Royalty book, Records of JW Arrowsmith Ltd. BRO: 40145/P/1a
32 Registration 1 July 1884; Title: Called Back. A play in a prologue and three acts; Author: Hugh Conway and Fred Fargus. Proprietor Edgar Bruce, The Prince's Theatre; First performance 20 May 1884, The Prince's Theatre, Coventry St, London W TNA: COPY 3/221
33 John Parker (ed), *Who's Who in the Theatre* (8th ed, Pitman & Sons 1936) 1687, 1821; Marvin Lachman, *The Villainous Stage: Crime Plays on Broadway and in the West End* (MacFarlane Publishers 2014) 173; 'News of the Day' *The Age* (Melbourne) 4 July 1884, 4
34 Fred Fargus to JW Arrowsmith, 14 Nov 1883, BRO: Records of JW Arrowsmith Ltd. 40145/P/61
35 Fred Fargus to JW Arrowsmith, 23 May 1884, ibid
36 Fred Fargus to JW Arrowsmith, 4 June 1884, ibid
37 Fred Fargus to JW Arrowsmith, 10 Jan 1885, ibid
38 Richard Altick, *Victorian People and Ideas* (Dent & Co 1974) 175
39 See Leonore Davidoff and Catherine Hall, *Family Fortunes* (U of Chicago P 1987) 207–208; Mary P Ryan, *Cradle of the Middle Class* (CUP 1981) 140–142; Tracy C Davis, *The Economics of the British Stage 1800–1914* (CUP 2000) 294
40 Royalty Book, Records of JW Arrowsmith Ltd. BRO: 40145/P/1a
41 Fred Fargus to JW Arrowsmith, 6 June 1884, Records of JW Arrowsmith Ltd. BRO: 40145/P/61
42 JW Arrowsmith to HR Fargus, 13 Nov 1885; Agreement between Frederick J Fargus and Henry Holt & Co, 13 Aug 1884, ibid
43 Law (n 29)
44 An author's film right is discussed in detail in Chapter 5, 118–9
45 Presumably the negotiation with Macmillan happened alongside that over *Dark Days*. Law (n 29)
46 Ibid
47 Fergus Hume, 'Preface' in *The Mystery of a Hansom Cab* (Jarrold & Sons 1896) 9
48 John Holroyd, *George Robertson of Melbourne 1825–1989: Pioneer Bookseller & Publisher* (Robertson & Mullins 1968) 56
49 Hume (n 47) 11
50 Ibid
51 Greene (n 2) 716
52 Imitation of the best European works was frequently advocated as the remedy, especially when travel abroad would not always be possible to refine one's education. Chairman Sir Redmond Barry, Second Progress Report of the Commission on the Fine Arts 1864–5 (Vic). SLV: MS 7855; MS Box 1199/2
53 Robertson did publish four Marcus Clarke titles and Rolf Boldrewood's novel *Ups and Downs* (The Squatter's Dream); Holroyd (n 48) 47–48

54 Garrison (n 11) 8
55 'A Successful Australian Author' *The Evening Post* (Wellington) republished in *Tuapeka Times*, 23 May 1888, 3. My emphasis
56 Half of the colonial Australian novels were serialised and many stories only appeared in serial form. The number of published books in Australia was, overall, very small. The top three book publishers in 1860–1899 were Sampson Low (UK: 15 titles; 4%); Richard Bentley (UK: 13 titles 3%) Chapman & Hall (UK: 9 titles); George Robertson (Aust: 9 titles; 2%); The Author (Aust: 9 titles; 2%); Tinsley (UK: 9 titles; 2%). Katherine Bode, 'Sidelines and Trade-Lines: Publishing the Australian Novel 1860–1899' (2012) 15 *Book History* 93–94; Katherine Bode, *Reading by Numbers, Recalibrating the Literary Field* (Anthem Press 2012) 44
57 Census of England and Wales, 1891, Preliminary Report and Tables of Population and Houses enumerated in England and Wales, and Islands in British Seas, Great Britain. Parliament. House of Commons, 1891; Census of Victoria, 1891, Robert S Brain, Government Printer, Melbourne, 1891
58 'The Author of Madame Midas' *Illustrated London News*, 6 Oct 1888, 410
59 Garrison (n 11) 10
60 Kristine Moruzi, *Constructing Girlhood through the Periodical Press, 1850–1915* (Ashgate 2012) 34
61 Garrison (n 11) 10
62 Fergus Hume, *Mystery of a Hansom Cab* (1st ed, Kemp & Boyce 1887), SLNSW: DSM C808-1; 823/H921/1A1
63 Michael Cannon, *The Land Boomers* (Melbourne UP 1967) 12
64 See Nathaniel Lindley et al, *A Treatise on the Law of Companies* (5th ed, Sweet and Maxwell 1889); John Waugh, 'Company Law and the Crash of the 1890s in Victoria' (1991) 15(2) UNSWLJ 356
65 Cannon (n 63) 12
66 Charles Hickson and John D Turner, 'Free Banking Gone Awry: The Australian Banking Crisis of 1893' (2002) 9 Financ. Hist. Rev. 155; Waugh (n 64) 357
67 Cannon (n 63) 12
68 Hickson and Turner (n 66)
69 Cannon (n 63) 18
70 Register of proprietors of copyright of literary, dramatic and musical productions (Victoria), NAA: A2389, 3036
71 There is no evidence that there was concern for piracies in circulation. Lucy Sussex suggests Hume's friend Alice Cornwell, part inspiration for Madame Midas, was a source of funds for some of his ventures but she was unlikely to have funded the whole printing. Sussex also speculates that Hume had worked as a bank clerk and may have been a personal friend of Jessie Taylor, a baker's wife (n 2) 121, 153–154
72 *Copyright Act* 1842 (UK), ss11, 13, 24
73 Register of proprietors of copyright of literary, dramatic and musical productions (Victoria), NAA: A2389, 3036b
74 Michael Cannon, 'G.N. Taylor and the Land Credit Bank' in his *The Land Boomers, the Complete Illustrated History* (Lloyd O'Neill 1972) 185–189; 'Land Credit Bank v Taylor' *The Argus* (Melbourne) 20 Feb 1892, 5
75 'The Courts' *Evening News* (Sydney) 3 Apr 1890, 6
76 Lucy Sussex suggests that this printing was at the instigation of Fergus Hume. If so, any friendship she surmised had existed between the banker's wife and the author must have deteriorated (n 2) 166
77 'A Publisher's Programme for 1889' *Pall Mall Gazette* (London) 29 Jan 1889
78 'A Successful Australian Author' *The Evening Post* (Wellington) republished in *Tuapeka Time*, 23 May 1888, 3
79 *Routledge v Low* (1868) LR 3 HL 100. See Chapter 4, 71
80 Trischler claimed he worked in San Francisco for AL Bancroft & Co, "the biggest publishing firm on the Pacific slope". He then moved to Melbourne to manage the branch

office which soon closed after Bancroft merged with a successful legal publisher, Sumner Whitney in 1886. Elede Toppy Hall, *The Bancroft-Whitney Company: Roots of a Legal Publisher* (California Historical Society 1981) 3; 'A Successful Australian Author' (n 78); 'A Publisher's Programme for 1889' *Pall Mall Gazette* (London) 29 Jan 1889

81 Sussex claims the offer was from Routledge for £100 – double what Hume got from Taylor/Trischler and would not have sold his copyright had he known. But Trischler does not date his information and cannot be considered a reliable source for business details, so the international interest may date from after the sale. The Routledge & Kegan Paul archives do not include any copy-books of general correspondence

82 This includes *A Woman Scorned* and *Dr Faustus* and *Little Don Giovanni* staged in 1886 by the Amy Horton Burlesque Company. 'A Chat with Mr. Fergus Hume' *The Maitland Mercury & Hunter River General Advertiser (NSW)* 18 Aug 1888; Veronica Kelly, *Annotated Calendar of Plays Premiered in Australia 1870–1890* (Department of English, U of Queensland P 1997) 251, 254–255

83 Fergus Hume, 'Letter to the Editor' dated May 4, 1887 'The Mormon' *The Era* (London) 18 June 1887

84 'A Chat with Mr. Fergus Hume' *The Maitland Mercury and Hunter River General Advertiser (NSW)* 18 Aug 1888

85 Whilst challenged by the quality of the reproduction and the lack of a population of signatures to compare, an experienced police forensic scientist advised that "The questioned signatures could be genuine, simulated or disguised . . . there is qualified support for the proposition that the writer of the Taylor signature at the apex of the form did not write the signature at the base". Private correspondence received by the author, 14 Dec 2015

86 'London Gossip' *Birmingham Daily Post* (England) 16 Dec 1887. My emphasis

87 Lindley et al (n 64); Book One: 68–81; Book Three: 345–379

88 'Anglo-Colonial Gossip December 14' *South Australian Register* (Adelaide) 17 Jan 1889, 6

89 Sussex notes that it was the same cover, but the text was reset, some errors were corrected and some of the language was toned down (n 2) 153

90 'Popular Fiction' *Jackson's Oxford Journal* (Oxford) 19 May 1888

91 'Publishing Extraordinary' *Western Mail* (Cardiff, Wales) 10 Mar 1888

92 'On Literary "Hits"' *The Leeds Mercury* (England) 24 Mar 1888

93 'Anglo-Colonial Notes' *Auckland Star* (Auckland) 2 Feb 1888, 5

94 'Civiana' *Otago Daily Times* (Otago) 15 June 1888, 3

95 Parodies include: 'The Mystery of a Handsome Man' Author/Composer: Walter Burnett, 15 Harold Rd, Upton Park, Essex: Author; Alfred Albert Lee, 15 Brunswick Terrace, Grosvenor Park, Camberwell. Composer; Proprietor: Harry Beaumont, 26 Dante Rd, Newington Butts, SE, William Feetham Fletcher, 49 Hayle St, SE; First performance: 15 Aug 1888 Montpeliere Music Hall, Walworth. TNA: COPY 3/221; W Humer Ferguson, *The Mystery of a Wheelbarrow; or, Gaboriau gaborooed: An Idealistic Story of a Great and Rising Colony* (Walter Scott 1888); W Humer Ferguson, 'The Mystery of a Handsome Cap' in R Andre (ed), *Plays for Amateur Actors* (Ward, Lock & Co 1890); 'Mystery of a Hansom Cab' words by EW Rogers; music by AE Durandeau, Francis Bros & Day, London, Undated; Public Notices, *Auckland Star* (Auckland) 18 Aug 1888, 1

96 Ignatius Feece, 'The Great Cryptogammon: Showing the Real Authorship of the "Hansom Cab"' *Otago Daily Times* (Otago) 11 Sept 1888, 3

97 'A Publisher's Programme for 1889 and Some Account of the Hansom Cab Publishing Co' *The Pall Mall Gazette* (London) 29 Jan 1889

98 'The "Jubilee Plunger's" Book' *The York Herald* (England) 10 Dec 1889; 'The Mystery of Mr Benzon's Book' *Lloyd's Weekly Newspaper* (London) 15 Dec 1889

99 The first press report that Hansom Cab Publishing company was ceasing to operate is dated August 1889, though works continued to be released for a short time after. 'Our Anglo-Colonial Letter'. London 16 Aug 1889 republished in *The Advertiser* (Adelaide) 23 Sept 1889, 6

100 Trischer & Co Ltd was incorporated in 1892 and went bankrupt in 1895. The seven subscribers self-described as two publishers, two solicitors, a clerk, a 'gentleman' and a 'traveller'. Trischler and Coy Ltd. Incorporated in 1892. Dissolved before 1916. TNA: BT 31/5324/36461

101 His passing in 1913 is noted in Parker (n 33)

102 Registration dated 24 Feb 1888, Title: 'The Mystery of a Hansom Cab' (Dramatic piece). Author/Composer: William Arthur Law, 223 Elgin Ave, Maiden Vale, Middlesex and Fergus Wright Hume of Melbourne in the Colony of Victoria; Proprietor Grace Hawthorne, Princess's Theatre, Oxford St, Middlesex; First performance 25 Feb 1888, Princess's Theatre, Oxford St, London. TNA: COPY 3/221. With no surviving contract it is not clear what royalty or fee was requested for the assignment to Hawthorne

103 ST Travers, Mystery of a Hanson Cab, unperformed dramatic work (Victoria) 20 July 1888, NAA: A2389, 3553; *The Colonist* (Launceston) 1 Sept 1888, 13; *Evening Post* (Wellington) 11 Dec 1888; Sussex (n 2) 167–168

104 'Long Runs on the London Stage' in Parker (n 33) 1749, 1832; Lachman (n 33) 12. Sussex suggests the play did not closely follow the novel and that Hume had little role in its writing. (n 2) 164

105 It ran at the Princess Theatre, Oxford St, London, a theatre managed by an American actress, Priscilla Cartland, whose stage name was Grace Hawthorne. Marieanne Collins and Dick Weindling, *The Marquis de Leuville: A Victorian Fraud?* (The History Press 2012) 191–192

106 'The Mystery of a Hansom Cab' *The Era* (London) 25 Feb 1888

107 'On Literary "Hits"' *The Leeds Mercury* (England) 24 Mar 1888

108 Agreement between Trischler & Co bankruptcy trustees George Marsden Esq & Alfred Saunders Walford Esq & Jarrold & Sons, dated 8 May 1894. NRO: JLD 3/3/4. They paid £125 for the entire copyright to *The Mystery of Landy Court*

109 Publications review scrapbook, 26 Feb 1891–17 Aug 1895. NRO: JLD 3/3/6/2/3, p376. Jarrold also sold the German translation rights for Landy Court for £10–4 in 1894, and soon after English rights edition rights to Wakefield Press for £5

110 Copyright & Royalty Payments books, 24 Apr 1896–24 Aug 1912. NRO: JLD 3/3/4/2/8. I could not discern from the records what the royalties amounted to; however, from accounts concerning printing and binding costs it appears that between 2,500–3,600 copies were still being printed in 1910, another 700 more in 1911

111 Another mystery or thriller writer of note published by Jarrold & Sons in the same period was Thomas Wilkinson Speight (1830–1915)

112 In addition to their own 3/6 edition, they sold the 6 shilling edition rights to C Arthur Pearson & Co in 1907 for a further £100 and there was sufficient trade that Pearson negotiated for 7 shilling edition rights in 1915 (the year that Ideal Films made a film of the story in Britain), initially anticipating continuing with both versions but later deciding against the purchase. Publishing Agreements. Authors O–Z, 1895–1932, NRO: JLD 3/3/4/1/3

113 The firm was established in 1899. See Curtis Brown, *Contacts* (Harper & Brothers 1935) 4

114 There are only incomplete receipts for the year 1916. Receipts for copyright and royalty payments A–Z, 10 Mar 1876–15 Jan 1918, NRO: JLD 3/3/4/2/4

115 'Fergus Hume Fund' *Truth* (Sydney) 6 Sept 1925, 12

116 *The Mystery of a Hansom Cab* (1911), Dir: WJ Lincoln (1870–1917), Prod: Amalgamated Pictures; *Called Back* (1911) Dir: WJ Lincoln (1870–1917), Prod: Amalgamated Pictures; *The Mystery of a Hansom Cab* (1915), Prod: Ideal Films (1915); *The Mystery of a Hansom Cab* (1925), Dir: Arthur Shirley; Prod: Pyramid Pictures

117 The contract provided that Jarrold & Sons were entitled to a percentage of gross receipts on hiring: 5% in the British Isles, 7.5% in countries who were signatories to the Berne Convention (including France, Germany, Spain, Italy and British dominions) and 3% elsewhere (such as in the United States). Publishing Agreements. Authors O–Z, 1895–1932, NRO: JLD 3/3/4/1/3

118 There is no reliable bibliographical study of this minor author and many unreliable ones
119 See Greene (n 2) 715
120 'Fergus Hume Fund' *Truth* (Sydney) 6 Sept 1925, 12
121 Ibid
122 'Novelist's Life-Long Dilemma: Condemned to Write Detective Tales' *Daily Mail Atlantic Edition* (London) 24 Nov 1925, 11. My emphasis
123 Probate records reveal that when he died in 1932 he left a modest estate of £201 6s
124 Michael Sims, *Arthur & Sherlock* (Bloomsbury 2017) 145
125 Arthur Conan Doyle, *Memories and Adventures* (Hodder & Stoughton 1924, OUP reprint 1989) 74
126 Sir Arthur Conan Doyle, *The Complete Sherlock Holmes Long Stories* (John Murray, 1929, 14th impression Jonathon Cape 1977) 100
127 Ibid 122
128 McDonald (n 5) 121
129 'A Dinner to Mr. Doyle' *The Critic* 1 Aug 1896, No 754, 78–79
130 McDonald (n 5) 125
131 'Literary Etiquette' *The Daily Chronicle* 7 Aug 1897, republished in John Michael Gibson and Michael Lancelyn Green (eds), *Letters to the Press: The Unknown Arthur Conan Doyle* (Secker & Warburg 1986), 52–53
132 Doyle (n 125) 74
133 'Literary Etiquette' *The Daily Chronicle* 7 Aug 1897, republished in Gibson and Green (n 131) 52
134 Doyle complained of the placing of book reviews by the same reviewer using non de plumes in numerous papers creating a false impression about interest in the title. 'The Ethics of Criticism' *The Daily Chronicle*, 16 May 1899, republished in Gibson and Green (n 131) 56
135 Doyle notes he received £4 for the first stories and £30 for *Captain of the Polestar* (n 132) 73; McDonald (n 5) 125
136 Doyle (n 125) 75
137 The plays were R Andre, 'Food for Powder' (who also penned a parody of *The Cab*) and CJ Hamilton, *The Four Leaved Shamrock* (Baker Street Irregulars 1960)
138 Martin Booth, *The Doctor and the Detective: A Biography of Sir Arthur Conan Doyle* (Thomas Dunne, St Martin's 2000) 110
139 Arthur Conan Doyle, *The Sign of the Four*, Shafquat Towheed ed (Broadview Editions 2010) 40
140 McDonald (n 5) 137
141 Douglas Kerr, *Conan Doyle: Writing, Profession and Practice* (Oxford Scholarship Online 2013) 10
142 McDonald (n 5) 139
143 His career as a short-story writer in 1883–1884 brought him an estimated £10–15 a year, with his medical practice improving from £154 in 1882 to £300 in 1895. McDonald (n 5) 126
144 Doyle (n 125) 95–96
145 Kerr (n 141) 9
146 Ibid 13
147 Peter McDonald, 'The Adventures of the Literary Agent: Conan Doyle, AP Watt, Holmes and the Strand in 1891' (1997) 30(1) Vic Period Rev 17, 19
148 McDonald (n 5) 140
149 Ibid 146
150 Reginald Pound, *The Strand Magazine, 1891–1950* (Heinemann 1966) 21, 34
151 McDonald (n 5) 154
152 Pound (n 150) 37
153 Booth (n 138) 145

154 McDonald (n 147) 20–21
155 Pound (n 150) 49
156 McDonald (n 147) 22
157 McDonald (n 5) 156
158 Andrew Lycett, *The Man Who Created Sherlock Holmes: The Life and Times of Sir Arthur Conan Doyle* (Free Press 2007) 189; McDonald (n 5) 119
159 Doyle (n 125) 102
160 McDonald (n 5) 158
161 Doyle (n 125) 100
162 Ibid 108
163 Ibid 97
164 See for example, McDonald (n 5) 122–123; Lisa Fluet, '"Distinct Vocations" and the Anglo-Indian in Sherlock Holmes' England' (1998) 24(2) Vic Rev 130; Angela Fowler, 'Arthur Conan Doyle's Spiritualist British Commonwealth: "The Great Unifying Force"' (2016) 59(4) ELT, 1880–1920 456; Susan Cannon Harris, 'Pathological Possibilities: Contagion and Empire in Doyle's Sherlock Holmes Stories' (2003) 31(2) Vic Lit Cul 447; Leslie Haynsworth, 'Sensational Adventures: Sherlock Holmes and His Generic Past' (2001) 44(4) ELT, 1880–1920, 459
165 See for example, Donald A Redmond, *Sherlock Holmes among the Pirates: Copyright and Conan Doyle in America 1890–1930* (Greenwood Press 1990)
166 Amnon Kabatchnik, *Sherlock Holmes on the Stage: A Chronological Encyclopedia of Plays Featuring the Great Detective* (Scarecrow Press 2008)
167 Denis Gifford's study of *Books, Plays and Films 1896–1915* lists an extraordinary 23 films featuring Sherlock Holmes. The first 11 were produced before the author's exclusive right to adapt a story for film was legislated, but it also likely that many were also unauthorised. Denis Gifford, *Books, Plays and Films 1896–1915* (McFarlane, Mansell 1991) 49
168 'Pastiches and Parodies' *The Arthur Conan Doyle Encyclopedia*, www.arthur-conan-doyle.com/index.php/Pastiches_&_Parodies; Martin Kaye, *The Game Is Afoot: Parodies, Pastiches and Ponderings of Sherlock Holmes* (St Martin's Press 1994)
169 'A Protest from Dr Conan Doyle' *The Critic* 2 Dec 1893, republished in Gibson and Green (n 131) 42
170 Doyle (n 125) 77
171 Alexander (n 25) 280–282
172 EJ MacGillivray, *The Law of Copyright* (John Murray 1902) 112
173 EJ MacGillivray, *The Copyright Act 1911, Annotated* (Stevens & Sons 1912) 20
174 Whether copyright protection of fictional characters is feasible, good policy or that this actually impacts upon the value and longevity of the franchise remains contentious. For the UK position see: *Tate v Fulbrook* [1908] 1 KB 21; *Corelli v Gray* (1913) 29 TLR 570; *Tate v Thomas* [1921] 1 Ch 503; *Bagge v Miller* (1917–23) MacG CC 179. For the US position see *Nichols v Universal Pictures Corp.*, 45 F.2d 119 (2d Cir. 1930), cert. denied, 282 U.S. 902 (1931); Zahr K Said, 'Fixing Copyright in Characters: Literary Perspectives on a Legal Problem' (2013) 35 Cardozo L Rev 769. For a discussion of copyright and fictional characters see, Heather Schubert, 'It's Elementary: Why We Need a New Copyright Standard, with Statutory Guidance, for Characters In a Series' (2015) 12 Rutgers JL & Pub Pol'y 216; Elizabeth Rosenblatt, 'The Adventures of the Shrinking Public Domain' (2015) 86(2) UCLR 561; David Lindsay, 'Franchises, Imaginary Worlds, Authorship and Fandom' in K Bowrey and M Handler (eds), *Law and Creativity in the Age of the Entertainment Franchise* (CUP 2014) 52
175 Law (n 7) 101
176 FW, 'An Interview with AP Watt' *The Bookman* Oct 1892, 20, 22
177 McDonald (n 146) 23
178 McDonald (n 5) 142

179 Doyle was not against advertising per se. He funded small advertisements for the book edition of *The Adventures of Sherlock Holmes*. McDonald (n 5) 126
180 Ibid 142
181 Ibid 138
182 Ibid 144
183 GK Chesterton, 'A Defence of Detective Stories' 22 June 1901 in his *The Defendant* (R Brimley Johnson 1901)
184 McDonald (n 5) 118–121
185 Dorothy L Sayers, 'The Present Status of the Mystery Story' *London Mercury* 23 Nov 1930, 47–52

4 Imperial copyright and its costs

The phrase "imperial copyright" immediately conjures an image of king and country, times of international piracy and geopolitical turmoil. It speaks first and foremost to the interest of the Crown and Empire and only secondarily to the author and publisher. Intuitively the entire concept of imperial copyright seems archaic and incongruent with modernity. This chapter looks at the reason why we have become so accustomed to thinking about copyright and modernity, blotting out the significance of it having an imperial legal heritage. It explores the legacy of author-centric advocacy in the late 19th century in building the legal infrastructure of international copyright. This advocacy profiled the importance of the celebrity author to civilised society, leading to the remit of copyright coming to be understood quite narrowly, in terms of its importance to a particular genre – the novel. A trans-Atlantic settlement over American piracy not only secured British copyrights in the US, but propelled the interests of established London- and New York-based publishing houses abroad, transforming them into multi-national publishing firms. This development has had long-lasting consequences for cultural production, consumption and distorted literary markets, dividing global book distribution into two spheres. This outcome has impacted the profitability of independent publishing in Australia, New Zealand and Canada, whilst also significantly increasing the importance of two related market sectors, educational publishing and academic and professional publishing, in these markets.

This chapter shows why international copyright is imperial by design. It does not create a level playing field when it comes to the distribution of opportunities for authors and consumers. Accordingly, understanding how to navigate this terrain is very important to survival as a professional writer, as well as the political significance of contemporary law reform advocacy that seeks to defend the status quo in the name of authors' rights.

The imperial legal foundations of British copyright

As discussed in Chapter 2, there are many conventional historical works that discuss the British origins of copyright in the English-speaking world. These writings treat copyright as first and foremost a legal phenomenon, where the rights defined in legislation have cultural consequences. In explaining copyright's progress, works usually trace the territorial expansion of control over the free movement of literary works through the strengthening of property rights across time and space, stretching from a metropolitan centre to the periphery. Anglo-copyright grows from a localised origin with the 17th-century trade practices of the Stationer's Company of London where it was claimed as a perpetual property, but of limited purchase. It comes to encompass all of Great Britain with the passing of the first copyright legislation, the *Statute of Anne* (1710), exporting copyright control to Scotland and Ireland where the Stationer's Company's writ did not run.[1] This statute is confirmed as the legal foundation for the modern right in *Donaldson v Beckett* (1774),[2] with a maximum term of 28 years. As Britain was also a colonial power, through this and related statutory reforms in the 19th century, copyright potentially reaches across all of the British Empire alongside the raising of the Union Jack.[3] Under an 1814 amendment, copyright in books was made applicable across the Empire and the copyright term was extended for the natural life of the author, if they had survived the initial 28-year term.[4] The *Copyright Act* 1842 further extended the copyright term for books for whichever term was longer – published in the life of the author for a life term plus seven years or a post-mortem term of 42 years.[5] In the *International Copyright Acts* of 1838 and 1844, Britain began to address the status of foreign imports and support the pursuit of reciprocal copyright agreements.[6] The *Copyright Act* 1842 also potentially applied to foreign authors, as works of foreign authors first published in Britain by British publishers could secure a British copyright.[7]

Colonial legislatures could, of course, also create additional or supplementary laws where these did not conflict with British legislation.[8] This was largely imagined as a tinkering with UK laws as fitted local circumstances and educational needs, nested within the larger framework of British design that sought to facilitate and strengthen Empire.[9] Until 1931 there remained a power to strike down colonial laws that were inconsistent with those of Britain,[10] though the political stakes in considering this with respect to copyright were high, with the danger of fuelling rebellion.

The 1842 *Act* also explicitly prohibited reprinting works in the British dominions without permission of the British copyright owner. Importation of other than personal copies into Britain and her dominions from America was also prohibited.[11] Catherine Seville notes, the "home and colonial markets were very different in their requirements and characteristics. . . . British Publishers seemed remarkedly unresponsive to colonial needs".[12] Nevertheless, in response to largely colonial Canadian objections to the prohibitions in the 1842 *Act*, the *Foreign Reprints Act* 1847 (10 & 11 Vict c95) permitted the rights of British authors to be suspended in the colonies, subject to the local legislature introducing a scheme to compensate affected authors, with only the Australian colonies not seeking to do so.[13] However, returns to British authors from these reprint schemes were notoriously low[14] and the law struggled with its interface with customs, responsible for seizing piracies when these were notified to them by British publishers.[15] Seville writes that the poor selection of titles led to some British publishers producing "colonial libraries".[16] However, the export of British fiction from London (rather than the US) was largely perceived as a mechanism for extending imperial control over its dispersed populations.[17] Selection was driven by considerations of what colonials "should" read. Light and low reading was not well catered for. Pirating stories in newspapers and importing American piracies into the colonies filled the void.

The idea that this was a one-way trade managed from London was reconfirmed with the 1868 House of Lords decision, *Routledge v Low*.[18] It determined that copyright only applied to works first published in the UK and to gain a British copyright the residency of an alien author need be in Great Britain. It was no longer treated as sufficient for foreign authors to temporarily reside in Canada or the British Caribbean to obtain a British copyright. This was an unwelcome decision for American authors and publishers but for them, Seville notes, it was manageable.[19] Less so for colonial authors who first published in the colonies. Unless writers had sufficient wherewithal to travel and contacts to facilitate a British publication, it left their works only protected in the local jurisdiction or entirely in the public domain, able to be pirated in the UK, all her dominions and the US. As such, testing interest with a local publication of a novel was not a stepping stone to larger success for colonial writers – more an obstacle to be avoided.

The UK Copyright Commission (1878) that sought to reform the law addressed Home, Colonial and International copyright as separate headings. "Home" set the main agenda and colonials were largely embraced within this, which left the separate heading of "Colonial copyright" constructing them as consumers of British publications,

> It must be highly desirable that the literature of this country should be placed within easy reach of the colonies, and that with this view the Imperial Act should be modified so as to meet the requirements of colonial readers.[20]

As Michael Birnhack observes, "When the British discussed colonial copyright, they meant *their own interests in the colonies*. They hardly referred to the local cultural and legal interests". Accordingly, he argues that colonial copyright is "a legal and cultural category about the diffusion and transplanting of the legal field that regulates some of the main institutional aspects of culture, under conditions of an imperial rule".[21] The notion of "their own interests" was a complicated multi-layered construct. Arguably much of the content of Britain's international copyright relations stemmed from attempts to maintain imperial control over legal developments and influence the culture and politics of colonies and British dominions.

Great Britain's signing of the *Berne Convention for the Protection of Literary and Artistic Works 1886* foreshadowed further international expansion of the copyright landscape. Article 19 provided that, "Countries acceding to the present Convention shall also have the right to accede thereto at any time for their colonies or foreign possessions". By general declaration the accession of Great Britain to the convention bound all colonies and foreign possessions of Her Majesty. The extent of British territories can be seen from Figure 4.1. Nevertheless, the British government asserted the liberty for India, Canada, Newfoundland, the Cape, Natal, New Zealand and the Australian colonies to make a denunciation at any time separately.[22] Section 9 of the *International Copyright Act* 1886 (49 & 50 Vict c 33) confirmed the power of the imperial Parliament to both enter into copyright agreements on behalf of her dominions, as well as declare they not apply. As will be discussed, the scope of this power would be challenged by Canada. Section 8 recognised the authority of dominion copyright registrations, meaning that rights first registered in a colony could be enforced in a British court if a copy made under seal could be produced as evidence. Details of colonial registrations were often re-entered by British publishers into the Stationer's Company register. It was not until 1928, following the Balfour Declaration of the 1926 Imperial Conference of the British Empire, that Australia, Canada, India, New Zealand and South Africa affirmed a commitment to the Berne Convention in their own right.

When copyright history is read through this legal lens – a focus on the positive laws created – the discussion fixates on the interests and motivations of those who are assumed to be the most important and powerful actors – the big nation states. Colonials are included in the discussion as markets fought over, more than as peoples. The right to control markets in the colonies and dominions is assumed to be part of any trans-Atlantic legal settlement, where a political settlement was required because the US had asserted its domestic cultural, educational and trade interests ahead of international copyright accord, electing not to sign the Berne Convention. The US did come to offer a precarious path for protection of foreign copyrights with the *Chace Act* (1891)[23] which is further discussed later.

Legal perspectives on copyright's global expansion focus on the technical imperfections and limitations of the right, suggesting a move toward a more expansive right – in territory, scope and time – is a natural progression rather than a political decision. With regard to Anglo-copyright, lawyers intuitively prioritise identification of the source of legal power that creates British property rights and in so doing they cannot but acknowledge the significance of the imperial power. Any basic legal education explains how English property rights in land were originally derived from feudal grants from the Crown. The right to seize Indigenous lands and reallocate them to settler owners relied upon this same doctrinal foundation. Early forms of intellectual property rights for printers, letter patents, were also derived from the Crown. The interpretation of the *Statute of Anne* in *Donaldson v Beckett* (1774) also further confirmed the constitutional power of Great Britain to determine the limits of any literary property right, notwithstanding any claim founded on natural law or the traditions of common law. It is the eternal and manifest power of the Crown that is

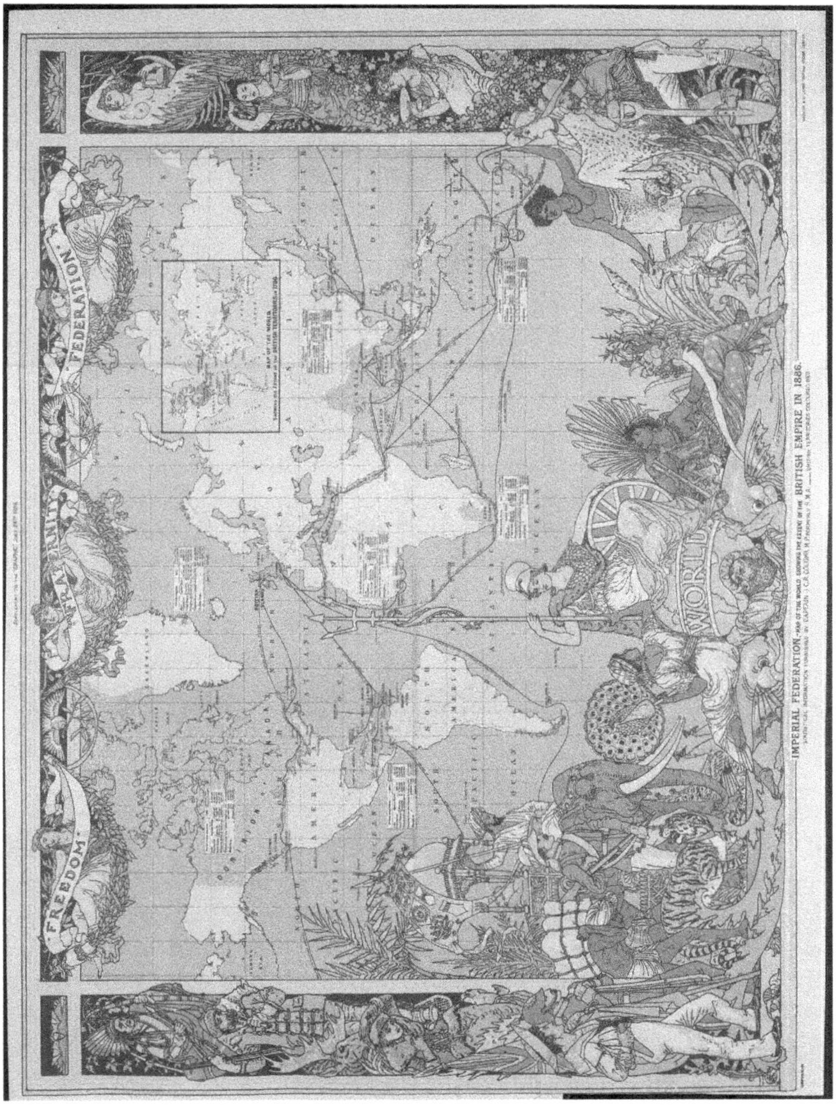

Figure 4.1 Walter Crane, Imperial Federation, Map of the world showing the extent of the British Empire 1886

Source: Supplement to *The Graphic*, 24 July 1886

not spoken of, when statutes acknowledge that Anglo-copyright is a creature of positive law.

But how do we get from this monarchical legal foundation to an effective justification for copyright in modernity, especially in former colonies? To understand how and why colonials supported imperial and international copyright, despite its imperfections, there is a need to consider economic, cultural and political perspectives of authors and readers. The legal framework of power suggests that colonial authors were disinterested in, unwilling or unable to assert their own interests because of their subordinate position within a monarchical structure. However, very little is conveyed of how copyright was understood across the Empire in the 19th century. There were actually good reasons for sophisticated professional authors in the colonies to support imperial law at that time, despite its shortcomings.

Routledge v Low (1868) was clearly unfair to colonial authors who were unaware that local publication affected their British copyright. However, a lively culture of newspaper republication was actively promoted in the colonies. In some Australian colonies a bespoke telegraphy copyright encouraged syndication of news and serialised fiction.[24] Through this mechanism, colonials were kept abreast of British and international political debates. Many understood how copyright functioned to their advantage and disadvantage.

In the aftermath of *Routledge v Low* a petition to the British Parliament protesting the state of colonial copyright was lodged in the Melbourne Athenaeum club for signatures, it being noted in the press that,

> The injustice of this state of the law is so patent that comment upon it is quite superfluous. . . . It may be that few of the works yet published in Victoria are of sufficient consequence to occasion us any concern as to the state of the law of copyright. Without discussing this view of the subject, I will simply direct attention to the fact that while the law stands at present it is very unlikely that any serious efforts will be made here to create a literature of our own.[25]

This echoed similar complaints in Canada, where the stakes were higher due to proximity to the US.[26] However, this petition was not a call to copyright independence. While recognising injustice in the current situation it is important not to forget that many colonial authors and readers culturally identified with British literary culture and some, *only* with British culture. There were sound reasons why colonial authors would have wanted their works recognised and respected in the Mother Country, regardless of copyright technicalities formally requiring first publication in the UK.

In the second half of the 19th century the number of books published in Australia and Canada was, overall, very small. In terms of bibliometric data on the Australian publications, half of colonial Australian novels were serialised and many colonial Australian stories only appeared in serial form.[27] At this time, newspaper serialisation did not necessarily imperil a UK copyright in the book.[28] Where a story had proven popular through serialisation in the colonies, it could still be offered to the British trade. If interest could be solicited and the logistics arranged, it made far more financial sense to publish in London from the start, where large established publishers facilitated staged exploitation of fiction, as discussed in Chapter 3.

By way of example, Rolf Boldrewood, a pseudonym for Thomas Alexander Browne (1826–1915), first published his story *Robbery under Arms* in serialised form in Victoria during 1882–1883 where the individual stories were protected under the colonial *Copyright Act* 1869 (Vic) (only). However, the three-volume edition was then published by Remington & Co in London in 1888 and this new literary compilation was governed by the *Copyright Act* 1842. This issue was subject to a profit-sharing arrangement with the publisher, with the author entitled to 2/3 gross proceeds minus advertising. Boldrewood retained copyright in the entire work. He then authorised a one-volume abridgement of the story by Macmillan. Macmillan also purchased Remington's reprinting right and the right to print cheap editions for £50 in 1889. Boldrewood was entitled to 4d per copy in England and colonies.[29] It is probable that the Remington publication in 1888 that occurred without first registration of any performance right would have extinguished the performance right in the UK. A performance right to the dramatic work was nonetheless first registered under the colonial *Copyright Act 1869* (Vic) by Alfred Dampier in 1890 and under the *Copyright Act 1842* (UK) in 1894.[30] As this example shows, Empire trade was not entirely one way, nor governed by strict adherence to legal technicality. It was supported by men of letters in the colonies for economic and cultural reasons, though rights management over the life of the copyright term from afar could prove difficult.[31]

The international advocacy of novelists

Hemmungs-Wirten's history of copyright draws attention to the political advocacy of authors in placing international copyright on a trans-national footing. The list of acclaimed novelists who were very successful commercially across many continents and also copyright advocates is very long, the best known being Daniel Defoe, William Wordsworth, Walter Scott, Edward Bulwer-Lytton, Charles Dickens, Mark Twain, Alexandre Dumas and Victor Hugo. Hemmungs-Wirten notes, "most of Europe read the same authors at roughly the same time. No wonder then, that successful novelists were highly invested in the quest for international copyright legislation and against infractions in whatever form".[32] The cultural esteem in which these particular writers were held at the time and the level of name recognition gained through a global readership, made them valuable advocates for the idea of a universal copyright.

This political activity was not limited to the assertion of a shared economic self-interest. As discussed in Chapter 2, there was a larger shared international cultural agenda. International copyright was linked to the virtue of Western civilisation. While copyright advocacy often coincided with public speaking tours and book promotion, it entailed men of letters claiming the right to speak for all men: "the extraordinary qualities that enable men of letters to put experience and existence into words is what makes them more universal than everybody else".[33] Through international copyright advocacy prominent authors promoted the need to find our better selves through art and literature, whether in Paris, London, Vancouver or in Melbourne. Linking international copyright to the cause of Western civilisation was particularly appealing in the colonies. It helped intellectually distance those who self-identified as civilised colonials from the grubby violence of ongoing dispossessions and genocides, and from the grasping commercial culture that underpinned the "progress" of its frontiers and port cities. Thus it was advocated in Melbourne that,

> All civilised nations of the slightest pretensions to literary rank, recognise this right, founded as it is on the first principles of natural justice, and in their legislation have provided for its protection. . . . Is it reasonable to suppose that a man will waste years of toil, of study and laborious research in the preparation of a work, which when published, a boon perhaps to the whole world, any fool may republish, deformed possibly and rendered worthless by his own ignorance and folly? Even supposing him to care nothing for the fair profits of his labour is it likely that he will be equally careless of what is dearer to him perhaps than life itself – his fame? The practice of all civilised nations is, fortunately, entirely against such a supposition.[34]

The appeal to a law that unites all civilised peoples through communion in copyright did politicise the question of access to literature in the colonies. It became a much bigger issue in Canada than the Australian colonies. Excellent detailed works by Eli McClaren[35] and Sara Bannerman[36] tell the story of the battle for Canadian copyright sovereignty from a nationalist point of view. However, what has not been accounted for is the degree of co-ordination between the old Empires and the new, to manage discontent and propel an imperial cultural agenda while masking this alliance amongst the most powerful.

The trans-Atlantic co-ordination of author, publisher and copyright associations

In the late 19th century many new organisations to promote author and publisher interests emerged in the leading centres of culture in Paris, London and New York to promote international copyright. The most important ones in the UK and US whose activities materially affected the book trade in British dominions arose from the activities of the Copyright Association, the Society of Authors, the American Copyright (Authors) League and the American Publishers Copyright League.

The Copyright Association (1872)

The Copyright Association was not the first British organisation of its kind. There were many similar bodies throughout the 19th century. The closest precursor to it was the Society for the Protection of Literature formed in 1843 at a meeting in the offices of Thomas Longman and supported by John Murray, with Charles Dickens serving as Chair. Their ambition was to influence the Board of Trade as it was making recommendations to free up the supply of cheap literature in the colonies in the 1840s, including considering import duties and reprinting. They failed.[37] Following the *Foreign Reprints Act* 1847 and internal divisions the organisation folded in 1849.

The new Copyright Association was mindful of this previous failure. Membership included authors: Robert Browning, Arthur Helps, Dr William Smith, Charles Reade, Charles Trevelyan; publishers: John Murray, Thomas Longman, Alexander Macmillan, George Routledge, Richard Bentley and Frederick Daldy. By this time Routledge and Macmillan had already established offices in New York with a view to directly participate in the American copyright system and to assist in co-ordinating printing with American publishers to secure both imperial and American copyrights.[38] In moving its first resolution Charles Trevelyan said,

> That it is expedient to form an association for the protection of copyright property, said that the highest interests of the human race were bound up in the prosperity of literature; consequently it was of the greatest public importance, on the one hand, that the claims of the owners of copyright property should not be pressed beyond their proper point and on the other, that the owners should no forgo any advantage to which they were justly entitled, and, which could be maintained consistent with the public good.[39]

Participants attributed the passing of the *Foreign Reprints Act* 1847 to a previously unsophisticated approach to lobbying, with the result that "the American publishers had got command of the [Canadian] colonial market". The strategy was one where gentlemen had merely passed private opinions to Parliament. While acknowledgement that the case for copyright protection "should not be pressed beyond their proper point" entails a concession that colonies and former colonies had legitimate cause for grievance, it was nonetheless argued that if lobbying had been more organised and strategic at the relevant time, the foreign reprint law might never had been passed in the first place.

An Eton and Oxford educated lawyer, Thomas Henry Farrer, who was serving as Secretary of the Board of Trade, was invited to join the meeting. This was a bold move. Farrer was not a believer in universal copyright or a supporter of authors and publishers. He would go on to describe the absolute right of the author "as fictitious as it is ingenious".[40] His view was that anybody should be able to republish whatever book they chose in the interest of improving access to cheap literature. Due to this opinion he is credited with advocacy of compulsory licensing schemes in the 1870s.[41] He also believed it should be lawful to import Canadian reprints into the UK.[42] Despite his opinions, his inclusion in the organisation was designed to facilitate a direct channel to the Board of Trade. The Association also created a new kind of copyright research position: "it would be more advisable to appoint a legal advisor to keep a look out, not only at home, but over the Acts of colonial legislatures, as well as with regard to the acts of foreign countries".[43] Frederick Daldy would come to serve in this capacity. He was also subsequently appointed to the 1878 Royal Commission, along with fellow Association members William Smith and Thomas Farrer. Charles Trevelyan, John Murray, Thomas Longman, Alexander Macmillan, George Routledge and Thomas Farrer also gave evidence to the commission.

What was most distinctive and important about the Copyright Association was the foresight in co-ordinating political activity where authors and publishers could present a common front to communicate directly with the Board of Trade on the subject of law reform. The Society of Authors would come to have a far greater public profile, but there were shared contacts amongst both bodies and co-ordination where author and publisher interests aligned.

The Society of Authors (1884)

At the time of its founding the three public objectives of the Society of Authors were:

1 The maintenance, definition and defence of literary property.[44]
2 The consolidation and amendment of the laws of domestic copyright.
3 The promotion of international copyright.[45]

It sought to represent all literary endeavours. The first president was Lord Tennyson and vice presidents were drawn from leading men of letters associated with poetry, science, history, theology, the army, fiction, dramatic literature and journalism. Sixty-eight paying members in 1884 grew to 870 by 1893, plus life members.[46]

In his account of the organisation's origin Walter Besant directly connected international copyright to earlier imperialism. His view was that due to a common English language, international copyright would facilitate a larger reach than the Romans,

> a writer of importance now addresses an audience drawn from a hundred million of English-speaking people. Remember that never before in the history of the world has there been such an audience. There were doubtless more than a hundred millions under the Roman rule round the shores of the Mediterranean, but they spoke many different languages. We have now this enormous multitude, all, with very few exceptions, able to read, and all reading. . . . Every day makes it plainer and clearer that we have arrived when the whole of this multitude . . . will very soon be reading books . . . they will prefer good books to bad. Let the work have a Message. Let it have a thing to say, a story to tell, a Man or Woman to present, a lesson to deliver, clear, strong, unmistakeable.[47]

The story that this Society chose to tell helped British and American interests come to dominate the growing world of English language readers dispersed across the oceans, whilst obscuring the imperial cultural and commercial logic that lay behind the position. As with the American bodies discussed next, the idea of universal copyright was linked with the progress of civilisation and the moral order of the universe, advanced through the novelist's pen, rather than by the sword.

American Copyright (Authors) League (1883)

As in the UK there were many American author and copyright organisations leading up to the signing of the Berne Convention on 18 September 1885. American activities intensified in the wake of President Cleveland's December 6th announcement that the US would reserve their position, as Congress continued to debate the merits of international copyright. The American Copyright League was the initiative of the clergyman and writer Edward Eggleston and *Scribner/Century Magazine* editor Richard Watson Gilder, with poet and critic George Lathrop as Secretary. Initial invitees included the founder of *Popular Science* magazine, Prof Edward Youman, novelist George W Cable, essayist and *Harper's Magazine* editor, Laurence Hutton and novelist and poet Henry C Bunner. The writer Henry James was also in attendance, but he promptly withdrew on realising that the discussion would centre on improving the situation for American authors, rather than redressing the injustice faced by English ones.[48] The organisation expressed their aim rather pragmatically as "to procure the abolition, *so far as possible*, of all discrimination between American and the foreign author and to obtain reforms of American copyright law".[49] Part of their law reform strategy was to use public readings by prominent novelists in the aid of international copyright to "first arouse interest in the subject itself, and next convince people that a wrong exists which our Government is bound to redress". These "author meets public" events were also an avenue to raise funds. Lathrop also went on a recruitment drive, leading to an initial membership of less than a dozen swelling to nearly 700 by 1885.

Though organisational membership drew from all men of letters, not all writers were affected by America's international copyright stance in the same way. An estimation of the size of different book market sectors in the US can been seen in Table 4.1.

Literary history and miscellany, biography and memoirs, description and travel, humour and satire, history and poetry made up a quarter of all books published in America, but these were also mostly works of American authors or of foreign authors published by arrangement. Very few science and theology books were ever pirated, and foreign-authored books were usually published in the US by arrangement between British and American publishers and through co-ordinating printing and copyright registration on both continents, foreign-authored works would be protected by US copyright. Education, language

Table 4.1 New book titles based on the annual list of new titles published in *The Publisher's Weekly*, 1882–1886

Analysis of new book titles published in the USA, 1882–1886	
Fiction	22%
Literary history and miscellany, biography and memoirs, description and travel, humour and satire	14%
Science (medical, physical, mathematical, political and social)	12%
Theology, religion, mental and moral philosophy	10%
Education and language	6%
Law	10%
Juveniles	9%
Et cetera	8%
Poetry and drama	5%
History	3%

writers and law books were nearly all locally produced. The juvenile market was the next largest sector, but here works of foreign authors were usually not sold for lower prices than those by American authors. Further, American publishers exported books for the young, and only imported them "to a comparatively slight extent".

It was US and British novelists who were most affected by the lack of agreement on trans-Atlantic copyright. British authors had their works pirated and American authors had to compete amongst multiple editions, ranging from 10, 15, 20 or 25 cent English novels,

> American readers were less inclined to read the novels of Cooper or Hawthorne for a dollar when they could buy a novel of Scott or Dickens for a quarter. . . . American men of letters, were therefore unable to rely on literature for a livelihood. Longfellow and Lowell were college professors; Hawthorne was in the government service; Emerson was engaged in lecturing. And American readers were weaned on a literature not their own.[50]

With international copyright "there would be but a single edition of the latest novels of the leading British story-tellers, and this would be offered at whatsoever a price the authorised publisher might choose to ask, sometimes much, generally little".[51]

American Copyright League writer and Columbia Law School graduate Bender Matthews stressed distinctively nationalistic reasons to support reform. A diet of English literature was antithetical to the very idea of American progress,

> A well-nigh exclusive diet of English fiction full of the feudal ideas and superstitions and survivals of which we have been striving for a century to rid ourselves, is not wholesome for those who need to be strengthened and enlightened to do their duty as citizens of a free republic.[52]

This perspective echoes that of American preacher, Rev Dr Henry Van Dyke, whose advocacy is discussed further next.

In November 1887 the American Copyright League Executive, and in particular Edward Eggleston, was authorised by members to pursue an international copyright bill, even where this might involve manufacturing clauses and other technicalities that were not felt to be in the true spirit of the universal right of authors. There was some anxiety that this position could alienate those more philosophically aligned with Romantic perspectives of authorship – those who felt similar to Henry James. It was considered desirable that authors present a unified front. Forming another body with a different public profile to take compromise initiatives forward thus felt opportune. The rallying cause centred on the need to raise "our own country to the standard of national morality of copyright and of international fair play maintained by all other civilised nations, now united in the International Copyright Union", as well as "justice to American authors".[53]

The American (Publishers) Copyright League (1887)

This organisation was established with a particular objective and membership: "The object of this Association shall be to co-operate with American authors in securing international copyright". Membership was limited to "publishers who favor international copyright". Many were recent converts,

> Their conversion resulted from a shift in perceptions of self interest. Increasingly, elite publishers faced competition from firms that utilized new technology to undersell them in the marketplace for cheap reprints of English novels. The prospect of international copyright, which once appeared as a costly imposition, began to look increasingly like a source of economic salvation: a mechanism by which elite firms, who could afford to license the copyright of foreign authors, could mobilise copyright law to exclude competitors from the marketplace.[54]

The term "publisher" was understood broadly, allowing for co-operation with "all members of the trade", including paper-makers, printers, binders and typesetter unions who had successfully opposed earlier reforms. The membership included the leading book publishers in New York.[55] It also included music houses, subscription book publishers and some reprinters. William Appleton was elected President, George Putnam as Secretary and Charles Scribner as Treasurer. The executives met at Appleton's Madison Avenue house. The International Copyright Association of New England was established soon after to support similar objectives in that state, with auxiliary leagues formed in St Louis, Cincinnati, Minneapolis, Denver, Buffalo, Colorado Springs – to do "missionary" work, as Putnam called it.[56] The Publisher's League also drafted an "Address to Booksellers" seeking to provoke that trade into forming a related copyright association, "working up public opinion in their respective towns in behalf of the desired reform, and the secretaries of which might bring influence to bear upon Congressmen of their States".[57] A "Conference Committee" was formed of the executive of the Author's League, largely led by Eggleston, and the Publisher's League: "[E]very subsequent step in the campaign, until the passage of the bill in 1891 was taken by this Committee".[58]

Putnam's use of the term "missionary work" was not accidental. As discussed in Chapter 2, British author advocacy profiled a modified form of Romantic spirituality that it was thought was inherent in all of mankind. The public circulation of the works of authentic souls was offered as a panacea to ward off the corruption and acquisitive culture that personified the modern city. The spiritual overtones of the American campaign were different, appealing to some amongst the political elites and their wives, as well as to the respectable middle class. By championing the moral issues at stake in the US, international copyright law reform was linked to God's plan for a strong and prosperous America.

Rev Henry Van Dyke's *National Sin of Literary Piracy* (1888), published as a pamphlet by Scribner, served to proselytise this case. His sermon was given at the Brick Presbyterian Church, New York and then repeated at the New York Avenue Presbyterian Church in Washington in the presence of First Lady Mrs Cleveland and "a fair representation of members of Congress" who had all been personally invited.[59] It linked the progress of civilisation to making of modern laws and the abolition of slavery. He then referred to the immorality of book publishing when it was supported by the unpaid labour of foreign authors. He warned "God judges nations, as well as individuals, by their moral qualities, and deals with them along inflexible lines of righteousness. Prosperity is a reward. Decay is a punishment". Van Dyke observed that God's wrath could be seen in America today in "the perversion of national taste and manners by the vast circulation of foreign books that are both cheap and bad". He lectured that this was leading to the

> decline of the American spirit in a certain class of our youth; the loss of simplicity and naturalness and independence; the failure of that lawful pride in American institutions and principles which alone can preserve the freedom of our republic.[60]

Putnam describes Van Dyke's sermon as an inspiration to other ministers across the country, as well as influencing the more intelligent of the journals.

Membership fees and well-publicised "author meets public" events built a fighting fund.[61] This supported proliferation of patriotic religious instruction, with messages reinforced by placing articles in "quality" newspapers such as the *Times*, *Tribune* and *Post* (New York), the *Sun* (Baltimore), the *Ledger* (Philadelphia) and the *Commercial* (Cincinnati). Key actors pursued direct trade negotiation with particular publishers across American states to build allies. These efforts, combined with skilful parliamentary management and personal influence amongst politicians, led to success where previous campaigns had failed. In his account of the strategy Putman presses that,

> A good share of the credit for the noteworthy change in the opinion of the House may, however, justly be claimed for the active "missionary" work which had been kept up by the league during the summer throughout the country, and especially in the constituencies of doubtful members, by means of the distribution of tracts and arguments, the preparation of material for the leaders of local newspapers, and also by reaching the personal correspondents of authors and the friends of authors.[62]

Though American author and publisher organisations did not necessarily share the Old World cultural justifications for international copyright,[63] there were still strong economic and domestic cultural interests that aligned American authors and publishers with the British cause. Nowhere were the implications of the strategy for other parts of the globe directly considered. However, behind the scenes it was apparent how further Anglo-American co-operation could be mutually advantageous as international trade grew.

The *International Copyright (Chace) Act* 1891

The *Chace Act* was the result of all this lobbying. The statute empowered the President to issue proclamations that would establish reciprocal copyright recognition with other states. President Cleveland's declaration of 1 July 1891 granted reciprocity to the original Berne Convention signatories including Belgium, France, Germany and the United Kingdom "and her possessions".[64]

Superficially, the terms seemed progressive in not including a citizenship or residency qualification for award of a copyright in the jurisdiction.[65] However, the *Chace Act* contained four significant technicalities that authors had to comply with: 1) registration of the title with the Library of Congress on or before the date of publication; 2) deposit of copies was required on or before the date of publication with no grace period allowed for in the 1891 statute, although as per previous acts some late deposit was allowed in practice; 3) the books had to be printed in the United States; 4) and a copyright notice had to be included on all copies. A report by the US Copyright Office from this time notes numerous "inequalities of exchange" in the internationalisation of rights, including that,

> there may be an important practical difference in the ease or difficulty of compliance with obligatory formalities, depending upon whether the author is a citizen or a foreigner. It is not as easy, for example, for a foreign as for a native author to arrange for the filing of his title page at Washington before publication, and it is obviously a much less difficult matter for

> an American than for a foreign author to arrange to have his book type-set in the United States before the day of first publication, which may mean for the alien author the burden of a double printing of his work, abroad and in the United States.[66]

The terms were especially difficult for foreign authors unknown to American publishers to comply with. Publishers were most unlikely to arrange publication and render logistical assistance to those untested in the market, unless the author paid for the publication. Compliance posed far less of a problem, however, for writers who had established trans-Atlantic connections.

The Canadian grievance

There was no effective regulation of the US-Canadian book trade. Ready access to American piracies undermined the concession made to Canadian publishers in the *Foreign Reprints Act* 1847 (UK) and it was ineffective in securing royalties to British authors and publishers following the *British North America Act* 1867 (30–31 Vict c 3) which created powers of the Canadian Parliament to address problems with the existing reprint scheme in 1872.[67]

From the British perspective the powers of the dominion Parliament to create its own laws remained limited where it involved conflict with imperial law. The *Colonial Laws Validity Act* 1865 (UK) (28 & 29 Vict c63) gave the British Parliament power to resolve "inconsistencies" between colonial and imperial laws. Colonial laws found to be "repugnant" to imperial law would be invalidated. The *Canadian 1872 Act* was disallowed by imperial authorities.[68] In 1875 Daldy helped negotiate a new arrangement that passed through both the Canadian and British Parliaments,

> The intention of the [Copyright Act][69] 1875 act was to encourage British copyright holders to obtain Canadian copyright, and exclude American-made reprints of British works in Canada. If the British copyright holder fulfilled the requirements to obtain Canadian copyright – including local publication – those works could be neither reprinted nor imported without permission of the copyright holder. However, as the Canadian act was held to be subject to the Imperial Copyright Act of 1842, together with its modification in the Foreign Reprints Act of 1847, United Kingdom copyright holders already enjoyed copyright protection throughout the empire, regardless. Reprinting privileges could be obtained only with their consent.[70]

The requirement of obtaining British consent before reprinting frustrated local ambitions. Britain's signing of the Berne Convention only further brought to the fore the question of Canada's sovereign copyright interests. And the threat of Britain striking down unwelcome Canadian laws had uncertain consequences not just for Canada but the whole of the Empire.

It was not the case that Canadian publishers were entirely anti-Berne or anti-copyright. As Sara Bannerman notes, "For many the Berne Convention symbolised the forward march of international law, civilization and progress".[71] Many Canadian publishers hoped that international copyright would mean that new opportunities would open up in the domestic market. As well as encouraging local publication by Canadians rather than publishing in London, they expected to be able to contract directly with British authors for exclusive rights to publish works of British authors in Canada, where they judged the title would do well in the local market. Canada considered that the declaration that created reciprocal copyright between the US and Great Britain was not a "copyright treaty", within the meaning of clause 8 of the *International Copyright Act* (1886) (UK).[72] Thus Canada was not obliged to respect American registered copyrights and Canadian publishers could directly negotiate with British publishers for a share of the North American trade.

The problem was, however, that trans-Atlantic publisher contracts had arisen, dealing with "North American" rights as a bloc. It was complained that,

> Canadian publishers are constantly endeavouring to enter into arrangements with authors and artists direct, but the English publishers looks upon us as mere colonials, steps between us and the author, and sells our market to the United States publisher.[73]

In addition to uncertainties about the legal status of trans-Atlantic bloc agreements, there were practical problems facing Canadian publishers in conducting business on an international scale. Canadian publishers did not have any practical capacity for doing business in London, whereas by the time the *Chace Act* was passed, American publishers were far better represented.

The very definition of a "United States publisher" was also changing,

> So thoroughly do the English houses understand this question, and in so many cases have they established branch houses here for publication of their own books, that a leading Boston author was tempted to remark to the head of a leading American publishing house that the chief effect of the International Copyright Act seemed to be to enable English publishing firms to establish branch houses here, manufacture duplicate plates, and flood the market with English books.[74]

American publishers could also copyright works by American authors in Britain and thereby assume direct control over the Canadian market for publications shipped from the UK.[75]

From a Canadian point of view, in addition to not considering Canada bound by the declaration of reciprocal copyright between Great Britain and the US, it was also legally possible for the imperial government to accede to a Canadian request to withdraw from the Berne Convention. Canada had accepted the signing of the Berne Convention with the understanding that it was possible to withdraw by giving a year's notice. No formal request was made; however a new law that asserted Canadian copyright sovereignty was passed in 1889. It included manufacturing clauses, requiring first or simultaneous printing in Canada within one month of publication elsewhere to achieve a Canadian copyright.[76]

This new *Act* was read as a denunciation of the Berne Convention, since it denied unconditional national treatment to works originating in a treaty state – the UK. It led to an intervention by the Colonial Office and another threat to invoke the *Colonial Laws Validity Act* 1865 (UK) to strike it down. Though this did not occur, constitutional disagreement remained about the extent of Canadian legislative power with respect to copyright. The 1889 *Act* never received royal assent.[77] The situation further energised Canada's copyright rebellion.

In 1895 a new bill emerged. It required British authors to arrange for Canadian printing of their works within a month of first publication or *thereafter be subjected to a compulsory license*, subject to the author receiving 10% of the retail price.[78] Most importantly, Canadian publishers would be free to set the retail price and determine the format and content of the work presented to the public.

This new draft was a major affront to well-known British authors. By the 1890s the standard royalty rate secured from US publishers by established authors was 15%, and not infrequently 17.5% or 18%. The popular romance writer Hall Caine reputedly obtained a 20% royalty for his North American editions from Appleton. A flat 10% rate was highly inflammatory.[79] It was even less than the royalty had been under the *Foreign Reprints Act* 1847.[80]

This political dilemma was described as one that "the Rosebery Government did not know what to do with". Joseph Chamberlain was an industrialist who served as President of the Board of Trade in 1880–1885. He became head of the Colonial Office in 1895, his central concern being the deterioration of Britain's international position due to the rise of the US and Germany. He thought competitive imperial expansion through the colonies was indispensable to Britain retaining influence and markets, redressing Britain's shrinking manufacturing base by drawing on the "natural advantages" of her tropical possessions.[81] Chamberlain was sent to confer with the representatives of the Author's Society in London and the Colonial Office in Canada.[82]

It was recognised that it was not just Canadian copyright that was at stake. The development had implications for the entire Empire,

> All the other colonial dependencies are intensely watching the result of Canada's attempt to override the Berne Convention. Imperial sanction of that act with its license clauses may be followed by similar legislation in Australia and other British colonies. *Copyright will cease to be an imperial principle.* The English author will lose control over his property in the colonies and the interests of the London publishers will be seriously affected.[83]

Reports of the controversy concede that "international copyright" was code for ongoing imperial rule of the book trade from London, regardless of colonies securing political independence.

The London publishers' response

London publishers understood well that the Canadian copyright proposal would stymy attempts to control the imperial and American book trade, organised through London. They complained that pricing concessions had historically been made in the Canadian market, in recognition that authorised works competed with American pirate editions. They had hoped that following the *Chace Act*, the trade could now prevent multiple competing editions from different sources servicing the Canadian reading public, except where the London publishers controlled the terms.

Macmillan and Co argued there were moral rights implications: Canadian publishers would be free to bring out inaccurately printed and abridged books, "purposefully mutilated", with illustrations that the author disapproved of and found repugnant. The royalty proposed was judged inadequate and difficult to collect, especially given the poor history of revenue collection that dogged colonial editions published under the *Foreign Reprints Act* 1847. The effects were also argued as particularly draconian for British educational and scientific works, which had notoriously slow sales and high production costs.[84] Publisher John Murray forewarned the broader implications across the Empire,

> The exclusion of pirated and unauthorised reprints of copyright works from our Australian colonies and India has, even in existing circumstances, been a task requiring the utmost vigilance and care. . . . The circulation of legalised Canadian reprints would render this work of exclusion well-nigh impossible. . . . If [Canadian demands] are granted, nothing can stop the extension of the concession to other Colonies, and any one who is at all conversant with the book market can foresee what a grievous injury would thereby be caused to owners of English copyright.[85]

In short, the Canadian bill was seen to fatally compromise the generalised universalism of the Berne Union and undermine the specific achievement for UK publishers represented by the *Chace Act*. Further,

> having given pledges to America that in exchange for the copyright she gives us, we will give copyright to her throughout British dominions, one of our colonies makes demands that it shall be allowed to break down the whole principle which during fifty hard years we have so laboriously built up.[86]

The degree of concern in Britain was such that there was again public discussion of the use of an imperial veto.[87] However, instead of continuing to battle it out in diplomatic exchanges and through parliamentary pressure, a cultural assault, building upon the successful missionary strategy that assisted the passage of the *Chace Act*, was let loose on the Canadian public. The campaign was co-ordinated in London by the Society of Authors, the Colonial Office and the Board of Trade with support by Appleton, on behalf of the American

Copyright League. It was led by a famous author who is little known today. At the time he was a household name across the English speaking world – the Victorian romancer Hall Caine.

The "English Tolstoy": Sir Thomas Henry Hall Caine (1853–1931)

Caine trained as an architect and journalist, finding fame as a Victorian writer and novelist. Born to a poverty-stricken working class background in Liverpool, he identified with his father's birthplace on the Isle of Man. The location and its people provided inspiration for many of his tales. His popular romances often explored tensions between fathers and children, brothers and their wives, with themes of marriage, adultery, wronged women and infanticide. In an age when Victorians were accustomed to biblical language and story "to an extent almost inconceivable today",[88] he also borrowed torrid themes of divine justice from biblical stories. The inclusion of religious themes was a tried method by which a novelist could claim respectability.[89] Adaptations of his stories were performed on the stage in London, New York, across Canada and the Australian colonies. He was recognised on the streets of London and New York.[90] His novel, *The Deemster*, alongside Rolf Boldrewood's *Robbery under Arms* and Conan Doyle's *The Firm of Girdlestone*, was listed in the *Daily Telegraph's* '100 Best Novels in the World' (1900).[91] If today his works can be located at all, they make for turgid reading.

Caine's personality and standing was such that he frequently featured as the subject of caricature. His wife, Mary, dutifully kept press clippings of these, as well as his copyright advocacy.[92]

The biography that accompanies Figure 4.2 describes him thus,

> *CAINE, THOMAS HALL M.H.K.:*
>
> Theologian and Manx legislator, born in Birchingham 1853, where one of his earliest feats was to discover Rosetti. It is true that whilst at school he became a champion of the 3 legged race, but it cannot be said that he takes his Manx proclivities so far that he has no tale. On the contrary, the contention set up by his critic, Miss Corelli, a gifted critic, is that he has too many. For the services rendered to the Vatican by Mr Caine's *Eternal City* – a Jesuit tract in disguise – the Pope made him a count of the Holy Roman Empire. Mr Caine's resemblance to Shakespeare is so striking that on his landing in New York, on a religious trip to America, the late Ignatius Donnelly, a total stranger, declared "Lord Bacon I presume".
>
> Mr Caine now lives at Greeba Castle, where his windows have recently been doubled to block out the booming of the Atlantic, which otherwise he considers a satisfactory ocean. The abnormal heat of the past few summers have been generally attributed to the fact that Mr Caine chooses August as his publishing month.[93]

Figure 4.2 A caricature of Thomas Henry Hall Caine, the Manxman

Drawing by Cosmo Hamilton, Source: Mary Caine Scrapbooks, Papers of Sir Thomas Henry Hall Caine (1853–1931).

Miss Correlli signs off with her motto, "Cave Cainem", Beware the Dog.

Caine was not acclaimed as the "English Tolstoy" by his literary peers but in the press, who were successfully encouraged to make precisely this connection by his publisher.[94] Discord created by Caine's self-promotion is indicated by Conan Doyle's negative comments about him discussed in Chapter 3.[95] He was also very unfavourably judged by George Bernard Shaw. The two corresponded over a review Shaw published of a play based on Caine's book, *The Manxman* (1894), written by the playwright Wilson Barrett. Shaw wrote,

> In my notice of it I said it was the worst play ever written – the worst that could be written – the worst that could even be conceived as unwritten. I cut that out for your sake. . . .
>
> I have formed the lowest possible opinion of you as an artist from "The Manxman"; and if you wish to retrieve the failure, you had better write another play and a good one. . . .
>
> You have probably even had your royalties . . . on such money that was actually paid to hear the play on the strength of your reputation before the theatre was closed, . . .
>
> Any fool can write a novel, though many wise men cannot. Very few people can write plays.[96]

Despite his detractors, Caine was well connected to literary elites and artistic circles. He was close friends with Dante and Christina Rosetti, sharing the Pre-Raphaelite Brotherhood philosophy that art should teach and present great moral truths that survive the artist's mortality. He gave public lectures on poetry, the arts, politics and corresponded with leading figures including William Morris, John Ruskin and Wilkie Collins. Bram Stoker served as his personal secretary and, in 1897, the then unknown author dedicated *Dracula* "to my dear friend, Hommy-Beg".

In many regards Caine was a perfect choice as spokesperson. He embodied the contradictions of his times. He saw himself, and his social circle, as leaders of an honourable profession where the literati instructed the reading public by appealing to their intellects, a Christian moral sensibility and emotions. He made a living as a professional author – a significant qualification,[97] and he appears to have enjoyed the fame linked to his literary achievement. Corelli's biographical note also alludes to two different senses in which the author personified religious fervour. In addition to his literary explorations of sin, the reference to his "religious trip to America" is an allusion to his missionary work in the service of international copyright.

As a member of the Society of Authors Caine was looked to in a leadership capacity by Besant. Though a staunch advocate for the natural rights of authors, he was also a pragmatist. His view was "[t]he Berne Convention is our ideal but when we cannot get the Berne Convention we are willing to accept what is not immoderately retrograde".[98] In July 1895 Caine was sent to Canada as a delegate of the Society of Authors and unofficially acting for British publishers. He also carried letters from the Colonial Office but was not officially acting for them. Though he admitted that he met with his American friend and publisher William Appleton in New York, including meeting with Appleton's neighbour, President Cleveland, he rather implausibly denied to the press that he ever discussed the very reason for his trip abroad, Canadian copyright. Letters to Appleton suggest otherwise. In those letters, approval was specifically sought from the American Copyright League to alternate copyright provisions he proposed to the Canadians.

"[Canada] carries his father's blood . . . the shame will be his father's no less than his" – Caine

Caine's speaking tour of Canada, which included addresses at the National Club, was reported in full in many newspapers. He repeated his spiel at dinners at Canadian publishers and bookseller associations. He lectured that,

> For fifty years we have been struggling – we and our great predecessors – Dickens, Thackeray, Carlyle, Lytton, and a host of others – for recognition of the principle that a man has a right to the commercial value of the property he creates in books. It has been a stiff fight but we have conquered all along the line. We have prevailed upon the chief nations of Europe to meet together in convention at Berne, and established once and for all the fundamental principle that without registration, simultaneous publication or any similar mummery, an author holds property in the children of his brain.[99]

However, he took great care to discuss far more than copyright. The copyright message was always embroidered with references to his famous works and plays, he gave advice to budding authors, commented favourably on the progress of Canadian and American society and arranged interviews with his wife. Public displays of happy Victorian domesticity, along with home furnishings that personified success, were an important part of the male image. The adage "a man's home is his castle" was literally true in Caine's case, and Mrs Hall Caine received journalists at Greeba Castle. (See Figure 4.3: Mrs Hall Caine at home).

Caine also spoke of the loyalty of Canada to Britain drawing on paternalistic themes familiar to those who had read his novels,

> Though you are independent of the old country. . . . You are in the position of the son, of a father who has many sons. . . . So the son goes off and marries himself, perhaps, to the strange woman. But because he lives under another roof he does not cease to be his father's son. He bears his father's name. He carries his father's blood. If he does wrong, the shame will be his father's no less than his.[100]

The discourtesy in linking Canadian copyright sovereignty to the sensibility of a "strange woman" was not commented on and perhaps the casual misogyny was muted by biblical allusion. As others before him had done, Caine's attitude toward copyright echoed the religious conviction that there was a moral arc to the universe. Despite limitations in the laws of man, copyright should be judged

by the sweet and dainty womanliness of 'tiful lake in Wordsworth homeland. | sessed superior durability to anythin

MRS, HALL CAINE AT HOME,

the famous author's wife, will be glad to know that she treasures as the happiest experience of bygone days the trip that she made through the United States. Much as the people of the United States were attracted by her sympathetic face and the brightness and geniality of her manners, however, to see Mrs. Hall Caine at her best, she must be seen at the pretty fireside of her own beautiful home. It was a long journey that I had to make over the mountains of North Wales, to Greeba Castle, in the most picturesque part of the beautiful Isle of Man, where I found Mrs. Hall Caine surrounded by the places of interest made famous by the pen of her illustrious husband.

Greeba Castle is almost as interesting as its owner, so before speaking of the warmth of the greeting which I received from Mr. Hall Caine and his wife, I should like to describe in a few words Greeba Castle and its approaches. One is struck

Figure 4.3 Mrs Hall Caine at home c. 1898

Source: Mary Caine Scrapbooks, Papers of Sir Thomas Henry Hall Caine (1853–1931).

in light of its movement toward eternal perfection. Obstacles, such as the US not signing the Berne Convention, were smoothed over. Despite the most obvious limitations of a manufacturing clause that Canada sought to emulate, Caine told all who would listen that we have secured "an even greater triumph in America" with recognition of British copyrights in the passing of the *Chace Act* 1891.

The author was encouraged by his public reception and its political consequence. He was especially pleased when Canadian-British historian and writer Goldwin Smith, who also led the Canadian Society of Authors, gave nationalistic reasons to support the British position. Canada, Smith explained, "is not a publishing country", there being little market for locally authored books in the English language, beyond Canadian biography, archaeology and topography. Smith suggested that the benefit of the draft bill would only accrue to "a few Canadian firms" while doing little to improve the market for local writers of works of general interest. The effect of the legislation would force these writers to publish locally, rather than overseas with the likely consequence that, following the passage of the Canadian law, other colonial jurisdictions would follow and every author would be required to print in each and every colony. He concluded, "The satisfactory settlement of this question would be the adoption of one copyright for the whole Empire. . . . If an Empire is an Empire indeed, why should not this course of action be taken?".[101] Canadian copyright sovereignty was taken to be a refutation of Empire.

Through his encounters Caine quietly judged the political climate in Canada, reporting back to London and New York. He advised that given the extent of Canadian feeling on the issue, political concessions would have to be made. At this time, the US had 65 million readers, whereas Canada had only 5 million. Even the imposition of an import tax would not prevent authorised editions flooding the Canadian market.

In a remarkedly candid private note (perhaps a draft of a cable), Caine informed the Colonial Office about the success of his missionary work. He believed his speaking tour had worn out public appetite for discussion of copyright altogether. The media had also become bored,

> How it is now. The public tired out – there is no doubt here. Colonial Office, Canadian cabinet, interested classes tired out. Therefore easy for me to do something. My task made easy.[102]

Though without legal training he drafted amendments to the Canadian bill to delay and divert attention. He suggested he would continue to profile the Berne Convention as the rallying cause: "They said it was impossible. It is done". No slouch in singing his own praises, he claimed he and Daldy had devised a proposal that could satisfy American authors, American publishers, observe the Berne Convention and be acceptable to Canadian publishers, authors and booksellers. He also claimed the Canadian Parliament was eager for a result.[103]

The compromise that was taken forward allowed for 60 days to arrange a Canadian publication, printed from London *or* American plates, where the

Canadian publisher was understood as an *agent* of the English or American publisher. The royalty was set at a *minimum* of 10%, allowing for the existing higher rates negotiated by established authors to stand.[104]

Caine's proposal was not ultimately accepted. The legislation that followed did, however, effectively cement the authority of London publishers over the Canadian market. While a 1900 amendment allowing Canadian publishers to apply to the Minister of Agriculture for an order to exclude importation of all copies first published in the British dominions (included those printed in London) superficially appeared to empower local publishers, in effect it only further facilitated the turning of independent Canadian publishers into agents of British firms, as Caine had advocated in his compromise.[105]

Australian copyright sovereignty

The federation of the Australian colonies in 1901[106] stimulated new discussions about copyright sovereignty. The first Australian *Copyright Act 1905* (Cth) provided that an author from any country was entitled to protection of their copyright where the work "was printed from type first set in Australia or published within fourteen days of first publication elsewhere in the world and the copyright was registered".[107] Customs officers were authorised to seize any works that conflicted with local registration of rights.[108] Following this legal change, the Sydney-based publisher, Angus & Robertson was floated as a public company in 1907.[109] However, this burst of copyright sovereignty was also short-lived. Copyright formalities such as registration were soon precluded in Article 4 of Berlin Revision of the Convention in 1908, coming into effect with the *Copyright Act* 1911 (UK).

No doubt under pressure from the Imperial Parliament, Australia then enacted the *Copyright Act* 1912 (Cth), which brought the *Copyright Act* 1911 (UK) into force.[110] Adopting the British legislation without any special protection of local interests was justified in the now familiar terms of copyright internationalism and membership amongst the "civilised world",

> a man who has copyright in Australia has a copyright over the greater part of the civilised world. He will gain the advantage of a uniform law on the subject, and the further advantage of enjoying the cheapest form of protection which was ever given to a property of this kind.[111]

Even where Canada and Australia briefly sought to assert political independence, the terms agreed to were insufficient to disrupt imperial control over English-language publishing markets. Power asymmetries within established Empire copyright markets continued with ongoing international reform further reinforcing these. Independent publishers in former colonies would struggle to obtain rights to the most lucrative titles whether these were locally or foreign authored, with market prospects largely limited to publishing locally authored works with far smaller distributions. If there was sufficient local acclaim, the local author was then also well placed to negotiate future rights abroad.

The missionary endeavours of celebrity authors and London and New York advocates of international copyright helped secure imperial control of the international book markets into the 20th century, in Canada and beyond. There was a natural alignment between the interests of established novelists identified with the "right" popular genres and those of large international publishers who promoted them. However, though not all authors or publishers are well served by this international publishing infrastructure, there was often a misidentification of the problem as being one of the local market size and late development of reading publics in former colonies. The lack of market opportunities were deliberately constrained by the proposals advanced in public and in private from London and New York. This legacy and its ongoing costs have not been well understood.

Understanding market distortions

There has long been a strong interest in explaining the challenges facing the Australian publishing industry. For a long time British cartel activity was identified as restricting a competitive import market, which had implications for support of local publishing, as well as leading to comparatively higher prices paid for printed matter by consumers.[112] More recent research complicates that argument, tracing in detail the transnational aspects of the trade where Australian works, in particular fiction, found markets in Britain[113] and America.[114] There are also more contemporary economic studies of publishing that seek to understand how Australian publishing operates in the global marketplace.[115]

What is somewhat frustrating about this Australian literature is that there is no serious discussion of the role of copyright at all, beyond acknowledgement that dating from the 19th century there was a division of the English language publishing world into British- and US-controlled spheres. Historians then trace how Australians placed themselves in relation to these divides. The ability of Australian writers or publishers to insert themselves into international publishing has become a source of national pride. My concern here is not to denigrate this accomplishment, or to dismiss the otherwise rich research about these publishing arrangements, but a larger one. In these accounts the international copyright infrastructure is always taken as a given without any discussion of power asymmetries, how they came about and how they continue to be justified. The enduring rhetoric of the universal right of authors fabricated in the late 19th century masks contemporary recognition of how historical disadvantage is perpetuated.

Ensor's impressive study of the largest Australian exporter, Angus & Robertson, does however discuss the role of another regulatory instrument in the book trade, tariffs. This is, in some ways, a de facto copyright discussion. The Federal Tariff Board was established in 1921 as a buffer between government and various interest groups demanding protection. In the 1930s federal tariffs were increased across a large number of areas aimed at protecting Australian industry, supporting employment at a time of depression and tackling balance of payments difficulties.[116] The Board discussed introducing a manufacturing clause or tariffs on imported books and magazines.[117] However, books and magazines presented a special case. Without it being explicitly stated, it was revealed that the significant trade imbalance in books came about because of the original design of international copyright, which affected the capacity to respond to support Australian industry.

In evidence given in the Tariff Board Inquiry into a Duty on Books in 1930, it was argued, as it had been put in Canada decades earlier, that tariff reform would cut off Australian authors from participating in international copyright markets, forcing them to publish locally, and also would drive up printing costs, retail prices and costs to libraries. There were also doubts in the ability of local publishers to recognise the value of worthwhile Australian publications, and thus a fear that it would lead to many worthy and important works never being published at all. For example, bohemian authors, such as Norman Lindsay, considered Australian publishing parochial, conservative and unwilling to support modern Australian writing.[118] With regard to freedom to manufacture British and foreign-authored works, due to international copyright it was argued that there was no ability to obtain these licenses competitively. Further, a high duty could freeze out British publishers altogether, leading to works not being licensed for publication in Australia at all. If, as a consequence of reforms, Australia was thrown out of the Berne Union as Canada had risked in the late 19th century, it was argued that works of Australian authorship would be free to be pirated internationally.[119] There was no confidence that Australian authors or publishers could routinely arrange for reciprocal printing in other jurisdictions to secure international copyright.

Tariff reform and manufacturing clauses did not proceed because they lacked support from local authors. Local publishers were relatively few. At this time only five or six firms published ten or more titles regularly each year and of these, only one, Angus & Robertson, published on a scale comparable with overseas houses, producing 25% of all Australian outputs, excepting pamphlets.[120] The main beneficiary of any tariff reform was identified as printers, although there was no significant evidence produced and printers gave conflicting evidence. The Board concluded that the overall employment benefit would be small.[121] It was recognised that it was not in the national interest to create additional obstacles and expenses that made it harder for the public to access knowledge, regardless of where the works originated. Accordingly, no tariff or primage duty was applied to imported British, Canadian or New Zealand books; books from other countries attracted a general duty of 15%; periodicals were free of duties, regardless of origin.

It was again noted in 1938 that imperial copyright not only privileged British publication, the lack of an import tariff for British imports meant that there was simply no advantage in firms assigning rights separately to Australian publishers. Net Price Agreements, first established by a cartel of London publishing houses in the late 19th century, effectively regulated wholesale prices and set minimum retail prices in Australia, although they were a subject of controversy.[122] There was little competition on price.[123] Further, syndicated works, including those of American origin, remained exempt from tariffs. This encouraged local magazines and newspapers to license foreign fiction at very cheap rates, rather than support publication of original work by Australian writers. Literary syndicates, mainly American corporations, also resold overseas fiction in Australia "at ridiculous rates", affecting pricing of works in the Australian market. Echoing the concerns of US authors prior to the *Chace Act*, Senator Cameron reported, "No Australian could afford to work for the rates offered through this competition, which is the equivalent of employing the cheapest possible labour".[124] Then there was also the dumping of "pulps" or remaindered works sold "at practically their cost as waste paper" through chain stores. This included magazines, comic books and music sheets. Overall, it was noted in the Australian Parliament that

> the Australian author is starved by English and American literature. . . . If everything that came into this country had to be translated, Australian literature would flourish and instead of buying English and American books and magazines, readers might be buying Australian printed books by Australian writers in the local language.[125]

Copyright reform was not investigated. The solutions mused over included local quotas of Australian content and ex gratia payments of public money from the Commonwealth Literary Fund to support impecunious but worthy Australian writers and publications, though the fund was recognised as only able to make a modest contribution.

Other regulatory tools were also looked at to indirectly tinker with market forces. Censorship regimes were recalibrated to try and impact on the trade imbalance, as well as to continue the cultural policy of trying to influence popular reading choices away from entertainment toward education. Australian and British content selected by established firms was often favourably defined in contrast to American "low" literature, especially periodicals.[126] This cultural discrimination was no doubt also impacted by the dominance of American film in Australia, a political problem discussed in the following chapter. Cheaply priced magazines featuring westerns, crime and sex, promoted by salacious covers and suggestive titles became a renewed target of revised censorship laws, but the numbers involved proved difficult to regulate.[127] These content concerns were alleviated somewhat when new wartime import restrictions prohibited non-essential imports from non-sterling countries, closing down the import of American periodicals.[128]

What an Australian publishing market might look like in the absence of international copyright agreements tying up rights can be seen from the effects of WW2,

> Its first effect was one of stimulus. British publishers, affected by paper shortage, currency difficulties, and enemy bombing, began to print in

> Australia books that formerly they would have exported here. In 1939 there were 486 Australian book publications; in 1941 there were 636. Local manufacturers began to produce comic books by scores of thousands.[129]

This led to significant investment in photo-lithography and the introduction of photogravure process, leading to cheaper access to colour printing. The difficulty of importing books from Britain or Canada led to Angus & Robertson producing 15% more new titles in 1940–1945 than in the previous five years, even though they faced paper rationing, a skilled labour shortage and had difficulties importing machinery. It was noted that there were "four times as many book publishers of any consequences as before the war", with the Commonwealth Literary Fund identified as assisting publications that might otherwise have been "fair risks for a commercial publisher".[130]

The biggest change was in the flourishing of local publishers producing colourful, disposable literature. The local titles were not necessarily all cheap and dirty generic substitutes for American publications. Further, crime fiction and true crime stories came to be set "where all the action took place in the country where they were devised, written, illustrated and printed: Australia". Some titles provided social commentary reflecting community debates about punishment and the death penalty and Franks also notes evidence of titles underpinned by original research.[131] Toni Johnson-Woods describes the period of import restrictions as "*the* richest period in Australian literary history; thousands of titles were produced, millions of copies sold and dozens of authors found gainful employment".[132] Most of these enterprises disappeared when restrictions were lifted in 1959. In opposing the lifting of restrictions author and journalist Frank Clune argued,

> Now that the war had ended, Australia is again faced with the threat of unrestricted overseas competition, and possibly with the 'dumping' of cheap mass-produced books from overseas including 'pulp' magazines and 'remaindered' fiction-lines.[133]

In this period television also came into the picture, sating public appetites in ways that magazines and other forms of cheap literature could not. However, arguably the larger impact that contributed to the demise of these firms came from the re-emergence of international copyright as it had been originally designed to function. It again became difficult to obtain the rights to reprint foreign publications domestically.

The right of international copyright owners to control the Australian domestic market was highlighted with the creation of a new provision in the *Copyright Act* 1968 which explicitly prohibited parallel importation of books, ostensibly designed to prevent dumping of excess stock produced overseas but also a means of supporting territorial price discrimination.[134] Consumers paid the cost. Following numerous subsequent reports and inquiries into the higher costs of books in Australia there has been a slow relaxation of parallel importation provisions on books with significant reform in 1991 and the total abolition of remaining restrictions recommended in the eighth review of the subject matter by the Productivity Commission in 2016.[135] In response, as in Hall Caine's time, internationally prominent authors including Peter Carey and Richard Flanagan have fronted the media claiming parallel importation restrictions support local publishing – again confusing their own and their publisher's interests with the situation of all kinds of writers and publishers. No further reform has been enacted.

Since the late 19th century a small class of celebrities have assumed the right to speak as representatives of the writing profession relatively unchallenged in public discourse. Adult fiction may be highly prestigious and important to a nation's imagination but in terms of volume of trade it is a relatively small concern. The biggest share of profit in Australian publishing comes from educational publishing that targets students as a market, and academic publishing that targets experts, including teachers, and the infrastructure that supports these endeavours continues to reflect the imperial ordering built into the international copyright regime from its inception.

The costs of education

Lewis writes that,

> There was practically no Australian book publishing industry in the 1950s, educational or otherwise. With the exception of Angus and Robertson, Australian publishers were essentially distributors of British publishers. This changed in the 1960s with the development of both general and educational publishing.[136]

With the post-war baby boom the school book market became the first big growth area, then as access to university education became easier, the tertiary book market grew in the 1970s. Following UK law, Australia did not develop a fair dealing right for educational purposes comparable to a US fair use right. Out of concern for the rise of the photocopier and the consequences for authors' incomes as educational institutions began providing tailored extracts from books rather than prescribing texts, copyright provisions were introduced and a collection agency was established to manage an educational licensing scheme.[137] The Franki Committee noted at the time that, "there is negligible copying from short stories, novels and other works of fiction and from biographies, histories and commentaries of a 'popular' nature".[138] Nonetheless, a test case was soon staged that concerned use of a university copier infringing the rights of an Australian fiction writer. It led to further reforms ramping up legal obligations on libraries, schools and universities.[139] In the 1980s there was a cycle of publisher take-overs and consolidation, with growing incorporation of smaller independent firms into trans-national ones. This led to the Big Five publishing houses: Penguin Random House, HarperCollins, Macmillan,

Simon & Shuster and Hachette. Combined, as much as 90% of the fiction market is published by these organisations, and there is inter-penetration into educational publishing and academic and professional publishing. For example, Macmillan is owned by the German company Holtzbrinck, represented in academic publishing by Springer. Penguin Random House is owned by the German company, Bertelsmann, which also owns Pearson.[140] The largest education publishers in the Australian market are Pearson Australia, Penguin, Random House Australia and Scholastic Australia, a subsidiary of the Scholastic Corporation (US), the world's largest publisher of children's literature and print and educational material for school students.

The educational and academic sectors combined completely dominate book publishing in Australia comprising over 40% of all sales (see Table 4.2). The tertiary sector is especially significant in terms of book buying (see Table 4.3). However, as noted earlier, profit is not merely generated from book sales, library purchases and subscriptions. They contribute funds generated to the Copyright Agency operating the educational licensing scheme established in 1980.[141] The school sector comprises roughly 60% of revenue, whilst the tertiary sector contributes about 30%. At a time of increased student numbers and declining

Table 4.2 Australian onshore sales by percentage of market share 2014–2015

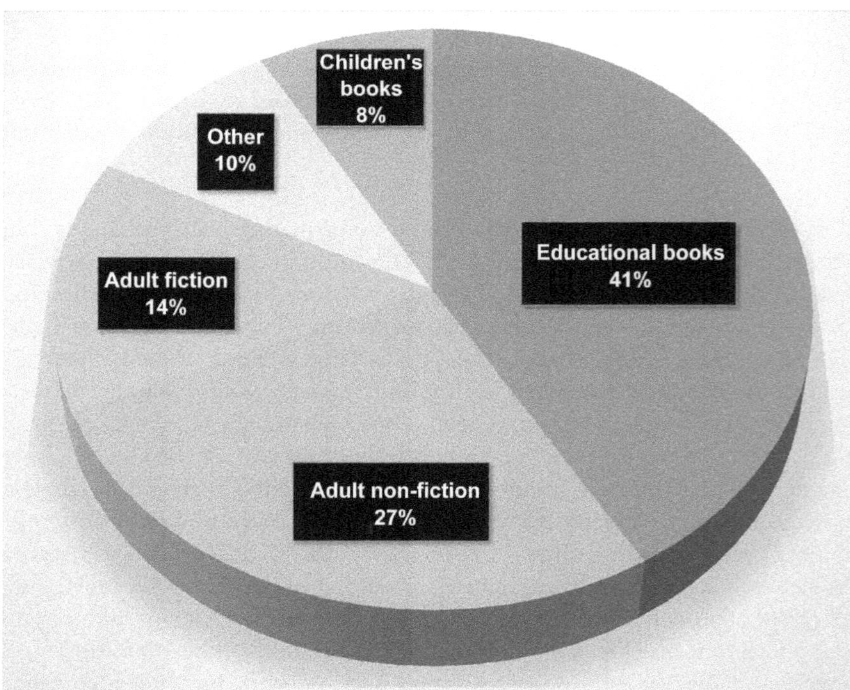

Source: Data derived from IBIS World, January 2016 in Throsby, Zwar & Morgan, *Australian Book Publishers in the Global Industry*, Macquarie Economics Research Paper, 1/2018

Table 4.3 Breakdown of Australian education sales 2015 (A$m)

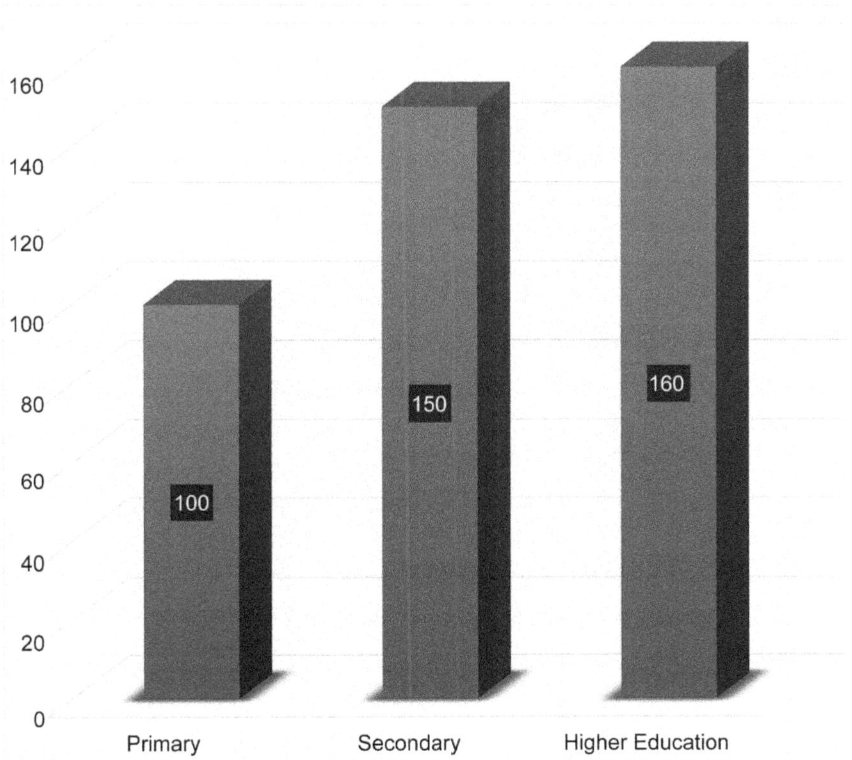

Source: Data derived from Australian Publishers Association January 2016.

public funding, license fees are slowly and very consistently growing, especially in the tertiary sector (see Table 4.4). The educational sector accounts for 71% of the income distributed by the Copyright Agency, meaning that this agency overwhelmingly collects and distributes funds amongst those involved in the creation, distribution and consumption of educational content. Their coding of distributions to the broad category of "educational content creators" amalgamates distributions to private-sector educational publishers, writers and illustrators. Data does not permit identification of the proportion of revenue that actually goes to Australian authors or academic institutional authors, compared to that which goes to Australian subsidiaries of multi-national publishing firms. One might imagine that if the data fitted the historical narrative about the proportional significance of this revenue to Australian and creative writers it would have surfaced long ago. A 2015 Australian study of 1,000 authors suggests that textbook writers receive the highest average payments from the agency (2015 A$1,400), followed by children's authors (A$600). Returns to other authors such as fiction and genre writers are not noted.[142]

Table 4.4 Distribution of educational license fees by Copyright Agency 2017–2018 (A$m)

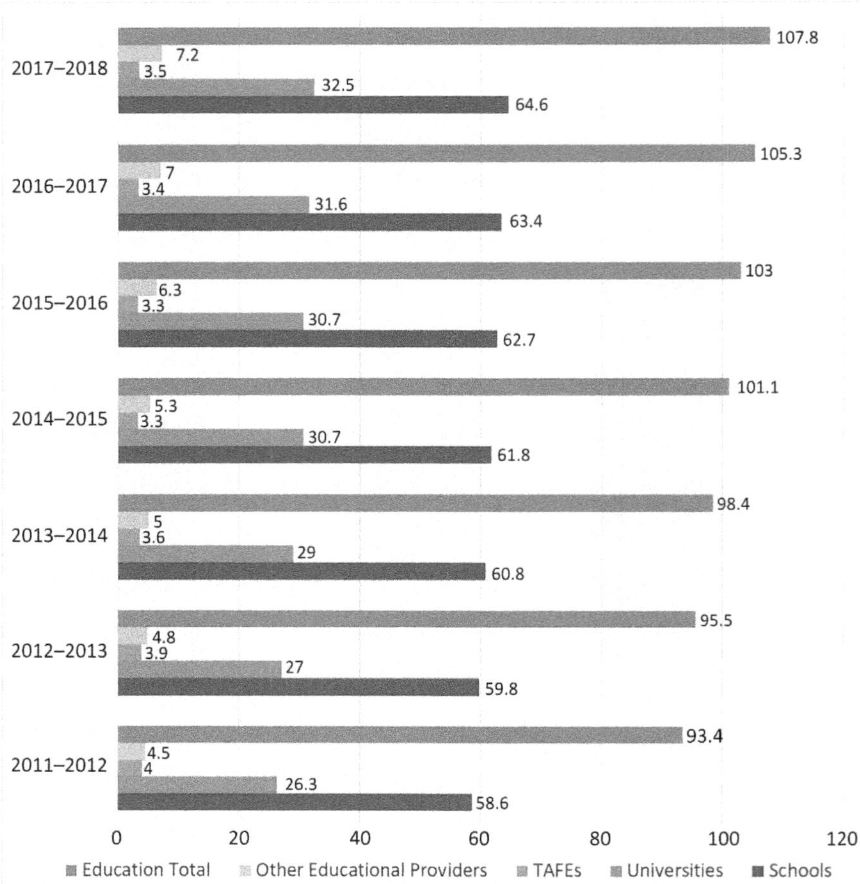

Source: Copyright Agency Annual Reports 2018; 2019

Digital technology has radically affected the delivery of education. Studies highlight that "virtually every stage of the traditional value chain in educational publishing has been disrupted in recent years". This includes the development of digital learning including Massive Open Online Courses, the decline of brick-and-mortar campus storefronts, textbook rentals and changing user behaviour including how titles are searched for or promoted to teachers and students, and piracy.[143] Given that the traditional value chain is essentially one that facilitates ongoing imperial copyright relations, this could be taken as a positive development. Technological disruption provides the opportunity to re-evaluate how copyright law should operate to support cultural and educational ambitions.

In Canada this has led to important public discussion leading to changes in how copyright functions to support education and the creative life of citizens.[144] However, attempts to reform Australian law and help address stresses on the education sector have been consistently blocked with emotional appeals by Australian celebrity authors fronting campaigns to retain the imperial status quo on behalf of the Copyright Agency, exhausting public interest and political will to meaningfully engage with expert reports.[145] Without an understanding of copyright history, well-funded propaganda that echoes of Victorian-era missionary work remains very effective in keeping the public in the dark.

Is international copyright still imperial in the age of transnational publishing?

Given the degree of consolidation in the publishing industry with transnational firms now dominating most market segments, there is no longer as clear a UK and US division of publishing markets, although identification of primary markets and rights management choices still orient toward traditional delineations. The belief in the value of authorial rights in supporting professional aspirations as well as national cultures remains strong. However, in recent years there has been a growing body of statistics on author royalties that should seed more critical discussion of how copyright works and for whom. Studies in both the UK and Australia demonstrate that on average, copyright persistently produces levels of income support below average minimum earnings, even where average earnings are distorted due to very unequal distributions within and across many classes of writer.[146] More fine-grained data relates to Australian practice. It underlines the reality that educational textbook writers and scholarly monograph writers are a class apart from literary fiction, genre fiction, children's, creative non-fiction writers and poets. This is due to the comparatively higher pay attributed to occupational roles that support their writing practice, as well as educational writers (but not scholarly writers) receiving much higher royalties on sales and also payments from the Copyright Agency than others, and still more from library-lending schemes than from educational licenses.[147] Although education writers do best overall as a class, it is interesting to note that educational and scholarly writers were also the most dependent of all classes of author on using established publishers.[148] On the whole, genre writers – crime/mystery/detective, action/adventure, fantasy, historical, horror, thriller, romance, erotica, science fiction and urban fantasy – do better than writers who do not identify with a particular genre, probably because having an identified genre helps reach audiences beyond national identifications. There is also the possibility of fan cross-over with some sharing of audiences with film, television and game consumers of the same genres.

The idea of the centrality of copyright to writing practice at large was promulgated by author's missionary work in the late 19th century to support their personal economic and cultural identifications across Empire as colonies and dominions started to exercise their independence. The spokesperson role of the creative fiction writer remains incredibly important when they are discussing cultural matters. Creative literature can inspire in ways that feeds the nation's imagination. It is important to the individuals who connect with the writing and their authors. But the idea that a few fiction authors today have some inherent greater wisdom or insight stemming from their particular experience in the publishing industry that enables them to speak for the profession of writing as a whole, and for copyright in general, is something that seriously needs reconsideration, in particular by them. They have no special insight into copyright in general and advocacy of the universal right of authors stems from an anachronistic imperial confection. Some celebrity novelists may have earned a position with some power within global publishing relations through making good publication choices as Conan Doyle did. However, in no way should celebrity writers be considered as representative spokespeople for a complex, transnational publishing industry. Economic studies consistently show that the fiction writer and the poet are, on the whole, now the *least representative* of writers *and* also the least favoured by the current international copyright system. In this regard the ongoing valorisation of nationally celebrated fiction writers as spokespersons for maintaining contemporary copyright relations does all writers a great disservice. It only helps sustain ongoing imperial power asymmetries into the 21st century.

Notes

1 Peter Prescott, 'The Origins of Copyright: A Debunking View' (1989) 12 EIPR 453
2 1 Eng Rep 837; 4 Burr 2408, 98 Eng Rep 257
3 The leading UK works include John Feather, *Publishing, Piracy and Politics: An Historical Study of Copyright in Britain* (Mansell Press 1994); Catherine Seville, *The Internationalisation of Copyright Law: Books, Buccaneers and the Black Flag in the Nineteenth Century* (CUP 2006)
4 *Copyright Act*, 1814, ss 4; 9 (54 Geo III c156)
5 *Copyright Law Amendment Act* 1842, s3 (5–6 Vict c45)
6 See Ronan Deazley, 'Commentary on *International Copyright Act* 1844' in L Bently and M Kretschmer (eds), *Primary Sources on Copyright (1450–1900)* (2008). www.copyright history.org
7 On appeal Jeffreys v Boosey (1854) 10 ER 681; 4 HLC 815 clarified that only resident aliens were covered by the Statute, but it remained unclear whether or not whether residency in a British dominion would suffice until Routledge v Low (1868) LR 3 HL 100 determined it was not
8 There was no imperial copyright law affecting artistic works until 1911. Thanks to Professor Lionel Bently for this point
9 The differences are however illuminating. See Lionel Bently, 'Copyright, Translations, and Relations between Britain and India in the Nineteenth and Early Twentieth Centuries' (2007) 82(3) Chicago-Kent LR 1181; Kathy Bowrey, '"The World Daguerreotyped – What a Spectacle!" Copyright Law, Photography and the Economic Mission of Empire' in Brad Sherman and Leanne Wiseman (eds), *Copyright and the Challenge of the New* (Kluwer 2013) 1
10 The *Colonial Laws Validity Act* 1865, (28–29 Vict c63). It was agreed this power would cease with the Balfour Declaration on 1926 and it was formally repealed by the Statute of Westminster 1931 (22 Geo 5 c4)
11 *Copyright Law Amendment Act*, 1842, ss. 15, 17 (5–6 Vict c45)
12 Seville (n 3) 81

13 There were however, failed attempts to legalise importation of foreign reprints in Australia. See Sarah Ailwood and Maree Sainsbury, 'The Imperial Effect: Literary Copyright Law in Colonial Australia' (2014) Law, Cult Humanit 1, 10–14

14 An early British treatise on international copyright refers to the rights offered to the British author under the reprint scheme as "an exceedingly empty thing". William Briggs, *The Law of International Copyright: With Special Sections on the Colonies and the United States* (Stevens & Haynes 1906) 607. See also Ronan Deazley, 'Commentary on the Foreign Reprints Act 1847' in L Bently and M Kretschmer (n 6)

15 Joseph J Beard, 'Good Hope and Great Expectations' (2008) 55 J Copyright Soc'y USA 589, 597–598

16 John Murray produced his first editions in 1843. See Angus Fraser, 'John Murray's Colonial and Home Library' (1997) 91(3) *The Papers of the Bibliographical Society of America.* 339. However, Catherine Seville notes that colonial libraries did not become commonplace until the late 1880s. (n 3) 83

17 Graeme Johanson, *Colonial Editions in Australia 1843–1972* (Elbank Press 2000) 2–5, 24–33, 272–273

18 (1868) LR 3 HL 100

19 Catherine Seville, 'Authors as Copyright Campaigners: Mark Twain's Legacy' (2008) 55 J Copyright Soc'y USA 283, 298

20 Copyright Commission, *Report of the Royal Commission on Copyright* (C 2036, 1878) [183]

21 Michael D Birnhack, *Colonial Copyright: Intellectual Property in Mandate Palestine* (OUP 2012) 1

22 Briggs (n 14) 695

23 *The International Copyright Act 1891*, ch 565, 226 Stat 1106

24 Peter Putnis, 'The Early Years of International Telegraphy in Australia' (2008) 129(1) Media International Australia 140; Lionel Bently, 'The Electric Telegraph and the Struggle over Copyright in News in Australia, Great Britain and India' in Sherman and Wiseman (n 9) 43

25 John Finnamore, 'Letter to the Editor: Colonial Author's Copyright' *The Argus* 10 Oct 1876, 6

26 Eli McLaren, *Dominion and Agency: Copyright and the Structuring of the Canadian Book Trade* (U of Toronto P 2011) 26

27 The top three book publishers in 1860–1899 were Sampson Low (UK: 15 titles; 4%); Richard Bentley (UK: 13 titles 3%) Chapman & Hall (UK: 9 titles); George Robertson (Aust: 9 titles; 2%); The Author (Aust: 9 titles; 2%); Tinsley (UK: 9 titles; 2%). Katherine Bode, 'Sidelines and Trade-lines. Publishing the Australian Novel 1860–1899' (2012) 15 Book History 93, 94; Katherine Bode, *Reading by Numbers, Recalibrating the Literary Field* (Anthem Press 2012) 44

28 Where a work was first published in a periodical the author could also reserve the right to publish the work "in a separate form" s18 *Copyright Act* 1842 (UK). There was no "originality" requirement in British legislation until 1911

29 See 'Introduction' and 'Adaptations'; Rolf Boldrewood, *Robbery under Arms*, Paul Eggert and Elizabeth Webby eds (U of Queensland P 2006); 'Mem. of Agreement Aug 23rd 1889 between Thomas A Browne and Messrs Macmillan & Co of London' Macmillan Archive. Vol. CLIV. BL: Add Ms 54939

30 A drama entitled *Robbery under Arms* no deposit Alfred Dampier, Alexandra Theatre, Melbourne, first published 1 Mar 1890. Register of Literary Copyrights (Vic), NAA: A2389, 4365; Registration No 4365, 18 Oct 1894, A drama entitled *Robbery under Arms*, Copyright Office Registers, Literary Works, TNA: COPY 3/40, 4365. For a discussion of the intersection between the performance right and publication, see Derek Miller, *Copyright and the Value of Performance 1770–1911* (CUP 2018) 183–203

31 Confusion as to who retained the film right to *Robbery under Arms* led to the collapse of Ken Hall's film of *Robbery under Arms* in the 1930s
32 Eva Hemmungs-Wirten, *No Trespassing: Authorship, Intellectual Property Rights and the Boundaries of Globalization* (U of Toronto P 2004) 17. The most comprehensive account of this activity is found in Seville (n 19)
33 Ibid 22
34 'Colonial Copyright' *Freeman's Journal* (Sydney) 21 Oct 1865, 664
35 McLaren (n 26)
36 Sara Bannerman, *The Struggle for Canadian Copyright: From Imperialism to Internationalism 1842–1971* (UBC Press 2013)
37 The *Colonial Duties Act* 1842 (5–6 Vict c49) reduced import duties, whilst the *Trade of British Possessions Act* 1845 (8–9 Vict c93) prohibited the importation of reprints into Britain. See Fraser (n 16) 339
38 Routledge in 1854; Macmillan in 1869, the latter being the most successful to do so. James LW West III, 'Book Publishing 1835–1900: The Anglo-American Connection' (1990) 84(4) Papers of the Bibliographical Society of America 357
39 'Copyright Association' *The Times* (London) 20 Mar 1872, 12 (emphasis added)
40 Copyright Commission (n 20) 12
41 The idea of allowing printing without permission of the author or publisher in the public interest was not entirely new. For example, Deazley notes Talfourd's bill of 1838 provided that when a copyright protected work had been out of print for five years or more, then anyone could give notice to the owners thereof, of their intention to publish that work. If, after 12 months no new edition had appeared, then the individual giving notice was not only free to republish the work, but upon republication the copyright in the work would belong to the new publisher for the residue of the copyright term. In the final version of the 1842 *Act*, after an author's death, should the owner of the author's copyright refuse to publish his or her work, then the Judicial Committee of the Privy Council were authorised to grant a licence, "in such manner and subject to such conditions as they may think fit", to ensure the publication of the same. See Deazley (n 6)
42 See Augustine Birrell, *Seven Lectures on the Law and History of Copyright in Books* (Cassell & Co, GP Putnam's Sons 1899) 207, 217
43 'Copyright Association' *The Morning Post* (London) 20 Mar 1872, 6
44 The notion of literary property advanced by the Society is discussed in Chapter 4, 78
45 Walter Besant, *The Society of Authors: A Record of Its Action from Its Foundation* (Incorporated Society of Authors 1893) 4
46 Ibid 7
47 Ibid 27–28
48 George Parsons Lanthrop, 'The American Copyright League: Its Origins and Early Days' *The Publisher's Weekly* 21 Jan 1888 [No. 834] 59
49 'The Reorganisation and the First Annual Meeting' *The Publisher's Weekly* 21 Jan 1888 (my emphasis)
50 Max M Kampelman, 'The United States and International Copyright' (1947) 41 (2) Am J Int'l L 406
51 Brander Matthews, 'Analysis of Book Titles Published in the USA, 1882–1886' in 'Will Copyright Reform Raise the Price of Books?' *Century Magazine* (1887) republished in *The Publisher's Weekly*, 21 Jan 1888 [No. 834] 77
52 Ibid
53 'An Open Letter to Readers of Books' *The Publisher's Weekly* 21 Jan 1888 [No. 834] 64–65
54 Peter Jaszi and Martha Woodmansee, 'Copyright in Transition' in Carl F Kaestle and Janie Radway (eds), *Print in Motion: The Expansion of Publishing and Reading in the United States, 1880–1940* (U of North Carolina P 2009) 97
55 A full list of members is noted in 'The American Publishers' Copyright League' *The Publisher's Weekly* 21 Jan. 1888 [No. 834] 66–70

General Tariff (applied to goods not from imperial countries) at 1/6 per dozen or 55% ad valorem, for each 3/per dozen or part thereof on the standard retail sale price in Australia or country of origin, whichever rate returns the higher duty. *Report of Evidence at the Tariff Board Inquiries into Proposal for Duty on Books, Magazines and Fashion Plates* (1930) 2. See further Ensor (n 110) 17–27

118 Norman Lindsay's controversial novel *Redheap* was banned by the censor in 1930, in part due to concerns about how Australia would be perceived in Britain. It was subsequently published by the new modernist press Faber. See Robert Darby, 'The Banning of Redheap: Sober Facts about Inflammatory Literature' (2013) 105 Labour History 171

119 The longest consideration of copyright is found in the evidence of former Melbourne University Law Professor, Sir William Harrison Moore, Director of Robertsons and Mullins, Melbourne, *Report of Evidence at the Tariff Board* (1930) (n 118) 64–71

120 Angus & Robertson, *Tariff Board's Report on Publishing Industry (1947)* (Commonwealth Government Printer 1946) 28

121 *Report of Evidence at the Tariff Board (1930)* (n 118) 54, 56

122 By the mid-20th century the export trade made up 50% of the British market. Ensor (n 110) 51

123 As Nile explains,

> In the years before the second world war, Australian publishers were intimidated by the ability of the British cartel to land books at cheap prices in a trade where a single ship load of stock was enough to sink even the most enthusiastic of local or nationalist sentiment.
>
> (n 113) 71–91

124 Senator Cameron, 'Revised Estimates' Australian Parliament, Senate 5 Dec 1939 [2040]

125 Ibid [2039]

126 See Cultural Defence Committee, *Mental Rubbish from Overseas: A Public Protest* (Cultural Defence Committee 1935)

127 See Toni Johnson-Woods, 'Pulp-Friction: Governmental Control of Cheap Fiction, 1939–1959' (2006) 30(2) Script & Print 103

128 s3 Customs (Import Licensing) Regulations 1939, Statutory Rules No 163

129 Jim Hagan, *Printers and Politics: A History of Australian Printing Unions* (ANU Press 1966) 266

130 Evidence of WG Cousin, representing Angus & Robertson (n 121) 14–15

131 Rachel Franks, '"A World of Fancy Fiction and Fact": The Frank C Johnson Archive at the State Library of New South Wales' in P Mountford (ed), *Peer Reviewed Proceedings: 6th Annual Conference, Popular Culture Association of Australia and New Zealand, Wellington* (PopCAANZ 2015) 13–24, 15–16

132 Toni Johnson-Woods, 'Pulp-Fiction in Australia 1949–1959' (2006) 20(1) *Antipodes* 63. There is a need for further research to be done here. Johnson-Woods notes the volume of imported books from the US actually increased overall during the war, but there is no breakdown of the data with reference to subject matter, Johnson-Woods (n 128) 118

133 Frank Clune, *Tariff Board Report*, quoted in ibid 117

134 Sections 37; 102 *Copyright Act* 1968 (Cth). Price discrimination did not necessarily lead to higher prices in all jurisdictions

135 Sections 44A; 112A *Copyright Act* 1968 (Cth); Australian Productivity Commission, *Intellectual Property Arrangements, Inquiry Report*, 2016

136 Glen Lewis, '"It's Academic": Imperialism and the Australian Tertiary Book Industry' (1990) 4(1) *Continuum: Journal of Media & Cultural Studies* 92, 100

137 Report of the Copyright Law Committee on Reprographic Reproduction (The Franki Committee) Australian Government Publishing Service, 1976

138 Ibid 1.17

139 The test case focussed on Frank Moorhouse's *The Americans, Baby: A Collection of Short Stories* (Angus & Robertson 1972). *Moorhouse v University of New South Wales* (1974) 23 FLR 112; [1975] HCA 26. See further Leanne Wiseman, 'Making Copies: Photocopying and Copyright' in Sherman and Wiseman (n 9) 197–220

140 Per Henningsgaard, 'Types of Publishing Houses' in Alison Baverstock, Richard Bradford and Madelena Gonzalez (eds), *Contemporary Publishing and the Culture of Books* (Routledge 2020) 35

141 *Copyright Amendment Act* 1980 No 154 of 1980

142 Jan Zwar, David Throsby and Thomas Longden, *Australian Authors: Industry Brief No 3. Author's Income*, Macquarie University, Oct 2015. www.businessandeconomics.mq.edu.au/our_departments/Economics/econ_research/reach_network/book_project/authors/3_Authors_Income.pdf

143 Jan Zwar, *Disruption and Innovation in the Australian Book Industry: Case Studies of Trade and Education Publishers*, Macquarie Economics Research Paper, 1/2016; Throsby, Zwar and Morgan (n 136)

144 Michael Geist (ed), *In the Public Interest: The Future of Canadian Copyright Law* (Irwin Law 2005); Rosemary Coombe, Darren Wershler and Martin Zeilinger (eds), *Dynamic Fair Dealing: Creating Canadian Culture Online* (U of Toronto P 2014)

145 Australian Law Reform Commission, *Copyright and the Digital Economy Final Report*, No 122, 2012; Australian Productivity Commission, *Intellectual Property Arrangements, Inquiry Report*, 2016

146 The Authors' Licensing and Collecting Society, *What Are Words Worth Now? A Survey of Author's Earnings, 2017*. https://wp.alcs.co.uk/app/uploads/2017/07/Authors-earning_2017-download-version.pdf; The Authors' Licensing and Collecting Society, *What Are Words Worth Now? Further Findings, 2017*. https://wp.alcs.co.uk/app/uploads/2017/07/Authors-earning-further-findings-2017-download-version.pdf; Zwar, Throsby and Longden (n 135)

147 Ibid

148 Jan Zwar, David Throsby and Thomas Longden, *Australian Authors: Industry Brief No 9. Authors and Publishers*. www.businessandeconomics.mq.edu.au/our_departments/Economics/econ_research/reach_network/book_project/authors/9_Authors_and_Publishers.pdf

5 Print capitalism meets Hollywood. The work of industrial authorship

New technology is often characterised as a disruptive threat to established copyright interests. This chapter explores how authors, playwrights and publishers responded to the emergence of film. The most popular narrative film titles were often based on well-known stories and plays. In the Victorian era, print and live performance markets were interconnected. Both markets were impacted by the international distribution of film, a business that steadily grew after 1896. Whilst the publisher might own a literary property right, authors often simultaneously arranged for a performance right for their stories. If success could be found on the London stage, international, provincial and colonial touring might also be arranged. As discussed in previous chapters, authors like Hugh Conway, Fergus Hume, Conan Doyle and Hall Caine all generated significant royalties from performance rights, in addition to money obtained by licensing or assigning the copyright to publishers. Once stories started to appear on film, many authors and playwrights sought to be paid for film adaptation. So did publishers. This chapter explores why authors, and especially playwrights, failed to significantly benefit from film rights.

The idea of authorial property, the widespread belief that private control over the circulation of the creative expression of authors is warranted, justified the need for copyright law reform to better protect authorial interests. However, while publishers were most effective in working with Hollywood to support the international infrastructure for exploitation of existing copyrights on film, traditional dramatic modes of experiencing stories were impacted by competition from the popularity of a spectacular new medium and, at the same time, authors and playwrights were cut out of meaningful negotiation over the terms of film adaptation. The early 20th century marks a fundamental shift in the industrial significance of authorship, as individual and family firms give way to multi-national enterprises, contractual terms become standardised and the negotiating power of any individual actor substantially diminished.

The emergence of film combines facilitated the rise of industrial authorship. Film combines sprang from the merging of film production, distribution and, to a lesser extent, exhibition interests. This development affected whose stories were produced, distributed and screened in cities, suburbs and small towns. Strategic pooling of patents, copyright licensing and imposing standard contractual arrangements were central to consolidation of Hollywood's bargaining power. Confidential business communications, contracts and evidence given to numerous Australian government inquiries into the national film industry are drawn upon to explain how Hollywood studios achieved a stranglehold over British and Asia-Pacific film production and distribution by the 1920s. I explore why the Imperial Conference 1926 solution to the problem of a growing international American influence – quotas for British and dominion films and restrictions on blind and block bookings of Hollywood content – failed, revealing for the first time the real extent of collusion to affect film markets outside the US facilitated through new industry bodies such as the Motion Picture Producers and Distributors Association of America (MPPDA). This chapter brings to light how quite limited copyrights and registration of patents could be used to secure market dominance and manage technological change. Though new players emerged once silent film came to be supplanted by sound on film, the international business infrastructure that concentrated power in a small number of multi-national firms survived into the talkie era. It was not necessary for Hollywood to own extensive film copyright or directly interfere in the running of domestic firms to control international film distribution and exhibition markets from an American base – a situation that radically disadvantaged independent and local film production across the globe.

The huge international appetite for American film raises concern for cultural imperialism; however the final part of this chapter complicates our understanding of an "American film". A very significant number of silent-era Hollywood films were censored, and not only by the state. For commercial reasons, and informed by box office data, the local distributor might rename, re-edit and reshoot a film to remove excessive references to American values and patriotism that it was predicted would jar audiences outside the US. It was not copyright, nor the director, producer or studio's vision that exclusively determined Hollywood content for overseas audiences. Though US foreign policy dictated that "trade follows the film" and the capacity for economic control afar was well developed, American cultural content would not be imposed on audiences judged as likely to be unreceptive. This chapter reminds us how and why cultural markets require a sensitive touch, where intellectual property rights are merely one of a number of complex factors that impact on the global circulation of a story.

Connecting cultural markets

Books and plays

The same story might be experienced through several mediums. While a book comes to life in the mind of the reader, the play offers a more social experience. In the mid–late 19th century successful books readily found an audience on the stage, and vice versa. However, although the author may also serve as playwright or lend name recognition as a "co-author" to a script penned by a more experienced playwright, the business of staging plays required significant capital and expertise. Many of the leading Victorian playwrights were associated with particular theatres and theatre managers. It was usually the theatrical entrepreneur, rather than the author or playwright, who facilitated touring of successful productions.[1] This was a trade based on links with leading performers, as well as controlling access to and circulation of the script, the necessary knowledge required to stage the play and essential unique props, scenery and costumes.

While copyright, where applicable, was licensed to facilitate dramatisation, it remained difficult to protect books and plays against competition from unauthorised dramatisation throughout the 19th century. There were different sources of right – a performance right under the *Dramatic Literary Copyright Act* 1833 (UK) and a literary copyright under the *Copyright Act* 1842 (UK). The rights were not formulated with the creator's interests in mind. What rights existed and the respective term depended upon whether a work was unpublished, printed or performed, and in which order the publication or performance occurred.

The manuscript of an unpublished and unperformed play was protected against both unauthorised publication and unauthorised performance in perpetuity. The *Dramatic Literary Copyright Act* 1833 created a performance right for works that were performed, capable of being printed but had not been printed, without prescribing a term. The owner of the performance right could assign that right in any part of the British dominions but, because the assignee was something less than an "owner", there were further steps that were necessary if the assignee wanted to sue for infringement in jurisdictions such as the colonies. Section 20 *Copyright Act* 1842 sought to equate the performance right to that of book publication, also requiring registration. This was effected by making the date of first performance the date of first "publication". For dramatic works that were performed, but not published as books, the term of the right was effectively reduced from an unlimited right to a term of the life of the author plus seven years after his or her death, or for 42 years from the first publication (whichever was longer). Copyright could restrain authorised printing of the manuscript.

This reform benefitted theatrical entrepreneurs interested in stockpiling rights to both published and unpublished dramatic works. The trade in unpublished plays was facilitated by the development of the innovative practice of "copyright performances". The copyright performance involved advertising and staging a first performance of an unpublished dramatic work specifically to secure the copyright registration – sometimes whilst the script was still undergoing further development, sometimes timed in conjunction with book publication. These performances could be little more than a reading of the story without staging.[2] What was secured by the registration was an exclusive performance right to the title of the dramatic work and theoretically the work itself. However, what was actually staged or toured later on could be further defined by contracts at the relevant date.[3]

While the practice of licensing dramatic works grew significantly in this period, the technicality of the legislation created great confusion. For dramatic works that were printed but not performed, the term of the copyright in the publication was the life of the author plus seven years after his or her death, or for 42 years from the first publication (whichever was longer). However, there was disagreement about how printing affected the performance right. The Copyright Commission 1878 doubted that a performance right could be gained where the story was first published as a book. Here "copyright performances" of plays also helped to secure a performance right in conjunction with book publication.[4]

Even with registration of the performance right and of a publication under the *Copyright Act* 1842, due to the test for copyright infringement being applied, it often proved difficult to protect the author's interest. As a leading treatise explains,

> The English law of Playright and Dramatic Copyright suffers from two great faults. In the first place, playright and copyright, which are merely protection of different modes of communicating the same intellectual results to the public are treated in different ways, and may begin and end at different times. Secondly, that tendency of the English law, which in questions of infringement seems rather to consider whether new work has been added rather than whether old work has been taken, is specially prominent in the case of dramatisation of novels.[5]

It was not necessarily a piracy to adapt a work for the stage afresh. Nonetheless there remained a distinctive market for the performance rights to particular plays. Further, the inclusion of a famous author's imprimatur could help attract interest in staging the work in a higher class of theatre, where success would increase the chances of touring.

Distribution channels for plays

Following the passage of the *Dramatic Literary Copyright Act* 1833, theatrical entrepreneurs sought the entire performance right to a play so that they might profit from licenses sold for touring the show to other major cities, provinces, North America and following the shipping route from Africa, across Australasia. The Dramatic Authors Society was established in 1833 as a rights management organisation to capitalise on these opportunities. The Society sought to assist members with negotiation and also with policing rights by contracting with agents who worked on a commission basis to collect fees and police infringements in far-flung places. By 1865 the Society would claim 2,000 plays under its protection. Leading playwrights, including Dion Boucicault and WS Gilbert, also exercised rights independently of the organisation.[6]

Colonial theatrical entrepreneurs closely followed London shows and sought to obtain exclusive regional touring rights to supplement performances and touring of works by colonial playwrights.[7] The enterprising colonial theatrical entrepreneur George Coppin (1819–1906) entered into an agency arrangement with the Dramatic Authors Society in 1865 and Irishman and writer Joseph Stirling Coyne (1805–1868) who was Society Secretary.[8] An exclusive arrangement purported to grant to Coppin the performance rights attached to a very large number of fashionable "tragedies, comedies, Plays, Operas, farces, melodramas, Burlesques and dramatic and operatic pieces" owned by society members for performance in the Australian colonies and New Zealand, initially for five years. In exchange Coppin retained 30% of all monies received from further assignments of rights for colonial touring and infringement actions pursued through the courts. Coppin had to cover his own costs including that of court proceedings, except for Appeals that required the consent of the Society Secretary. In 1878 the Dramatist's Society informed the Royal Commission into Copyright that legal technicalities affected the ability to enforce society members' copyrights in the colonies. For example, whilst the agreement with Coppin sought to create a general power of attorney so that he could sue on behalf of the Society, Coppin did not have power of attorney from the individual playwrights or a registered assignment of rights to individual works. Technically this should have frustrated infringement actions; however surviving colonial case law suggests a more nuanced picture. Both Coppin and JC Williamson successfully pursued alleged infringement of performance rights in plays by British authors in the colonies, even where doubts had been raised about their legal capacity to bring the action.[9] Presumably the courts preferred to support the ideology of a theatrical trade regulated by copyright to such a degree that they overlooked that the plaintiff actually had no standing to bring the litigation.

The Dramatic Society's agency and rights management arrangements fell into disarray in the 1880s leading to the interests of playwrights being taken over by the newly formed Society of Authors in 1884. With this development the specific issues concerning playwrights came to be merged with author interests in general. The collective and distinctive interests of playwrights and theatrical entrepreneurs became less visible. As is discussed further later, playwrights lost significant capacity to impact on the development of British copyright policy and industrial practice. This led to limitations in protecting their markets from competition with film, even though eminent playwrights would continue to independently advocate their own interests in Parliament and the courts.[10]

Book, plays and film adaptation

Films were generally based on stories that had originated in other mediums and films were commonly exhibited alongside traditional theatrical, music hall and vaudeville acts. Film historian Denis Gifford has compiled a catalogue of 2,774 silent films released in the UK, US, Germany, France, Scandinavia, Canada, Japan and Australia from 1896–1915 tracking the underlying works from which the films were adapted.[11] Though there are always issues with archival work on silent film related to the fragility and survival of these works, the sample is large enough to reveal something of the new financial opportunities for authors and playwrights created by the new entertainment medium.

Keeping in mind that this catalogue does not seek to cover "actualities" – documentary, news or sports-related films – the data analysis represented in Table 5.1 reveals the different types of creative subject matter underlying the first wave of silent films indexed by Gifford. Table 5.2 maps that data across copyright categories. Novels, followed by short stories, were overwhelmingly utilised as source material, with literary works inspiring 70% of all film adaptations; 26% were based on plays, 4% on cartoons.

It is a misapprehension to think that film-makers needed to obtain a license from literary copyright or performance right holders for all the films catalogued. Some of the underlying literary works were clearly in the public domain. For example, there were 75 films listed as based on the plays and poems of William

Table 5.1 Subject matter analysis: literary, theatrical and artistic sources of the first 20 years of motion pictures, 1896–1915

Source	*Number*	*Percentage*
Ballet	2	
Biography	5	
Cartoon	104	4
Character	18	
Novel	958	35
Non-fiction	2	
Opera	48	2
Play	672	24
Poem	186	7
Short story	772	28
Song	7	
TOTALS	**2,774**	**100**

Table 5.2 Rights analysis: literary, theatrical and artistic sources of the first 20 years of motion pictures, 1896–1915

Copyright work	*Number*	*Percentage*
Literary works combined:	1941	70
Biography, characters, novels, non-fiction, poems, short stories		
Musical and dramatic works combined:	729	26
Ballet, opera, plays, songs		
Artistic works:	104	4
Cartoons		
TOTALS	**2,774**	**100**

Source: Data derived from Denis Gifford, *Books and Plays in Films, 1896–1915* (McFarland/Mansell, 1991)

Shakespeare – works that pre-dated British copyright legislation. There were 26 that featured the character of Sherlock Holmes, but not all were necessarily based on a Conan Doyle story, where the mere idea of character was not protected by copyright. Further due to US-UK copyright technicalities, many works first published in Britain before 1891 were not protected in the US, a major source of films and it was unclear if screening these stories in the UK constituted a copyright infringement.

Many authors and playwrights were aggrieved by stage and film reimaginings of their work without consent, leading to pressure for further reform to extend the definition of infringement to clearly encompass all kinds of unauthorised adaptations.[12] Unsurprisingly, there was also litigation to test whether a film did infringe the performance right in a dramatic work. An example is *Karno v Pathé Frères London* (1908).[13] Karno managed a troupe of comedians, including Charlie Chaplin, who specialised in music hall sketches. Pathé Frères London had been established in 1902 by the very successful French film equipment, production and distribution company founded by the Pathé Brothers in 1896. The dispute concerned the "sole rights" to the vaudeville act, *The Mumming Birds or Twice Nightly*, and potential infringement of the performance right by *At the Music Hall*, being a film of the same vaudeville show. The show involved performers on and off stage. A male vocalist, a lady vocalist, a conjurer, a wrestler, a quartet and a soubrette were on stage. "Audience members" included a boy in an Eton suit, his guardian and an intoxicated swell. Performers were asked to "extemporise", responding to various scenes read out from cards, the humour based upon the incompetence of the acting, various pranks and the personas, such as "Deadwood Dick". The pantomime had been much performed in America and England. At the time of the litigation it was being performed by three companies in England and was touring abroad. No written script was used in the UK but Karno claimed in evidence that all the stage directions and words were "carefully rehearsed" and performances staged under license were essentially the same.

The Mumming Birds was registered as a dramatic work in the UK on 15 January 1906, noting its first performance in Britain at the Star Music Hall, Bermondsey, 14 April 1904. A silent film, which, according to the report, copied the essential particulars of the skits, started being exhibited in provincial theatres in advance of the tour of the live performance, spoiling interest in the show that might otherwise have drawn an audience.[14] On hearing the evidence, Mr Justice Jelf found that the lack of connecting words, the absence of reliance on printed stage directions precluded protection under the *Dramatic Literary Copyright Act* 1833. However, he tentatively suggested that had the pantomime involved more "literary elements" the performance right may have been infringed by the film because the new medium involved more than mere pictures or stationary tableaux vivants. Film captured the essence of the live performance – "figures moving about", just "like living persons", where they could be "seen by spectators".[15] Film appropriated many of the unique features that made live theatre a popular pastime. There was a clear sympathy to protect established theatre and restrict market interference from cinematic interlopers.

The Berlin Revision of the Berne Convention (entered into force 9 Sept 1910) placed authors' and publishers' rights on a firmer foundation. Article 12 clarified that writers of original works should be entitled to control who made dramatic adaptations of their stories. Article 14 clarified that this included a right to represent the story on film. However, it was also recognised that film adaptation was no small task. Plot and emotion were conveyed through inter-titles, music (also licensed), cinematography and effects (including colourisation, used to signal appropriate emotional responses and night and day), as well as the performances and expressions captured by the cinematographer. Sometimes, in place of inter-titles, actors provided "lectures" accompanying the screening. The makers of cinematograph film (along with gramophone companies), were also recognised as deserving protection for their investments and awarded an exclusive copyright to film productions.[16] The UK ratified the revised convention on 14 June 1912 and this change was enacted in British law in the *Copyright Act* 1911 (UK).

After the *Act* was "modernised", it took a number of cases to clarify the essential features of dramatic copyright infringement, with basic principles only becoming clear in the 1920s. Even with the technical clarification, stock theatrical features, characters and plots remained unprotected in the UK.[17] Whether the alleged infringement involved reproduction of the literary or dramatic work on film was a complicated matter. Whether or not there was an infringement depended upon complex technicalities as to who owned which specific rights at what times, and the specifics of the similarities alleged.[18] Litigating after a film was released was soon understood as a poor way to determine the scope of exclusive literary and performance rights. Licensing adaptation rights from likely potential claimants was one way of managing legal risks. This led to a practice of film companies licensing underlying rights for strategic reasons, regardless of the source of inspiration for the film production script.

Given the number of film adaptations based upon literary works and a situation where theatrical performance markets were transforming into "exhibition" markets, an alignment between film production companies, established publishers and author societies made commercial sense. Copyright in the underlying literary works could be drawn upon to better manage potential competition across mediums and support synergistic marketing between new editions of books and authorised feature films inspired by the same or similar stories. A specialist film rights clearance agency, the Author's Cinematograph Copyright Agency, was established in the UK around 1913. The Society of Authors also established a Cinematic Sub-Committee around 1914.[19] The Society of Authors and film production companies worked together to limit the prospects of competing film versions of the same story coming out at the same time in the same geographical markets. The Society sought to extend its existing author/publisher mediation service to disputes over film rights. There were also initiatives to restrain the unauthorised use of known book titles as film titles. Sometimes the film version was, in actuality, based on an entirely unrelated story. By appropriating a well-known title a film could draw an audience while the potential film market for a licensed work would be spoilt. Copyright did not easily extend to titles. Between 1911 and 1914 there were inconclusive attempts to use the tort of passing off to reduce competition between the titles of plays and film. However, this remedy was only available *after* the competing film had been made and distributed.[20] Members of the Cinematic Sub-Committee sought to share news of titles for which the rights had been sold, and film production companies advised them of film titles in development to help all parties manage potential conflicts.[21]

The journal *The Author* provides an indication of the value of adaptation rights for film in the first decade of the 20th century. Payments for US rights were generally higher than in Britain, with a custom of paying £200–£400 on account of royalties, running from 5–15% on the producer's share of receipts. It was common for American film-makers to pay £100 outright for UK rights for a copyrighted novel, but there is also reference to a playwright receiving £200 outright for moving picture rights, another author accepting £500 for entire "world rights" to a play, and a famous writer receiving £750 on account of a percentage of the gross receipts.[22] These are not insubstantial payments to authors, though the scale of production costs and potential returns would also vary greatly depending upon the fame of the story, whom the film producer was and the extent of national and international film distribution.

The decline of the author-playwright

Though the noted playwright Bernard Shaw gave evidence, author-playwrights and theatrical entrepreneurs were not represented in the Commission of Inquiry that recommended copyright reform to keep pace with new technologies.[23] Section 24 and the First Schedule of the *Copyright Act* 1911 (UK) determined that where a story and play had previously been made public, the new film adaptation right belonged to the owner of the copyright in the literary work. The owner of a pre-existing performance right did not gain any new or enlarged right under the Act. This development placed established playwrights and author-playwrights at a distinct disadvantage to book publishers. Plays were now directly competing for venues and audiences with film affecting the contemporary value of dramatic copyright, but neither author nor playwright could prevent an unwanted film adaptation or benefit from it unless they had also retained the copyright in a book publishing agreement made at the time before film had been invented.

Some authors became personally involved in film rights negotiations – seeking to assert rights the law did not afford them. Hall Caine approached film rights as an opportunity to propel the acting career of his under-occupied son, Derwent. Employment of Derwent was treated as part and parcel of a film licensing arrangement.[24] Caine believed retention of performance rights entitled him to ownership of any new film right, notwithstanding his assignment of copyright to publishers. He argued with the Author's Cinematograph Copyright Agency that,

> The facts of the case are so absolutely plain that they can hardly need a moments consideration for anyone who knows what a drama is in the making and what a film is in the making, and what both are in their effects upon each other.
>
> They are both forms of dramatization, and as such have been recognized by the law of every civilized country in which they exist together . . . I myself . . . am under interim injunction . . . in Australia, not to sell the film of the *Eternal City* until I have satisfied, or defeated, the people to whom an agent leased the play made from the same book. . . .
>
> I reserved the dramatic right in my novels. It is absolutely impossible for anybody to make films from them without reproducing some of the scenes which I alone have a right to present for public exhibition in any form whatever.[25]

Caine's understanding of the law was based on a logical reading of whose labour value and market was being appropriated by film-making given the similarities between film and drama. It was also based on his understanding of Australian legal practice but, as is discussed later, this was anomalous. Though active in the organisation, Caine had not been advised by the Society of Authors about the actual technical content of the recent law reform. Nonetheless, presumably due to his past service to the Society as a copyright missionary and his impressive capacity to publicly propel his own interests, Caine had his way. He obtained a personal concession that the London Film Company would not be sued over a production based upon his purported assignment of a film adaptation right in *The Deemster.*[26] However, the value of this concession is unclear. The film itself does not appear to have been distributed.

While, after 1912, authors and playwrights might have sought to retain a film adaptation right or negotiate an appropriate royalty rate for a new film production, playwrights now had to operate in a far more confined market. In terms of employment as a writer in the film industry, a new professional, the film scenarist, was also beginning to step in to replace the role of the theatrical playwright in visualising the story for public entertainment. The scenarist/film writer was a mere employee of the film production company, not an owner of a dramatic copyright entitled to a royalty. Theatre might continue to thrive in the large metropolitan cities that were famous for it and London and New York hits could fill theatres as they toured the globe; however the playwright's opportunities for theatrical employment became far more constrained outside of these centres, and especially so abroad.

The theatrical entrepreneur as film-maker

Whilst authors and large book publishers were potentially useful friends and allies to the larger film-makers, theatrical entrepreneurs who controlled access to leading exhibition spaces were potentially a threat. Though in Britain film exhibition took longer to displace the dominance of theatre, in Australia theatrical venues came to be associated with independent film production and distribution companies in the very early 1900s.[27] Theatre managers who controlled access to the leading exhibition spaces understood the strength of the consumer demand for film and the profits to be had by servicing an increasingly large audience. Diversifying into film production, building new higher quality cinemas, upscaling amenities and extending control over film distribution was a logical step. When it came to licensing of film adaptation, the traditional practice of theatres first obtaining a performance right to exhibit the dramatic work was retained in Australia. Large Australian film production companies such as Amalgamated Pictures Ltd licensed the right to adapt a story for film from the playwright – often without any consideration of the ownership of the original literary work. This legal practice was entirely contrary to the 1912 reform.[28] The practice appears to have continued till as late as the 1930s. The penny dropped during production of the Ken Hall/Greater Union film of Rolf Boldrewood's *Robbery under Arms*. In 1933 it emerged that despite expending £3,600 on purchasing the film adaptation right from Ray Longford (1878–1959), Longford had only ever held a performance right. Boldrewood's British publisher, Macmillan, wrote to the relevant copyright holder, the author's daughter, Rose Browne, to alert her to the situation. The matter took several years to resolve. In 1937 Greater Union's Stuart Doyle (1887–1945) travelled to Browne's home town of Melbourne to obtain the right to make a talkie of *Robbery under Arms*; however by this time Greater Union was abandoning feature film production to focus more exclusively on distribution and exhibition profits. The film was never made.[29]

Perhaps in light of Australian legal practice, restrictive clauses started to appear in US-issued contracts over performing rights after 1912. For example, a 1915 contract between Australian theatrical entrepreneur JC Williamson and Americans Winchel Smith, Victor Mapes and David Belasco over the touring of the Broadway comedy, *The Boomerang*, explicitly reserved the motion picture rights. This was to ensure that the JC Williamson Film Ltd, a new Australian film production company that emerged in late 1914,[30] did not film the stage show, interfering with American plans to distribute their own version of the title on film the following year.[31] However, the key to controlling exhibition markets was not to be achieved through non-compete clauses in international licensing of dramatic works. A more important priority for film companies was to consolidate control by building a new business infrastructure to support international film distribution.

The rise of film combines in the early 20th century

American film combines, originally based on patent pools, began to emerge in the early 20th century.[32] In 1907 American litigation gave Edison a monopoly over "the design of most practical cameras in use" in the trade.[33] As a result of this litigation, the world's largest international film distributor, Pathé agreed to become an Edison licensee, "Once Pathé fell in line, most of the producers followed. Vitagraph, Kalem, Lubin, Melies, Selig and Essanay joined Pathé to form the Edison Licensees".[34] Initially the party that lost the litigation, American Mutoscope and Biograph Company, did not. Instead, they sought to enhance their own patent position. Biograph owned the Pross patent on projector shutters and the Latham loop patent (purchased in February 1908), both essential to the projector and useful in cameras. Like Edison, they licensed these to equipment manufacturers and constructed their own alliance of firms.[35] The Motion Picture Patent Company (MPPC) was formed when Biograph came to terms with Edison in 1908. Anyone anywhere on the globe keeping abreast of the technological developments and improvements related to patents over film stock, cameras and projection would have been aware of the American litigation and company consolidations and their potential significance for the film producers and distributors.

American film scholars argue that one outcome of the creation of the patent pool was the spread of the idea of using available intellectual property rights as well as tying arrangements, as leverage, alongside a strategy of vertical and horizontal integration of film companies. The emergence of MPPC also encouraged a collective identity amongst smaller companies who came to self-identify as independents. But as Staiger notes, it is simplistic to consider the MPPC as monolithic, and the "so-called independents" as immune from adopting similar corporatist practices and litigation strategies. Staiger tracks the development of cartel behaviour operating amongst the "independent" distribution companies that sprang up to distribute members' films. By 1912 this behaviour had led to four distribution combinations in operation – General Film, Mutual, Film Supply and Universal. As well as the "independents" adopting the same corporate strategies of combination – vertical and horizontal integration, diversification, interlocking directorships – there was also collusion to disrupt the gathering of evidence about patent infringements and co-operation in sharing costs in defending actions against the MPPC.[36]

Explanations for the sharp demise of the MPPC suggest that it was falling apart well before anti-trust litigation led to a decision to dissolve it in 1915.[37] Stagier notes that take-up of the innovation of multi-reel films completely disrupted the existing pattern of distribution and exhibition arrangements. The higher costs associated with feature-length stories, stars and elaborate sets made the pricing of films per foot as set out under conventional distribution contracts unattractive. National feature film distribution alliances, such as Warners, Paramount, World and Fox's Box Office, sprang up from 1914 to ensure a regular schedule of feature films and an assurance of a return on increasing costs. Feature films, and in particular the "super films which most exhibitors must take to maintain their clientele",[38] produced higher returns for the distributor.

One method of maximising profit was to combine feature films with block and blind booking – take studio and star power and other production matters into account in pricing license bundles, using demand for distinguished "A" features to drive the bulk purchase of sight unseen blocks of "B" and "C" grade films. "A" films were usually 90–95 minutes in length. "B" films were a maximum of 65 minutes, i.e. six reels (three spools). "B" productions were not necessarily B grade or lower quality films but they were always booked as the supporting feature to the "A" film, because of their length. Only the "A" film was usually promoted. "C" films were mainly actualities, that is short non-fiction films, typically news.[39] Film copyright made possible a new method of "wholesaling" films. With block and blind booking, films could be stripped of their distinctive authorship and intrinsic cultural qualities that created ephemeral demand and leased alongside films without underlying copyrights. The commodity form was aggregated in terms of exhibition needs, graded and priced as suited the distributor negotiating with exhibitors. To maximise return and for sake of efficiency, the international trade was managed through territorial agency arrangements, but these agents and subsidiaries did not simply handle the logistics of distributing celluloid. The backbone of their business was underpinned by contracts and bundles of assorted patent and copyright licences.

The value of international copyright to American film companies

The US had elected not to secure international copyright protection by joining the *Berne Convention for the Protection of Literary and Artistic Works (1886)*. However, many American firms achieved "backdoor" international copyright protection. Article 6 of the Berlin Revision to the Berne Convention (1908) provided that automatic protection would be afforded to works published simultaneously in another country with first publication in a Berne country. American authors could qualify for full Berne Union protection by issuing identical release dates for a book publication in the US and a Berne Union country, usually Canada or Great Britain. By creating a Berne Union nationality for these works, Americans could obtain the new film adaptation right in many major countries of the world, including the UK and dominions.[40] In addition, as discussed previously, many American films were adaptations of stories or plays by Berne country authors, especially British fiction writers.[41] Permission was also needed to distribute an American film adaptation of these works in any country that was a signatory to the Convention. Thus, due to the copyright status of the underlying works, various mechanisms operated to offer American film adaptations valuable copyright across the globe.

The practice of blind and block booking provided an additional layer of protection for American films that were not protected by copyright in foreign territories. From 1916 American agents started to resist the practice of throwing in distribution rights to Australia, New Zealand and the South Pacific, alongside distribution rights to Great Britain.[42] This allowed for a recalibration of contractual conditions taking into account the geographical and cultural particularities of a film market, drawing upon the more detailed knowledge of local distributors about demand and exhibition profits. By the mid-1920s the

Australian film market required approximately 600–650 films a year, 90% of which were supplied from America.[43]

A consideration of a 1920s three-year contract between the US giant First National and an Australian distributor, Harry Musgrove (1858–1931), principal of a newly formed company, the First National Exhibitors of Australia, clearly demonstrates the power dynamics in play. The transaction was indirectly controlled by the Hollywood film producer, who maintained the freedom to attach conditions for the exhibition of particular films. This meant that, if desired, "A" films, with the capacity to generate the highest profits, could be transacted separately to the "B" and "C" films sold as part of the block. The contract did not grant Musgrove a similar right to cherry pick and transact any individual films with Australian exhibitors. He was *only authorised to make contracts for block bookings*. This meant that in order to obtain the crowd-pulling "A" film, the exhibitor would have to purchase a block of undifferentiated "B" and "C" films, whether or not they wanted to screen them. This was greatly resented. For example, as Harold Harvie, a picture showman who screened films at the Soldiers' Memorial Hall in the tiny outback Victorian towns of Healesville and Yarra Glen complained, "Paramount will not book us single features unless we take a contract". This led to the theatre being unable to screen a 'Know your own country' film that had been produced in the area in conjunction with the Tourist Association and the Commonwealth Immigration Department. In order to screen it Paramount required them to purchase the rights to a package of 52 "scenics" which they could never fit into their programming.[44] Tying in exhibitors this way made it especially difficult for any independent film productions to be placed.

While only able to contract film in blocks, all contracts Musgrove entered into had to be *individually approved in writing by the American distributor*. The US distributor retained the right to *approve all terms of the contract* between Australian distributor and any exhibitor. As a consequence the US distributor could not only control the trade from afar regardless of whether or not there were underlying copyrights engaged, they could also extract very valuable trade information about the size, scale and value of the enterprises comprising the local exhibition market. Having access to this intelligence eased the American take-over of Australian businesses. The first contract had provided Musgrove with one "A" film a week at the average price of £1000. However,

> When I got the business on a footing they increased the price, and I had to put the company into liquidation. They then came out and took control themselves like every other American has done since 1912.[45]

Adolph Zukor's Famous Players-Lasky had been the first of the Hollywood studios to establish a subsidiary distribution arm in Australia, Paramount, in 1917. As the cartoon (Figure 5.1)[46] indicates, this was recognised as a bold move. The new company reported to the trade press that from 1917–1920 it had grown in size from four to 100 employees, with a rise in market share from 6 to 60%.[47] Paramount and Universal dominated the Australian distribution

Figure 5.1 Excerpt, "Moving picture world news reel for February"
Source: *Moving Picture World*, 10 March 1917, 1551

market; however in November 1917 an Australian-based distributor, Australasian Films, supported by its production arm, Amalgamated Films, and its extensive exhibition interests, Union Theatres, fought back. Australasian Films joined the First National Exhibitors' Circuit. Due to their market dominance Australasian Films were afforded the same status as American members, which included Vitagraph and Pathé, amongst others. Australasian Films also bought the right to distribute First National Circuit films to Fiji, the Far East, New Zealand, British New Guinea and Java.[48] Presumably this arrangement was one reason that Australasian Films emerged as the only Australian firm to be included alongside American subsidiaries when an "Australian" film industry association was established in the 1920s.

International trade follows the film

The early 20th century was a time when American firms were becoming more international in ambition. This activity was supported by the US government.

In 1918 legislation was passed that encouraged US industries to form new trade associations with the aim of increasing exports, freed from domestic prohibitions on collusion, price-fixing and other forms of anti-competitive behaviour. Corporatist behaviour that was illegal under American anti-trust law was actively encouraged abroad to help strengthen export markets for American manufactures.[49] Cultural trade, in particular trade in American films, was promoted because films were carriers of the American dream. In 1922 the Motion Picture Producers and Distributors Association of America (MPPDA) was formed. The head of the organisation, Will H Hays, proclaimed,

> Members of our Association have taken . . . definite steps to make certain that every film that goes from America abroad, wherever it shall be sent, shall correctly portray to the world the purposes, the ideals, the accomplishments, the opportunities, and the life of America.[50]

These public sentiments are suggestive of a political agenda for film; however, the practices put in train ultimately served another purpose. "Correct" portrayals were promoted by "the Formula" – an MPPDA self-regulatory code designed to ensure that "only books or plays which are of the right type are used for screen presentation".[51] The Hays strategy was to develop an infrastructure that facilitated industry self-regulation to forestall greater government oversight of the film industry, not only through censorship laws, but especially inquiries into oligopoly and unfair trade practices. The Formula and successive productions codes were enforced through industry contracts.

Soon after the MPPDA was established in the US, a similar, deceptively named organisation emerged in Australia – the Motion Picture Distributors Association of Australia (MPDAA). As mentioned, with the exception of Australasian Films it was constituted by the local branch offices of the large American film studios. The objectives were to grow the Australian industry through promoting the interests of members, to lobby government, specifically with regard to taxation and censorship, and to share information with a view to promoting mutual trade interests.[52]

The Empire responds

After the First World War British film-making was in a very poor state. American influence being wielded through film was seen as a threat to Empire. British industrialist and politician Sir Alfred Mond said,

> When I think of Empire I never think of Great Britain and Empire, I think of Empire with Great Britain in it, therefore, when I think of films of the Empire, I do not merely conceive our going round the Empire showing people things we do here, but I conceive of films of Imperial character, showing the people of Canada what is being done in Australia, and the people of New Zealand what is being done in India; what I call really

> representing in the film the whole activities of that enormous territory and diversified in people, in race, in religion, which makes a great complex under the British flag.[53]

However, in terms of Empire trade policy, a significant legal change had occurred in 1926. In what is known as the Balfour Declaration of 1926, the Imperial Conference of that year noted,

> nothing would be gained by attempting to lay down a Constitution for the British Empire. Its widely scattered parts have very different characteristics . . . very different histories, and are at very different stages of evolution. . . . They are autonomous Communities within the British Empire, equal in status, in no way subordinate one to another in any aspect of their domestic or external affairs, though united by a common allegiance to the Crown, and freely associated as members of the British Commonwealth of Nations.[54]

Following the Balfour Declaration and the Statute of Westminster 1931, former dominions sought to assert an independent international legal identity, albeit as part of a Commonwealth of nations. Political independence was expressed through affirming the commitment originally made by Great Britain that bound her dominions to the *Berne Convention for the Protection of Literary and Artistic Works (1886)*. The Australian government issued a Declaration of Continued Application in April 1928, leading to Australia's full participation as part of a Commonwealth or "Antipodean" bloc at the Rome Convention that opened in May 1928.[55] Legal co-operation was to be retained throughout the Commonwealth, but it was understood that countries would determine their own political and economic interests. However, this did not preclude co-operation to support Empire trade and protect British culture from American influence.

The UK proposed a solution to the powerful influence of American cinema across the Commonwealth at the 1926 Imperial Conference. It was "to develop the industry in this country [Great Britain] on a sound economic basis". The UK Parliament soon passed legislation requiring British cinemas to screen a quota of British and dominion films (with annual increments in the quota over ten years), and to restrict blind and block bookings of films.[56] The discussion paper tabled at the Imperial Conference suggested all Commonwealth countries should likewise consider quotas to boost the sale of British productions in the Commonwealth, and if necessary, also introduce domestic legislation to address the objectionable problem of block booking.[57] However, much to the annoyance of Australian film-makers, there were no initiatives that reconceived of British relations with her dominions to support preferential treatment of Australian films. Australian films were not exempt from British tariffs so they could better compete with American films within the UK, whilst British films attracted few tariffs in Australia. Accordingly, in terms of cultural policy, even after the Balfour Declaration, Australia retained the historical disadvantage of being a former colony of the UK, with cultural trade only imagined as emanating from a London centre to Commonwealth periphery.

Australia held a Royal Commission into the Film Industry (1926–1928).[58] The Commissioner, Walter Marks, was a wealthy solicitor and member of the Nationalist Party elected to the House of Representatives in 1919 as member for the Sydney seat of Wentworth.[59] Marks had visited Hollywood several times in the mid-1920s to study film-making and meet with producers. He was rumoured to have taken a lead role in a private film production. Due to his attachment to Hollywood and his looks, Marks gained the nickname the "Political Douglas Fairbanks".[60] Like the Managing Director and a chief spokesperson for the Australasian Films combine, Stuart Doyle, Marks enjoyed owning and sailing yachts. Both men were members of the Royal Motor Yacht Club of New South Wales. *Rydge's Business Journal* would come to describe Marks as "a great personal friend of Mr SF Doyle".[61]

The Royal Commission heard evidence from 253 witnesses representing a wide range of interests including producers, actors, distributors, exhibitors, musicians, journalists, educators, religious and various judicial offices. All witnesses, except for four British, were Australians. Evidence was taken on questions of duties and taxes, censorship and access to capital for film production and quotas. However, the most significant inquiry was as to whether or not a combine was in operation.

Australian representatives of the Australasian branch offices of the large American firms were directly questioned about their loyalties and the real degree of local control. Much of this evidence was heard in-camera. Under questioning the Secretary of First National Pictures (Australasian) agreed with the proposition that despite the engagement of Australian company directors who held nominal shares, this was "purely an American company".[62] Executives for Fox Film Corp Ltd, United Artists (Australasia), Selznick Pictures (Australia) and Famous Lasky Film Service made similar admissions. Most of the American branch offices also noted that they returned between 50–65% of gross earnings for film hire untaxed to the US.[63] But not all witnesses were so frank. Thomas Ferguson, Secretary for Metro-Goldwyn-Mayer Limited, claimed at first that his company was not an American company. He told the Commission "practically all the shareholders" were Australian. It took persistent questioning before he was forced to acknowledge that what the Australian employees held were "dummy shares".[64]

Overall, approximately a quarter of witnesses directly addressed whether or not there was an American and/or an Australian combine operating to the detriment of local film producers and exhibitors. Of these 65 witnesses, 37% agreed with the proposition there was one in operation, 5% explicitly designating it as American and 10% as an Australian combine.[65]

Changes in ownership and alliances between particular firms obscured the broader industry dynamics. For example, in his in-camera evidence, John

Winterflood, General Manager for exhibition company Birch, Carroll and Coyle Ltd told the Commission that the entry of the Hollywood studio "pup companies" had reduced the control of Australasian Films/Union Theatres in the Australian market.[66] He suggested that rather than there being an American stranglehold or an Australian/American combine, shifting alliances created active competition. His company, which had a strong penetration of the Queensland exhibition market, had benefitted from this situation by joining with Union Theatres in 1926.

Australasian Films/Union Theatre executives William Gibson and Stuart Doyle deflected concern over US control, telling the Commission that their organisation "was an all Australian one, with Australian directors, staff and shareholding, . . . [with] a natural inclination and leaning towards British and Australian pictures". Doyle also highlighted the Anglophile culture of Hollywood, listing 206 stories by English authors currently in production; a further 97 where rights had been purchased for future production; eight English authors engaged by Hollywood firms to supervise productions so that the pictures "were produced in a manner in accordance with English ideas, ideals and traditions"; and listing by name 154 important artists and technicians from across the British Empire currently working for American studios in the US.[67]

The Royal Commission concluded that while 90% of films imported into Australia were produced in the US and the film industry had become the eighth largest industry in that country,

> It is abundantly clear to your Commissioners from the evidence adduced that there is no American combine in existence in Australia exercising a stranglehold over the motion-picture industry. The film distributors have formed themselves into an organization termed "The Motion Picture Distributors of Australia". This is clearly a trade protective association, and in no way controls or directs the selling operations of the respective companies. Outside the organisation, the members display the keenest rivalry in their attempts to place their products.[68]

Had the commission sought to view the minutes of the MPDAA, a different conclusion about combine behaviour and US control may have been more apparent.

Collusion within the MPDAA

The minutes of the MPDAA show that distributors colluded to establish a "standard contract" controlling the entire Australian exhibition market. Clauses were crafted concerning payments to distributors, delivery and return of films, admission prices, duty and taxes, insurance, advertising, switching, equipment, non-delivery penalties, transferring contracts, special circumstances and issuing court proceedings. It was recognised that the existing contracts contained semantic differences. Historically these had come about due to the engagement of different firms providing legal expertise. Retaining these cosmetic differences was judged important because,

> Even if distributors agreed to a uniformly WORDED contract, it would not be a wise thing for distributors. *It would lend too much colour to the suggestion of a "combine".*[69]

It is interesting that the MPDAA remained concerned about being seen as a combine in light of the weakness of Australian competition law of this era.

In the US the Federal Trade Commission had demonstrated it was possible to investigate, and if necessary, break up forms of combination. In Australia the *Industries Preservation Act* 1906 (Cth) was framed along similar lines to the *Sherman Act*; however it was never used against American firms. The legislation also had one major difference. Section 4(1)(a) required proof of intent to restrain trade or commerce *and* proof of an intent to cause detriment of the public. The US *Act* had no similar requirement of proving an intention to cause detriment to the public. This created a very high burden on the Crown. It led to consideration of the "reasonableness" of the restraint of trade, providing those engaged in anti-competitive conduct the opportunity to justify combine activity.[70] Despite this significant legal challenge, had the Royal Commission asked pertinent questions of witnesses about the film distribution and exhibition contracts in use and properly evaluated the significance of the terms of trade, it is still possible they could have compiled considerable evidence to support an action against MPDAA members under Australian competition law.[71]

The terms of trade between distributors and Australian exhibitors were finally scrutinised by Commissioner Marks when he was appointed to an Inquiry into the Film Industry in New South Wales (1933–1934). The terms of reference directed him to consider contracts as one of the "Undesirable Features Associated with the Film Industry in New South Wales". Marks noted,

> Most of the contract forms closely resemble each other in general effect while differing in detail. . . . A number of the forms of contract tendered as exhibits contain provisions which I consider to be unduly onerous, and some are inequitable. . . . The contract forms in general use throughout Australia and New Zealand are, in my opinion also, "definitely one-sided". *I consider certain of the conditions would not be tolerated were it not for the position of advantage enjoyed by distributors in contracting with the majority of exhibitors.*[72]

Nonetheless, despite finding exhibitors were subjected to "humiliating conditions", Marks advised the government against regulation. Instead he suggested that the Motion Picture Exhibitor's Association work with the MPDAA on developing a standard contract, so that distributors could avoid "adverse criticism at the forms now in use".[73] Rather incredulously, Marks suggested there was an incentive for distributors to give up their restrictive terms of trade because of their interest in generating "better feeling" and improving the "measure of public repute and esteem" directed toward distributors. More scandalously the Australian parliamentarian also suggested that New Zealand and US government scrutiny of the terms of trade and censure could ultimately ameliorate the situation for Australians. In his treatment of competition issues the report very clearly demonstrates submission to US distribution interests and Marks's complete disregard for fair trade, to the cost of Australian independent distributors, exhibitors and the Australian public. Marks's service to Hollywood was so well received by industry interests that it opened up the opportunity for him to "investigate" film production in Canada, the US, England and France: "Everywhere the industry put out the red carpet for him and he received 'unstinted praise' for the [Royal Commission] report".[74]

Outwitting the censor

In the first three decades of the 20th century, religious and social reform bodies continually lobbied for a stronger censorship regime. This advocacy was often reported as "wowserism" in newspapers; however films were also censored during wartime. Wartime regulation softened broader public opposition to film censorship.[75] Further, in the absence of any classification or advisory information provided as to the intended audience for a film, respectable audiences could be unwittingly "embarrassed",

> One point is clear – no showman should present the naked Truth to an audience without fair warning. Men and women stroll into picture theatres with their children haphazard, and should not stumble unwarned on pictures of a lady in tights who has none of Lady Godiva's objection to peeping Toms.[76]

In 1918 regulations were passed in Australia under the *Customs Act* 1901 (Cth) that required all *imported films*, rather than just synopses, to be submitted to the Commonwealth Film Censor for registration. Section 7 allowed for refusal to register a film which, in the opinion of the Commonwealth Board of Censors,

(a) is blasphemous, indecent, or obscene; or
(b) is likely to be injurious to morality, or to encourage or incite crime;
(c) is likely to be offensive to any Ally of Great Britain; or
(d) depicts any matter the exhibition of which is undesirable in the public interests.[77]

Following the Imperial Conference of 1926, s7(c) was amended to read "is likely to be offensive to any friendly nation". Oddly for a modern reader, and reflecting the competing pulls Australia felt toward the US on the one hand, and British Empire on the other, it was felt necessary to supplement this with a new clause: (d) "is likely to be offensive to the people of the British Empire". The Chief Censor was granted the right to hear appeals from decisions made by his staff. Appeals from the Chief Censor were heard by the Minister. Applicants were also required to deposit specimen advertising – posters, press-books, photographs and sketches – material that was largely produced by the US studios. Applicants needed permission to later amend advertising content. For constitutional reasons it remained impossible for the Commonwealth to censor local film production directly; however films came under Federal Customs oversight if exported.[78]

Within the Chief Censor's office staff inspected comedies, documentaries (scenics) and topical items (gazettes). The Chief Censor personally inspected all the feature films. The Chief Commonwealth Censor, Cresswell O'Reilly was described by one who observed him in action as "a hard-faced, stiff, cold public servant".[79]

> Cresswell O'Reilly. He's got a name that suggests anything but Methodism, but he was a Methodist. And I remember when I first went to sit beside him – because the Distributor was allowed to have one representative beside the Censor – and he'd switch on his light, and you knew you were gone. Every time he switched on his light, he wrote a note, an "excision" as he called it, or an "elimination".[80]

Working for First National (Australasia) at the time, Ken Hall (1901–1994) described part of his job was to "outwit the censor",

> I would take the film away, re-edit it, and put new titles into it. We had title writers here who would copy the American title. We had labs that could get the same tint because lots of films were tinted. We could tint it up, run the new title in, and you couldn't tell. So I wrote many times: AND SO THEY MARRIED.[81]

Other film-makers such as Charles Chauvel (1897–1959) routinely included extra scenes in anticipation of eliminations, in the hope that other shots might slip through.[82] Hall also recalled his First National boss, John C Jones sending him by fast yacht to New Zealand to recut "hot films", like *The Private Life of Helen of Troy*, a satire of ancient mythology with sober Spartans and scantily dressed Trojans – before the film arrived in Sydney.[83] This regulatory loophole was soon closed. Thereafter films were to be inspected in Australia before the studio made any alterations.

O'Reilly told the Royal Commission he inspected on average 14 feature films a week and found problems with nearly half of these. Hall attributed the practice of re-editing and, on occasion, shooting new footage, such as close-ups of wedding bands, to saving a significant number of First National films from being refused certification during the 1920s. Over one in ten films was refused certification. Only a paltry number of appeals to the Minister were filed. These met with some success. O'Reilly was not exaggerating in claiming

Table 5.3 Australian Censor Decision on Feature Films 1925–1927

Censor decision on feature films	*1925*	*1926*	*1927*
Passed unconditionally	45%	52%	45%
Passed after eliminations	46%	36%	43%
Rejected in first instance	9%	12%	12%
Number of Appeals to Minister	1%	2%	1%
Appeal: Censor's decision upheld	86%	67%	50%
Reconstruction allowed	1%	33%	50%

he objected to almost half of the films he saw. An analysis of figures reported to the Royal Commission in 1928 reveals that between 1925–1927, 9–12% of films were rejected and a whopping 36–46% re-edited, the majority being of American origin (See Table 5.3).

One of most active policy areas for both the MPPDA and the MPDAA was to meet public concerns about the moral censorship issues, which included promoting "wholesome advertising", so as not to draw the wrath of the local censor. For example, Hoyts Theatres were chastised for advertising a film with the by-line, "he flirted with his mother". The MPDAA sent letters to the American industry association asking them to address the supply of salacious and unusable advertising copy. Censorship was a sensitive issue, not just in itself, but because it was feared as a gateway to broader regulatory scrutiny of the terms of trade.

The optics and sounds of cultural imperialism

While working to outwit the censor, Ken Hall gained an excellent education that would inform his later career as the leading film director for Union Theatres/Cinesound. He recalls that commercial considerations routinely took precedence over the political ambition to "showcase" American life and manufacturing. He observed that making pictures is not a matter of geography, rather,

> Largely – a matter of good sense – show sense and a knowledge of what the public will accept, a sense that will stand square against foolish and misguided criticism, and any other kinds of "isms", doing a commercial job and trying, honestly, to do a national job as well.[84]

Hall did not just use his intuition to inform decisions about what appealed to particular theatre-goers and what might be a turn-off. Though he did not identify it as data analytics, from the start of his film career working for First National he engaged in careful interpretation of daily box office returns to better understand and calibrate audience demand across the cities, suburbs and rural locations. There was a quasi-scientific and commercial logic that underpinned his role as editor and as film-maker. Overtly jingoistic titles, flag-waving and other obvious patriotism was unceremoniously excised,

> We had to take miles of flag-waving out of American pictures. I did this. Because we knew what would happen to them in the theatres. I titled one of their pictures for them. . . . It was a story called *The United States Flavour.* Well I wasn't going to put that in. All they could tell me was that it was about the steel industry. So I called it *Men of Steel.* [In Hollywood] They called it *Men of Steel.*[85]

Once film reels left Australia they continued to circulate in international markets and were further duplicated and exchanged. Given that somewhere up to one-half of US films were recut in Australia due to the censor, and a further unknown number were also re-edited, including retitling, for commercial reasons, this raises the problem of defining an "American film" abroad. Despite an American imperialist ambition for film, reliance on American stars, locations, original direction and stories, censorship – as mandated by government and also practiced with an eye to the local box office – there was dilution of the American imagery and ideals screened across the British Empire. A propagandistic display of the virtue of an American identity was doctored for commercial reasons. This reality, coupled with the Anglophile origins of many of the silent film era adaptations, makes it hard to directly account for American political influence on Empire cultural values exercised through the medium of silent film and to a lesser extent, also the talkies.

In the mid–late 1920s many inventors across the globe were working on sound technologies. That the American technology succeeded, and, for example, British photophone did not,[86] is at least in part because of the international film distribution practices and infrastructure that were already set in place. Sam Warner had not been a big player in the silent-film era. However, in 1925 Warner purchased Vitagraph to enter the distribution market and help secure greater access to exhibition spaces for Warner films. Warner also operated a radio station to promote their films. As a cost-saving measure, he sought to replace the cost of orchestras in smaller venues by using sound recordings and began recording eminent singers, demonstrating developments in sound projection technology. Through operation of the radio station Warner had formed a relationship with Western Electric, the holder of important sound patents and soon, also, with William Fox (Fox Film Corporation), owner of additional Swiss-origin sound-on-film patents marketed as "Fox Movietone". Initially, the larger studios were dismissive of sound. As with the gramophone discussed in the following chapter, sound was considered a novelty. There was also considerable cost and risk in making talkies, not just in shifting technologies for production but also because screening required an expensive fit out of theatres that might be independently owned or owned by rivals. A turning point came in October 1927 when Warner Bros presented Al Jolson in the "Jazz Singer" to massive acclaim. In 1928 Warner and Fox agreed to shift to the production of talkies. In July 1928 only 500 out of 20,000 American cinemas had sound operators – a mere 2%. A year later the figure was 5,000 or 25%.[87] The rise of the talkies heralded new rounds of shifts in ownership and alignments amongst the large Hollywood companies. The desire to hear familiar accents and sounds on screen also led to a blossoming of Empire film-making.[88] However, corporate strategies and contractual terms helped reinstate and even further extend the consolidation of Hollywood's cultural and economic power.

In addition to their distribution contracts, exhibitors also now needed contracts and licenses to use some sound recording and, especially, sound projection technology. Projectors were not made available for outright purchase. The technology was only available by signing up to a two- to three-year lease. By only leasing equipment, under the auspices of quality control clauses, a strict regime of equipment servicing using only Western Electric technicians could be mandated. Exhibitors soon began making familiar complaints concerning the imposition of standard oppressive conditions attached to the hire agreement; however respect for the principle of freedom of contract meant that individual attempts to set aside these oppressive contracts were not successful.[89]

Technological disruption and the rise of industrial authorship

With the development of film, new communications technologies disrupted established cultural markets. In the film trade, improvements in cameras, projection and sound created opportunities for new entrants in the US and abroad. New company formations and alliances facilitated the consolidation of ownership of relevant intellectual property rights. But regardless of the corporate identity of the particular players, it led to a film trade defined by the persistence of a small number of actors who participated in take-over activity, vertical and horizontal integration and tying arrangements to consolidate industrial power. Information sharing, often occurring in secret, and industry collusion facilitated through trade associations, expanded the global footprint of Hollywood while standardising international terms of trade.

Print markets were disrupted by the rise of Hollywood. So were author interests. However, the profits of publishers were never directly imperilled. Film and publishing representatives crafted mutually beneficial legal and business strategies. Author interests fared far less well. Without a seat at the table, fiction authors and playwrights emerged with little more than a right to negotiate with publishers over the applicable royalty for a film adaptation, if, and only if, they could assert a film right at all. The problem was not that creators were simply missing in action. With the shift to international corporatism, authors came to be excluded from the most important sites where the broader terms of their participation in the new cultural markets was being determined. A global cultural belief in the importance of intellectual property rights to the entertainment industry and an ideological preference for private negotiation and industry self-regulation insulated these business and legal affairs from serious scrutiny. As intellectual property rights management matured, it was the new multi-national companies and cross-industry alliances that were empowered while the natural rights of the author were de-natured, diluted, and copyright's ideologically celebrated characteristic property – primarily rewarding creative, as opposed to commercial, endeavour – was fundamentally disrupted. The figurehead of the author was called into service to support relatively small law reforms that obscured much more significant changes to business practice in the publishing and film industries, affecting the direction of cultural production and the value of a popular story. Similar dynamics in relation to the music industry are explored in the next chapter, but here there is no commodification of a story penned by an author. Rather what influenced law reform with regards to sound recording was respect for the fame of a celebrity performer – a party not awarded a copyright at all, allowing us to trace the significant distance travelled by copyright law in the 20th century from the conventional idea of it as a form of protection of an author's literary property.

Notes

1 Tracy C Davis, *The Economics of the British Stage 1800–1914* (CUP 2000) 335–342

2 For example, having learnt of the significance of the copyright performance from Wilkie Collins in 1888, Hall Caine presented a copyright performance that was simply a reading of his story *The Christian* in 1897 for which audiences paid £1. Vivien Allan, *Hall Caine: Portrait of a Victorian Romance* (Sheffield Academic Press 1997) 256

3 For this reason historians need to take care in relying upon the copyright registration as an accurate reflection of the work. For a detailed account of copyright performances and the role of contract with respect to trans-Atlantic trade see Derek Miller, 'Performative Performances: A History and Theory of the "Copyright Performance"' (2012) 64(2) Theatre Journal 161

4 Sir Thomas Edward Scrutton, *The Law of Copyright* (3rd ed, William Clownes & Sons 1890) 75–76. United Kingdom, Royal Commission on Laws and Regulations relating to Home, Colonial and Foreign Copyrights. c2036 (1878) xv

5 Scrutton, ibid 72, 189. See for example, *Chatterton v Cave* (1874–75) LR 10 CP 572; (1877–78) 3 App Cas 483; *Tate v Fullbrook* (1908) 1 KB 821; *Scholz v Amasis Ltd v Fenn* (1909) MCC 216

6 Martin Banham (ed), *The Cambridge Guide to Theatre* (CUP 2000) 302

7 For an overview of works being performed in the colonies see Veronica Kelly, *Annotated Calendar of Plays Premiered in Australia 1870–1890* (Department of English, U of Queensland P 1997)

8 (Duplicate) Grant of License from the Dramatic Authors Society to George Coppin, 23 Nov 1865, V&A Theatre & Performance Archive: THM 123 Samuel French Archive

9 John Palgrave Simpson Esq, Minutes of Evidence, *The Royal Copyright Commission* C 2036 (1878) 2414. Cases include *Boucicault v Bennett* (Unreported) *The Argus* (Melbourne) 27 Feb 1875, 9; *Williamson v Kelly* (Unreported) *Sydney Morning Herald* (Sydney) 11 Aug 1879, 7

10 Barbara Lauriat, 'Charles Reade's Role in the Drama of Victorian Dramatic Copyright' (2009) 33 Columbia Journal of Law & the Arts 1; Eric White, *A History of English Opera* (Faber & Faber 1983) 324–334

11 Denis Gifford, *Books and Plays in Films, 1896–1915: Literary, Theatrical and Artistic Sources of the First Twenty Years of Motion Picture* (McFarland, Mansell 1991)

12 See United Kingdom, *The Royal Copyright Commission* C 2036 (1878) xiv
13 *Karno v Pathé Frères London* (1908) 99 LT 114
14 'Kings Bench Division' *The Times* (London) 4 Apr 1908, 3. Chaplin played "Mr Rowdy" (a drunken bum), "Mr Pest" (a tuxedo wearing drunk) and directed. See Paul Matthew St Pierre, *Music Hall Mimesis in British Film 1895–1960: On the Halls on the Screen* (Rosemont Publishing 2009) 196–197. Charlie Chaplin reprised the role of the inebriated swill in the Karno and Charlie Chaplin film adaptation, *A Night in the Show* (Essanay 1915)
15 *Karno v Pathé Frères London* (n 13) 119
16 *Berne Convention for the Protection of Literary and Artistic Works*, opened for signature 9 September 1886, 1161 UNTS 30 (entered into force 29 Jan 1970) Art 14
17 *Tate v Fulbrook* [1908] 1 KB 21; *Corelli v Gray* (1913) 29 TLR 570; *Tate v Thomas* [1921] 1 Ch. 503; *Bagge v Miller* (1917–1923) MacG CC 179
18 *Ganthony v GJR Syndicate Ltd* (1915) MCC 247; *Barstow v Terry* (1924) 2 Ch 316; *Schofield v Welsh Pearson & Co Ltd* (1924) MCC 61; *Sutton Vane v Famous Players Film Co Ltd* (1928) MCC 374; *Kelly v Cinema Houses Ltd* (1932–1933) MCC 362; *Dagnall v British and Dominions Film Corp Ltd* (1933) MCC 391; *Bolton v International Pictures* (1936) MCC 20; *De Manduit v Gaumont British Picture* (1939) MCC 292
19 Society of Authors Archive. Vols. CCC, CCCI. Cinematic Sub-Committee; 1914–1917, nd BL: MS 56874-56875
20 *Glenville and Others v Selig Polyscope Co* (1911) MCC 18; *Menchen v Denvile* (1913) MacG CC 166; *Raleigh v Kinematograph Co* (1914) MacG CC 185; *British and Dominion Film Corporation v Fred D'Albert Repertory Company* (1928) MacG CC 346 (Ch. D); *Samuelson v Producers Distributing* (1932) 1 Ch 201
21 Society of Authors Archive. Vols. CCC, CCCI. Cinematic Sub-Committee; 1914–1917 (n 19)
22 'Moving Pictures' (1913) 23(8) *The Author* 233–235
23 United Kingdom, Report of the Committee on the Law of Copyright (Gorell Committee) Cd. 4976, 1910
24 Vivien Allen, *Hall Caine. Portrait of a Victorian Romancer* (Sheffield Academic Press 1997) 360
25 Hall Caine to Mr Spalding (Author's Cinematograph Copyright Agency) 6 Apr 1915. Hall Caine Correspondence, UoR: CW 3/11
26 Mr Spalding (Author's Cinematograph Copyright Agency) to Hall Caine, 12 May 1914; 30 Mar 1915; 4 May 1915. Hall Caine Correspondence, ibid
27 For example, Amalgamated Pictures came about through an agreement between "Theatrical Managers", John Henry Tait (originally a law clerk) and James Nevin Tait (originally a stockbroker), and Australian pioneers of film processing and photography, the "Biograph Proprietors", Millard Johnson & William Gibson (originally chemists). The new enterprise followed on from earlier successful releases and touring of films including Gibson's highly successful *The Story of the Kelly Gang* (1906), advertised as 40,000 feet and credited by Australians as the longest narrative film in the world for its time. Amalgamated Pictures Limited, SRO, Vic: VPRS 932 P1 Unit 63 File No. 4751
28 No doubt Caine's Australian experience led to his confusion as to the ownership of the film adaptation right. As noted earlier (n 25) he reported an injunction preventing his assignment of a film right due to prior licensing of his dramatic work
29 Robbery under Arms: Letter Regarding Disposal of Rights to Cinesound Productions 14 Mar 1933, NFSA: 447544; Undated letter, Rose Browne to Macmillan, BL: Macmillan Archive. Vol. CLIV Correspondence With: 1. Thomas A Browne, Al. 'Rolf Boldrewood'; 1889–1903; Graham Shirley, George Miller and Phillip Noyce, 'Ken G Hall Oral History' NFSA:9843
30 Graham Shirley and Brian Adams, *Australian Cinema. The First Eighty Years* (Angus & Robertson, Currency Press 1983) 46

31 Contract between Winchell Smith, Victor Mapes and David Belasco and JC Williamson Ltd, dated 24 Nov 1915, JC Williamson, Agreement for Plays, 1884–1929, Box 440A, NLA: MS5783
32 Ralph Cassady Jr, 'Monopoly in Motion Picture Production and Distribution 1908–1915' (1959) 32(4) S Cal LR 325; Jeanne Thomas, 'The Decay of the Motion Picture Patents Company' (1971) 10(2) Cinema Journal 34; Janet Staiger, 'Combination and Litigation: Structures of US Film Distribution, 1896–1917' (1983) 23(2) Cinema Journal 41, 47; Martin Sopocy, 'The Edison-Biograph Patent Litigation of 1901–1907' (1989) 3(1) Film History 11
33 Staiger, ibid 46
34 Eileen Bowser, *The Transformation of Cinema, 1907–1915, Vol 2, Part 2* (U of California P 1994) 23
35 Staiger (n 32); Sopocy (n 27)
36 Staiger, ibid 51–55
37 *US v Motion Picture Patents* Co 225 F 800 (ED Pa 1915); Thomas (n 32)
38 "Exhibition within the Empire of Empire Films". A discussion document prepared for the Imperial Conference of 1926. Reproduced in full in Ian Jarvie, *Hollywood's Overseas Campaign, the North Atlantic Movie Trade, 1920–1950* (CUP 1992) Figure 2A, 70
39 Thanks to Graeme Shirley for this point
40 *Copyright Act* 1911 (UK) s 35(3) provided that the simultaneous publication had to be in sufficient quantity to satisfy the reasonable requirements of the public and that no more than 14 days had elapsed (unless further time was permitted by Order of Council) between dates of publication in one such place and the other. Although there had been some dispute in Berne countries over the "genuineness" of the alleged simultaneous publication, there was no real retaliation. Richard Colino, 'Copyright Protection Abroad for U.S. Cultural Exports' (1962) Duke Law Journal 219
41 The popularity of British fiction in the US is discussed in Chapter 4, 80
42 Kirsten Thompson, *Exporting Entertainment. America in the World Film Market* (BFI Publishing 1985) 30
43 Report of the Royal Commission into the Motion Picture Industry of Australia, Commonwealth of Australia, 1928, [16]. Hereafter, 'Film RC Report'
44 Harold Harvie, Minutes of evidence. Royal Commission on the Moving Picture Industry in Australia, Commonwealth of Australia, 1927. Hereafter, 'Film RC Evidence' [3555], [3572]
45 Evidence of Harry George Musgrove, 7 August 1925, Tariff Board Inquiry and report file concerning films. NAA: B1/152
46 A similar excerpt first appeared in Thompson (n 42) Frontispiece
47 Ibid 73
48 Ibid 81–82
49 Eliot Jones, 'The Webb-Pomerene Act' (1920) 28(9) Journal of Political Economy 754
50 Will H Hays, 5 October 1923, cited in John Trumpbour, *Selling Hollywood to the World* (CUP 2002) 17
51 "The Formula" (1924) was a forerunner to the "Don't and Be Careful" code (1927) and the more familiar MPPDA "Production Code" (1930). Richard Maltby, 'The Production Code and the Hays Office' in Tino Balio (ed), *Grand Design: Hollywood as a Modern Business Enterprise, 1930–1939* (U of California P 1996) 43
52 Founding participants included: Australasian Films, Fox Film Corporation (Australasia), Famous Laksy Film Service Ltd, First National Pictures Ltd, Universal Film Manufacturing Co Ltd, Imperial Films Ltd, Co-Operative Film Exchange Limited, and Selznick Pictures Ltd. Memorandum of Association, 7 Jan 1925, Motion Picture Distributor's Association of Australia Records 1924–1926, SLNSW: MLMSS: 8708
53 Cited in Jarvie (n 38) 59
54 'Balfour Declaration' Imperial Conference. Inter-Imperial Relations Committee Report. Proceedings and Memorandum, 18 Nov 1926, E (IR/26) Series, 1–2

55 See Benedict Anderson, *The True History of Copyright, the Australian Experience 1905–2005* (U of Sydney P 2007) 155–157

56 *Cinematograph Films Act* 1927 (17–18 Geo.V)

57 "Exhibition within the Empire of Empire Films". A discussion document prepared for the Imperial Conference of 1926. Reproduced in full in Jarvie (n 38) 68–74

58 The Film RC was tasked

> to inquire into and report on the moving picture industry in Australia, and, without limiting the generality of the foregoing, to inquire particularly into: – The importation, production, distribution, and exhibition of moving picture films; The incidence and effect of the Customs Tariff upon the importation of such films and the sufficiency or otherwise of existing duties of Customs; The sufficiency or otherwise of the existing income tax law of the Commonwealth in relation to persons firms and companies engaged in the industry; and In connexion with any or all of the foregoing matters, the income, profits, expenditure and losses of such persons, firms and companies derived from, or incurred in connexion with, the industry, and the amount of capital invested in the industry.

59 The other Commission members were Senator Walter Leslie Duncan, (Nationalist), interested in supporting the cause of White Australia within Empire and suspicious of American power, Senator John Grant (Australian Labor Party), a tax reformer interested in governance, Senator Herbert Hays (Nationalist Party; United Australia Party), a Tasmanian mainly interested in local politics, Francis Michael Forde MP, (Labor), a Queensland protectionist, the Henry Gregory MP, (Country Party), opposed to Nationalist tariff policy and Lewis Windemere Nott MP (Nationalist), a doctor and hospital superintendent

60 Marks, Walter Moffitt: *Scrapbooks* 1924–1929, NLA MS 3676

61 Gordon M Smythe, 'Stories of Successful Men – Stuart Frank Doyle' Rydge's Business Journal 1 Oct 1929, 832

62 Sargent John Gambier, Secretary, First National Pictures (Australasian), Minutes of Evidence Given in Camera between 19 Apr 1927, 3 June 1927; NAA: A11636/ 3/2 at [67]; [72]

63 American subsidiary could fabricate an accounting entry for any film as they liked: "They can say the value is £100,000, and if it earns only £90,000 they show a book loss of £10,000". The Royal Commission concluded that once duties, the cost of carrying on the exchange, and censorship charges were debited against the American subsidiary company's share (the remaining 35–50% income on gross receipts), there were very low profits against which any Australian income tax could be extracted from American subsidiaries. Report of the Royal Commission into the Motion Picture Industry of Australia, Commonwealth of Australia, 1928, [149], [153]

64 Thomas Edmund Ferguson, Secretary and Treasurer, Metro-Goldwyn-Mayer Ltd, Minutes of Evidence Given in Camera between 19 April 1927, 3 June 1927; NAA: A11636/ 3/2 at [226]-[229]

65 Data analysis by the author. Film RC Evidence

66 John Winterflood, Film RC Evidence [5301]

67 Stuart Frank Doyle, Film RC Evidence [11337]

68 Film RC Report [59]

69 Confidential correspondence, 'Report on Uniform Contract' 13 May 1925. Motion Picture Distributor's Association of Australia Records 1924–1926. SLNSW: MLMSS: 8708. My emphasis

70 Sir Charles G Wade, 'Australian Anti-Trust Legislation' (1919) 1 *Journal of Comparative Legislation and International Law*, 196–205, 3rd series; Martin P Hanahan and David K Round, 'Serious Cartel Conduct, Criminalisation and Evidentiary Standards' (2009) 51(6) Business History 875

71 Proof of intent could be found in the confidential minutes of the MPDAA

72 Inquiry into the Film Industry in New South Wales, Final Report Part IV 1934 [93], [95], [141]. My emphasis
73 Marks also noted a large number of film exhibitors are prejudiced, "some seriously" by protection periods that consolidated the power and profits of the "first run" houses controlled by the merged Hoyts/Greater Union company. Here again Marks also advised against regulation, at the expense of independently run suburban and rural cinemas. Ibid
74 Dagmar Carboch, 'The Fall of the Bruce-Page Government' in Aaron Wildavsky and Dagmar Carboch (eds), *Fall of the Bruce-Page Government/the 1926 Referendum: Studies in Australian Politics* (Cheshire 1958) 163
75 Ina Bertrand, 'The Woman Suffers' in Geoff Mayer and Keith Beattie (eds), *The Cinema of Australia and New Zealand* (Wallflower Press 2007) 22–23
76 'The Cinema World' *Punch* (London) 13 Jan 1916, 16
77 S7 Customs (Cinematograph Films) Regulations 1918 (Cth)
78 Customs (Cinematograph Films) Regulations 1926 (Cth). The main local productions continued to be regulated by State Offices, and it took many years for the states to delegate this function to the Federal censor. Ina Bertrand, 'Film Censorship-"Paternalism"'? (Nov 1976) XI(2) *Politics*, 205–208 (n 15–16)
79 Graham Shirley, Interview with Ken Hall, 2 Aug. 1976. NSFA: 326468; Joel Greenberg, 'O'Reilly, Walter Cresswell (1877–1954)' in *Australian Dictionary of Biography* (Australian National UP). http://adb.anu.edu.au/biography/oreilly-walter-cresswell-7920/text13779
80 Philip Taylor, 'Ken G Hall. Interview' (1975) 1 Cinema Papers 73–74
81 Ibid 75
82 Conversation with Anthony Buckley, 21 Nov 2016
83 'Review: The Private Life of Helen of Troy' *Variety* 31 Dec 1926; Mordaunt Hall, 'The Screen' *New York Times* 10 Dec 1927; Ken G Hall, *Directed by Ken G Hall* (Lansdowne Press 1977) 31
84 Ken G Hall, 'A Country NoBody Knows' *The Film Weekly* (Sydney) 9 May 1935, 5
85 Graham Shirley, Interview with Ken Hall, 2 Aug 1976. NSFA: 326468
86 There was advocacy to link use of Empire quotas in conjunction with mandating use of British sound technology. See 'Commonwealth to Face Big War over "Talkie" Machines!' *Smith's Weekly* (Sydney) 11 May 1929, 1
87 Brian Yecies, *Wiring up the "Talkie War": The Coming of Sound to the Australian Cinema* PhD Thesis, La Trobe University 2001; Professor Toeplitz Lecture – The Advent of Sound, NAA: C5247, 1378531
88 'The Talkie Problem' *Smith's Weekly* 2 Mar 1929, 11
89 See e.g. *Western Electric Company of Australia Ltd v Adams* (1933) 50 WN (NSW) 197; NAA: A10071, 1933/44; *Western Electric Company of Australia Ltd v Hornsby* (1934) 34 NSWSR 73; NAA: A10071, 1934/7

6 Why does a gramophone maker deserve a copyright? The role of celebrity, women and consumer markets in the recording industry

American rapper Megan Thee Stallion,[1] Kesha[2] and Taylor Swift[3] are three of the latest high-profile artists involved in ugly contractual disputes with recording labels, involving clashes about control over artistic expression, image, royalties and back catalogues. The power of the recording company comes about through ownership of copyright in the music and sound recordings. This chapter explores how this right originated, exploring one of the earliest sound recording contracts in existence, the contracts between the British Gramophone Company (1897), a firm linked to the larger US company, His Master's Voice (HMV), becoming EMI (1931–2012), and Australian-born opera diva Dame Nellie Melba (1861–1931). From the earliest of days, the commercial and legal focus of the sound recording company has been to capitalise on the commercial value of a celebrity woman's image, a matter that through advanced commodity relations has become barely separable from appreciation of a performer's musical talent.

In the first years of the 20th century, Melba was pursued by senior executives of Gramophone and Typewriter Ltd[4] in London who were seeking to engage her talents as a recording artist. This chapter explores the reasons why and exposes the extraordinary personal pressure and illegal acts orchestrated by the company to "get Melba". In so doing, the chapter offers a critical feminist reading of the history of the international recording industry and the role of intellectual property rights in supporting innovation. It relates legal developments to a social history of cultural consumption and the advancing economy of fame, showing why authorship and inventorship are not the drivers of technological and social change in the way this is often conceived.

The chapter sets out the ambition of a feminist history and briefly demonstrates some of the flaws in conventional histories of the recording industry with respect to their analysis of the role of key actors and the function of intellectual property rights. It then advances a feminist reading of the industry. It exposes the invasions of privacy and other abuses involved in the effort to recruit Melba and why she overcame reservations about "canned music". While previous chapters have explored the strategic use of an author-centric notion of copyright to help grow an infrastructure to support global exploitation of stories in print and on film, this chapter discusses how a diva's celebrity could be used in a similar fashion helping justify a novel kind of copyright for recording companies – an exclusive right to their sound recordings. In conventional histories, Melba would not normally be considered relevant as a modern copyright subject because she has the legal status of a mere performer. Performers are not copyright owners. However, Melba's unique talents, voice, gendered abilities and restraints were used to bridge the category of invention and authored works.[5] Melba's celebrity helped reposition a novel technological artefact into the mainstream of cultural consumption, and along with this, the sound recording right came to sit alongside the copyright in sheet music. The analysis reveals the fluidity of intellectual property taxonomies, subverting attention from their technical legal distinctions to better consider the connections that facilitate cultural commodification.

The paper then shifts register to connect a feminist history of the gramophone to contemporary research into the lack of gender diversity in popular music and the ongoing constraints on women's capacity to lead and contribute as creators and performers. To address gender inequity in the music business, there is a need to more critically evaluate what is transacted in the industry. As is discussed, the orthodox history of intellectual property law is conceived in line with a masculinist norm – where men of action create, make deals and earn rewards. This draws attention to the making of the licensing deal as the heart of the business and conceives of the relevant factual context very narrowly. As a result, the role of intellectual property in social reproduction is hidden from view because of a decontextualisation of the social relations at stake. Decisions made about what intellectual property involves reproduce existing world views about the qualities of celebrity, creativity and invention in ways that are antithetic to addressing sexism in the music industry. To disrupt a gendered status quo we need to change how we tell stories about the relationship between the music industry and its artists, mindful that how we describe intellectual property and what we assume as the subjects and objects of the law has real-world effects.

The orthodox attribution of success

Why is there a need for a feminist legal history of the recording industry?

Feminist scholarship asks readers to think more deeply about the social and interpersonal relations that underpin business and legal transactions. It is hoped that we come to a better understanding of social life by considering the perspectives of multiple actors, with a range of different backgrounds and experiences, and of how ascription of a gendered identity affects individuals' understandings of opportunities, interactions with others and outcomes. Feminism seeks to "offer a better understanding of the social world by addressing aspects which have hitherto been ignored or misrepresented, while, at the same time, countering the ideological effects to which such misconceptions give rise".[6] In the legal domain, feminism considers the way that gendered fictions about how the world operates influence our understanding of how legal, economic and social relations function. The political interest is not merely in exposing sexism. It is recognised that gender produces real-world outcomes because fictions can underpin constructions of our social reality. It is difficult to redress injustice without disrupting the ongoing reproduction of gendered world views in law and society.[7]

This chapter challenges conventional histories of the sound recording industry. Such works are relatively few, and (overwhelmingly) they are written by men. They present the view that the industry developed from the creativity and efforts of male protagonists, including composers, music publishers, men of science and entrepreneurs. Armed with patents and copyrights, and assisted by the negotiating skills and business acumen of their lawyers and their friends in positions of power, new and enduring enterprises brought new kinds of cultural consumption to the public.[8] In adding to these existing histories, my interest is not simply to include women by bringing to the surface new or previously overlooked historical details.[9] As an intellectual property lawyer, I want to critically examine the significance being ascribed to the role of men in business wielding private property rights in the formation of the recording industry. The uncritical, and perhaps unwitting, reproduction of key tropes affects our understanding of what the industry is or does, and of the constitutive relevance of intellectual property rights within society. A feminist history entails evaluating, in light of the available evidence, a number of inter-related ideological presumptions that permeate the way writers talk about key players involved and the role of law in the industries' history.

Conventional writing about the origin and growth of the sound recording industry reproduces "common-sense" economic ideas about intellectual property that warrant closer interrogation. One idea is that intellectual property rights support innovation by rewarding those who invest in scientific and creative endeavours by preventing free-riding by competitors. Or as Richard Posner more philosophically puts it, "If you cannot be assured of being able to reap where you have sown, you won't sow, and the land will lie fallow".[10] It is recognised that the creation of intellectual property monopolies can create conflicts between private actors, including between different scientists working on related inventions, and between the content owners and the technology makers proposing new distribution formats. Monopolies that impose false scarcities through creating exclusive rights in intangible knowledge can lead to market inefficiencies by diverting limited resources "into the creation of intellectual property, and away from other socially valuable activities".[11] Expansive rights can retard the ambition of other innovators, affect downstream markets, and deny consumers access to the "best" products available at the lowest price. Thus the first assumption, that there is a need for exclusive rights to provide incentives to create, leads to a second one that modifies it: legislators and judges may be called upon to calibrate intellectual property rights to balance private rights and social advantage. However, the legislature is often characterised as unable to comprehend intellectual property subject matter and as beholden to particular influences. A third related premise concerns the role of the consumer in the production/commodity cycle regulated by intellectual property laws. It is imagined that the consumer benefits from a competitive market created by well-calibrated patent and copyright laws, with benefit defined by there being an ongoing supply of technological innovations and cultural works. Likewise, it is presumed that trademark and competition law assists consumers to make rational choices, by preventing their decisions from being corrupted by deceptive practices. In a well-functioning competitive market, consumers can sate their desires and make choices with reference to the inherent qualities of information goods, while also taking into account other factors common to all markets including past experience, trust in the source, convenience, pricing and so on.

Not all industry histories set out to tell an intellectual property story in any detail. However, in explaining that the major modern sound recording companies arose from late 19th-century scientific discoveries, they make constant references to patenting. An original interest in patenting then gives way to discussion about how music copyrights were affected by the development of new sound technologies by the end of the 19th century. Here histories shift to focus on key industry actors, such as the Music Publishers Association and the Gramophone Company, and their lobbying of Parliament for favourable reforms.[12] Company trademarks might also be casually mentioned along the way, but brand signification is not seen as doing a lot of work. Further, consumers are also usually only included as relatively passive, powerless, and disengaged participants who express their interest in the products marketed at them mainly by purchasing decisions. Performers, who were awarded no intellectual property rights by the legislature, barely feature in the discussion at all except as a source of the sound on cylinders or discs. It is as if the sound recording industry developed from the technology, the creation and commercialisation that was dependent upon rebalancing intellectual property protection, while industrialists were able to take for granted the support of performers and their fans.

The following section discusses many of these presumptions seeking to disrupt the conventional understanding of what the recording industry is or does, and how intellectual property operates within it.

Reconsidering what we think we know about the history of the gramophone

The role of patents

Most histories acknowledge that the gramophone was developed in North America, where the grant of patent rights complicated the terrain for inventors. It is accepted that patents blocked some fruitful innovations and delayed developments, in some cases until rights in question expired. For example, Cambridge historian, Peter Martland's *Recording History, The British Record Industry 1888–1931* notes the intense scientific and commercial competition that marked the 19th-century origins of the industry. He goes on to explain the links between the British firms that were successful and their licensing of rights to use foreign inventions. The conventional story is that the rise of the Company originated from the efforts of the American sales manager William Barry Owen, who was sent to London tasked with licensing Emile Berliner's US patents into the British and European markets. Throughout the late 19th century, patenting had been used extensively in the US in the gramophone industry, often as an economic weapon to stifle competition. The Victor Talking Machine Company had spent over a million dollars buying and defending Berliner's pivotal "flat disc" patents in the US. In 1901 the Company came to an arrangement with Victor Talking Machine Company's Eldridge Johnson, leading to the world market being controlled by these two firms.[13] Although executives in the US, UK and France continued to work together on technical refinements to improve the quality of the gramophone experience,[14] national offices were run separately throughout the early years of the 20th century. An English solicitor, Trevor Williams, provided the original capital for expansion in the UK, including funding the purchase of rights to Berliner patents in 1899. Further funds were then sought within Britain.[15] The firm was in some ways a typical British-based multi-national of the pre-WW1 era, with manufacturing plants in Austria, France, Germany, India and Russia. However, it was also atypical due to its reliance on American connections,

> Although the firm was formed with British capital, all its products and technology and most of its senior management originated in the United States. The company's growth in its first twenty years rested on an extensive licensing and marketing agreement with the Victor Company of the United States.[16]

Here patent filing and commercial licensing strategies operate hand in hand. Effective international management of legal rights is presented as the foundation of multi-national success.

Although there were significant international patent law reforms following the *Paris Convention for the Protection of Industrial Property (1883)* that improved foreign patent filing between US and the UK,[17] this does not necessarily mean that patent ownership and licensing was playing the regulatory role imagined by historians, especially in jurisdictions outside of the US. UK patent searches suggest that the significance of patent ownership and licenses in the British industry might be somewhat exaggerated given the absence of many key patent filings.

The most detailed research into gramophone patents is the work of Allen Koenigsberg, who traces the filing and ownership of 2,118 US sound recording patents from 1877–1912.[18] In his book, *The Patent History of the Phonograph 1877–1912*, an essay by sound engineer Raymond Wiles identifies the most commercially important patents were five Berliner patents and two American Gramophone Co patents. These patents were subject of an agreement between the American Gramophone Co and the Victor Talking Machine Co in 1903.[19] However, a search of UK patent records shows that not all these relevant US patents were ever filed in the UK. In fact, it appears that only two of the five Berliner patents were ever valid in the UK.[20] This raises a serious question about the validity of the Company's claim to own and control Berliner patents in the UK, and more importantly, of foundational claims about the importance of patent ownership and licensing in the gramophone industry in the UK.

The absence of key patent filings in the UK – and hence a rather incomplete legal protection of the related American inventions – suggests a need to reconsider what we think we know about the commercial logics surrounding international patent licensing and their importance to the industry at this time. The discussion of the role of patents in supporting innovation imagines a legal infrastructure that did not in fact exist at this time. Patents were important to the trade, but not because of the disciplinary power of law protecting bundles of exclusive monopoly rights that were carefully prescribed in registered patent specifications. Patents, as a form of intellectual property, had a symbolic and pragmatic importance. What was being transacted was more a cultural attachment to the productive idea of licensing patents, than a package of enforceable rights. There is a sound business logic here. Having a business relationship with a major US innovator suggested the creation of a pipeline to future technological innovation from the same source. Patent activity signalled technological progress. The connection helped build confidence around investment in a very new industry at a time of growth where further investment was needed. A business connection with the Victor Talking Machine Co created an optimistic environment supportive of domestic innovation and licensing from other sources. This activity could proceed with less threat of American-instigated litigation from other US gramophone makers, including the Victor Talking Machine Co, as had impacted on other gramophone makers.

Nonetheless, it is doubtful that patents did have the regulatory importance at this time that has since been imagined for them. After all, the Company did not employ a patent agent or lawyer until 1909.[21] It was more the commercial appeal of relying on the idea of patenting to organise the expansion of international trade than the creation and licensing of exclusive rights that mattered.[22] The philosophy of intellectual property supported an idea that had its own value in the marketplace – that the Company was an international "technology company" supported by the management of intellectual property rights. In fact, it was shared belief in an imaginary of intellectual property rights that advanced the Company's progress. Its executives did not need to bully competitors or litigate to control the trade. But they did need to propagate belief in what a technology company comprises, and as part of this, reinforce trust in the value of intellectual property rights and their capacity to protect Company interests and expand business internationally.[23] This belief was especially important because the Company did not have a British manufacturing plant until 1907 and protectionist tariff policies impacted on the viability of global expansion of manufacturing enterprises.

The Company's broad ideological commitment to intellectual property protection placed them in a difficult negotiating position when, in the first decade of the 20th century, there were calls to reform copyright law. Music publishers sought the right to control the recording of their musical works on mechanical contrivances, threatening the autonomy of the Company to pursue their future commercial interests on their own terms. The Company needed to develop a strategic negotiating position on copyright that did not cede too much control to the music publishers, or impact on their public image as a technology firm to whom intellectual property protection was important.

The role of copyright

In the early 20th century gramophone companies were free to record whatever sheet music they wanted royalty-free, much to the chagrin of authors, composers and music publishers.[24] Unsurprisingly, music publishers agitated for law reform. This led to an international agreement in 1908 that prohibited the recording of music without licence from the copyright owner of the composition. However, the convention, to which Great Britain was a signatory, left it up to states to determine how this new right would be implemented.[25]

Although not a party to the treaty, the US enacted a law in 1909 whereby music copyright owners were giving an exclusive right of mechanical reproduction which was exhausted with the release of the first authorised recording of a composition; thereafter recording companies could "cover" that composition by complying with a few bureaucratic requirements and paying a prescribed fee. This came about after Congress, whilst wanting to protect the rights of composers and authors, intervened to prevent the largest pianola firm, the Aeolian Company, from obtaining a monopoly on "canned music" through a secret contract with US Music Publishers' Association.[26] At this time Germany also supported a system of compulsory royalty payments to composers, in the interest of fostering competition in the player market.[27] Similar concerns over monopoly power and the need for a legislative solution were also evident in Britain, with approximately 80% of the relevant copyrights in Britain having been assigned to music publishers.[28] The solution that was eventually devised was a compulsory licensing scheme whereby any musical work could be mechanically reproduced, subject to a fixed rate percentage, overseen by the Board of Trade.[29]

The next step was the recognition of positive intellectual property rights in favour of phonogram producers themselves. Johnson Okpaluba argues that the inception of a copyright for the phonogram came about due to "vested interests and seized opportunities",

> The rights granted to phonograph manufacturers under the Copyright Act 1911 were a precursor for dealing with new technologies. Authors were granted exclusive rights to reproduce or disseminate the work and analogous rights granted to those responsible for reproduction and

> dissemination. Economic self-interest, as seen with the phonogram manufacturer, became equally as influential as any natural law concept of copyright, as the legislature was reluctant to concentrate powers in the hands of authors without limitation.[30]

Though less balanced in treatment, music publisher William Boosey, who had lived through these events, paints a similar picture,

> The gramophone companies, who have always been very ably represented in the House of Commons, brought forward a pathetic appeal that if the unhappy composer were to be allowed to be properly remunerated for the records of his composition, which were obviously going to seriously affect his profits on his printed copy, a grave injustice would be done to the workmen who were engaged in the manufacture of mechanical instruments. The Labour bugbear, as usual, terrified the Government.[31]

He went on to complain that Winston Churchill, President of the Board of Trade, failed to grasp that the gramophone was actually reproducing the musical work, because, unlike the pianola roll, the cylinders could not be read by experts.[32] He further blamed Josiah Wedgwood for brokering a compromise that led to the adoption of a flat rate for use of musical compositions. He notes this calculation ignored that the value of the recording varied greatly, depending upon who recorded it,

> artistes like Melba and [Enrico] Caruso could command thousands of pounds from the sale of records of Puccini's music, while the wonderful Act of 1911 only permitted Puccini to draw hundreds of pounds upon the same records.[33]

The value of the recording was co-dependent on the virtuosity of the performer and the merit of the composition. As a commodity, the recording was much more than a mere technological artefact. A flat-rate ignored these cultural variables.

Conventional historical discussions relate copyright law reform to a culture of deal-making – from international agreements in Berlin to parliamentary deals in the US, Germany and the UK. Implicit in this is the idea that the detail of law reform ensues from the efforts of powerful men whose source of agency and power needs little explanation, beyond noting for posterity biographical details of those credited as important actors representing "key" interests.[34] This dubious and blinkered approach has political, psychological and policy dimensions.

First, the landscape of the law is presented as a field of contest, with winners, losers, supporters and bystanders. It is primarily those who compete as invested stakeholders that are seen to be affected by the outcome, leaving the impact of laws on the rest of society a secondary consideration (at best). Second, negotiating skill and the personal capacity to draw other men to one's corner is presented as highly determinative of the legislative outcome. Key events are explained in light of the active/passive personality traits of participants: persuasive/easily swayed; strategic/outmanoeuvred; practical/philosophical; master of the subject/disappointing. There is an elision between having highly gendered personal qualities and possessing the agency to influence others. Dominant personal qualities are taken to prevail, regardless of the constitution of the decision-making forum and its communicative practices. The cultural, ethnic and educational backgrounds and other markers of identity of those involved are not assumed to be relevant. Third and finally, we are led to believe that the technology company won a compulsory license, rather than needing to negotiate permission to record with rights holders directly, and additionally, a copyright in their sound recordings, through outmanoeuvring opponents. Though they did not "deserve" it, Parliament felt a compulsory licence was necessary to avoid the chilling effect of the music publisher's monopoly and a sound recording right was created notwithstanding the conceptual confusion created by its owner being an industrialist, as opposed to being a creator. Given the reductionism of the explanation of the outcome and the (ir)rationality of Parliament, it is not surprising that copyright law and law-makers come to be viewed with derision.

A gendered framework leads to significant narrowness in understanding legal power, the measure of rationality, industry logics and legal synergies between actors and sectors. This has broader implications for our understanding of law and its relation to culture and society. The limited depth of the contextualisation serves to further reinforce the ideological function of intellectual property. In explaining how the industrialist negotiated copyright reform there is propagation of the fiction that there is such a thing as an international "technology company" brought about by adept negotiation. This idea comes to be personified in the gendered identity of "the entrepreneur". In copyright scholarship the "technological" entrepreneur is also distinguished from the publisher (whether of texts or – as here – of music), who is denied a similar designation as "innovator" through the author-function.[35] The publisher, seen as deriving copyright from the original author, is seldom figured in cultural history as an innovator, despite creating significant new practical and legal structures to exploit international cultural markets as the 20th century progressed. By contrast, the conventional characterisation of the originary technological "genius" plays into Romantic ideals of authorship. Further, by assuming that the music publishing and gramophone sectors are locked in a fight against each other, because technological innovation is presumed to "disrupt" the "old media" market, other more complex synergies between them, such as shared investments in the idea of intellectual property and co-operation and co-ordination in legal practice surrounding the management of rights (not requiring law reform) pass without scrutiny.[36]

The role of trademarks

An inordinate focus on the significance of the inventor and his patent encourages a "light-touch" reading of the function of trademarks. This follows because the trademark is constructed as a later-stage consideration associated with marketing the particular goods, rather than being identified as playing a foundational role in the broader cultural positioning of the company associated with the innovation from the outset. The company histories of Jones and Martland discuss the role of trademark only briefly, but Martland does note that in the early days of the business, Company executive Theodore Birnbaum designed "The Recording Angel" mark – a cherub seated on a disc record holding a quill pen inscribing a recording (see Figure 6.1).[37] He goes on to note that the company's second mark was far more important, largely because it endured for centuries. This was "His Masters Voice" mark featured the dog Nipper and a gramophone, based on a painting of the subject and of same name by Francis Barraud, a former student of the Royal Academy of Art and scenic artist of Prince's Theatre (Bristol) (see Figure 6.2).

Barraud's artwork took inspiration from his brother's dog Nipper who was puzzled as to the source of the sound coming from the phonograph. The original painting was of an early Edison machine and the artist acknowledged that the horn was ugly and black. Barraud was advised that if could repaint the

Figure 6.1 Gramophone and typewriter company Melba label recording featuring "Recording Angel" trademark (1905)

Credit: Emile Sarlija

Figure 6.2 Gramophone Monarch label recording featuring "His Masters Voice" trademark (1909)

Credit: Emile Sarlija

horn in gold it may improve saleability. He attended the Company offices with a photograph of his painting, and requested to borrow a brass horn. Company manager, Mr. Barry Owen.

> asked me if the picture was for sale and whether I could introduce a machine of their own make, a gramophone, instead of the one in the picture. I replied that the picture was for sale and I could make the alteration if they would let me have an instrument to paint from.[38]

On 15 September 1899, the Company sent Barraud a letter making him a formal offer for the picture, which he immediately accepted. He was paid £50 for the painting and a further £50 for the full copyright. The deal was finally confirmed on 4 October 1899 when a representative from the Company saw the amended painting for the first time. The next year "Nipper" made his first appearance on advertising on needle tins and was then used on promotion novelties such as playing cards. The Nipper trademark was registered by the Company for use on devices in 1901 and for recordings in 1910.[39] Both Martland and Jones suggest the "His Master's Voice" mark was the most important trademark asset of the Company as it provided a well-recognised global identity for the multi-national corporation that emerged.[40]

From the beginning it spoke to links with American research and innovation. Martland notes,

> relations between the Victor and Gramophone Companies [were] governed by a series of agreements concluded over the period 1901 to 1919. These were based on the joint ownership of patents and trademarks, the worldwide division of trading territories and the licensing deals to share each other recordings.[41]

Similarly Jones says,

> the British and American companies shared a common trademark and research laboratory, and had an understanding not to compete with one another in the world's markets. The Gramophone Company did not manufacture anything in Britain.[42]

This interpretation of trademark resonates with the significance attributed to patent in supporting the international growth of a technology company, as discussed earlier. However, the "His Master's Voice" trademark did not displace the "Angel" mark until 1909–1910, when problems arose in enforcing it.[43]

What is missing from Jones's and Martland's discussions of trademark is that there is no reflection on the signification of the two marks chosen or the commercial relevance of the uses to which they were put. For example, the "Angel" mark links a heavenly origin to the technological function of the gramophone. What was compelling about this messaging? What logic stood behind the ultimate choice of a sentimental association between a complex piece of machinery and a companion animal in the "His Master's Voice" mark? If one looks beyond the legal origination of trademark ownership to consider the function of marketing significations in light of the social context in which goods circulate, a different understanding of the industry and the sound market emerges. A feminist reading of the Company's history opens up this inquiry. Rather than presuming that the subject matter of intellectual property rights derives from the "ground-breaking" technologies and deal-making by Parliaments and men of business, the emergence of new rights is considered in light of the interaction between much larger ideas about technology, art, law and society.

A feminist reading of the origins of the recording industry

Cultural perceptions of sound recording technologies

The Gramophone Company was in the business of supplying an emerging British market for recording machines, and also maintained offices in France, Germany and Russia. Martland notes, however, that in 1902, when Sydney Dixon was appointed as Managing Director in London, the management structure changed. The size of the organisation was such that more formal lines of communication were needed between the US, UK and the European offices. London became the head office, with power concentrated in the hands of the Managing Director. In addition, a British branch was established to manage domestic sales organisation. As Managing Director of a more tightly structured company, with his own authority over British and European offices, Dixon could implement his own idea about growing the international trade.[44] While the gramophone trade was very small compared to cylinder and the flat disc technologies, all these contraptions shared a problem that also affected the player piano.[45] Despite extensive investment in technology, manufacturing plants overseas, establishing sales offices and international distribution agreements, the aura of patented technical innovation was not sufficient to overcome public scepticism about the value of new musical contraptions. Where devices for home use were concerned, technical excellence was not necessarily the driver of consumer choice. Potential purchasers needed to be convinced that the equipment was culturally significant and the recordings of artistic merit.

Mechanisation, in the form of the player piano, had allowed for democratisation of music, "Mechanization, however, replaced the unique with uniformity and made reproduction and duplication of experience a commonplace".[46] While opening up access to music to larger audiences without requiring the necessity of music training, "easy-to-play technology" and "canned music" designed for "amateurs" was regarded as encouraging a broad deterioration in public taste. The music showed "no variation, no soul, no joy, no passion".[47] The situation was not helped by the problem that in the early years the music selected also pandered to mass taste. Like pianola rolls, early cylinder and gramophone recordings reproduced familiar and well-known dance music, hymns and popular songs. Likewise, early recordings were not only limited in reproductive fidelity, many featured "lower-paid local talent secured from the beer gardens and street corners".[48] Serious audiences believed the moral lessons of music were imperilled by technologies that trivialised and debased the musical experience.[49]

To expand the market for gramophones, recording quality in both the technical and cultural senses needed to improve. One way of achieving this, beyond further refinements to the equipment, was to reconsider the calibre of the artists recorded.

There was a natural synergy between the technology of voice recording and opera singing as,

> those who represented the "greatest living voices" – the "master voices" – also possessed the type of *technical* ability for voice production that meshed with the available recording technology. As Berliner explained, "[with] loud-talking machines . . . the voice is expected to do considerable mechanical work. Its whole energy, if possible, must be collected and brought to bear on the [recording] diaphragm, and this with as little inconvenience as possible to the speaker or singer". . . .

> In Western European culture, particularly in opera, singers were trained to be both loud enough and articulate enough for the audience to be able to hear and understand the words of the libretto. In other words, the same trade-off – fidelity versus volume – that haunted the development of sound recording had also been tackled through compositional and vocal techniques for live performance.[50]

In 1903 the Company made its first recording of Enrico Caruso. Although the EMI Trust artist files on Caruso from this early period have not survived, the sound recordist Fred Gaisberg's biographer notes that it came about at the technician's initiative when Caruso was singing at La Scala in Milan. Gaisberg recollected that the fee demanded of £100 for ten songs was originally considered unacceptable by the Company, which telegrammed "Fee exhorbitant forbid you to record". Gaisberg ignored this command, given the great opportunity that was presented to him. A pressing was arranged for sale in time for Caruso's Covent Garden season and he later believed these records made a profit of £15,000.[51] While Caruso was readily persuaded to record for the Company, there is no evidence he was ever approached to help market the technology. Melba was originally not especially interested in personally releasing recordings on what remained a novel platform. However, for reasons explained later, Melba remained an obvious choice for the Company to pursue.

The gender of music

Women's affinity for music and its moral function was much discussed throughout the Victorian era.[52] Musical accomplishment was not seen as merely ornamental. Rather, music was idealised as an artform capable of disciplining the emotions, reconciling passion, intellect and theological meaning. It supported the "cult of domesticity",

> The woman headed the family and the home and was responsible for social stability, morality and the transmission of culture. . . . Part of the moral value of music lay in its socializing effect, and part of the moral power of woman lay in her ability to integrate man socially and restrain him from antisocial behavior. Music "carefully played" compels listening, aids conversation, and soothes the troubles of work, claimed "the matron" who wrote *The Habits of Good Society*. A husband or brother "may be made almost domestic by the cheerful notes".[53]

Alongside this, the piano became a significant marker of social status in the middle-class home.[54] Piano teaching and piano sales prospered in this context.

Women could perform in private and for charity, but composing, playing instruments (beyond the piano) and subjecting oneself to the male gaze outside of private vocal performances amongst family and friends was considered as (at least potentially) morally dangerous. These attitudes reflected a general scepticism about public performance. Adam Smith claimed in *An Inquiry into the Nature and Causes of Wealth of Nations* (1776) that performing involved "as a sort of public prostitution" and thus Smith believed the high fees earned by famous actors, opera singers, and dancers to be compensation not only for years of training, but also "for the discredit of employing [these skills] in this manner".[55] Along with the famous castrato of the 18th and early 19th century, divas were often characterised as "divine monsters" threatening the social order.[56] Even after the emergence of divas represented as ideal, hard-working women, prejudice against women performing in public lingered.[57]

Melba's contemporary, Luisa Tetrazzini (1871–1940), faced intense scrutiny of her private life,

> she was widely rumored, for instance, to have had a voracious sexual appetite, and she was involved in relationships, occasionally scandalous ones, with a variety of men.
>
> [H]er stoutness, her financial extravagance, her tendency to cancel appearances, her affection for lap dogs and boy toys – traits by no means shared by all divas – have all become cemented into popular mythology.[58]

However, prima donnas were also cosmopolitan and had a worldliness that carried a certain cachet. But in other ways, they were "other worldly". They sang in foreign tongues, did not utter words realistically and their hours of practice to attain vocal artistry was invisible. Such characteristics made them particularly alluring, in ways that set them apart as less threatening and sexually available as "low" theatrical women.[59] By mid-Victorian times prima donnas also could be admired for their personal qualities and assessed for the virtues they projected, as well as for their singing talent.

Major divas such as the "Swedish Nightingale" and "Queen of Song" Jenny Lind (1820–1887) and the Covent Garden favourite, the "Queen of Hearts" Adelina Patti (1843–1919) enjoyed positive public notice and were rewarded with significant performance fees.

The rise of pictorial magazines also helped portray theatrical personalities in idealised ways. Published from 1842 onwards the *Illustrated London News* became the most popular and comprehensive picture newspaper throughout the Victorian era. This was reading material for "the respectable families of England". It sugar-coated social issues and, subverting the verbal with the visual, it focussed on the "beautiful" at the expense of the artistic freedom of illustrators.[60] The magazine carried regular and extensive coverage of the London musical season, including portraits of the stars and articles about new musical inventions.[61] In her study of visual representations of divas represented in the *Illustrated London News* Montemorra Marvin notes,

> Female singers . . . were seemingly aware of the need to place their private personas on public display as a means of gaining social respectability, and to some extent, they themselves actively endeavored to do so. . . . During

> much of the Victorian era, conventional thinking suggested that a woman's moral and mental condition was reflected in her outward appearance.[62]

She observes many of the portraits of divas in pictorial newspapers resemble images of royalty.[63] This idealisation may have helped disrupt notions about the social and moral acceptability of prima donnas as theatrical women.

What did Melba represent?

Helen Mitchell Armstrong (1861–1931) was initially trained by Italian opera teacher Signor Cechi, who taught out of the premises of the Melbourne music sellers Allans and Co, where Melba had also taken piano lessons.[64] After she married and moved to a drought-stricken farm in Queensland she determined to take up music as a profession,

> My husband is quite agreeable. . . . I do not mind telling you that times are very bad here, and we are as poor as it is for anyone to be. We have both come to the conclusion that it is no use letting my voice go to waste up here . . . I must make some money.[65]

Acting, musical performance and music teaching were among the few professions, outside of nursing or education, where women were able to excel at this time. The aspiration of a talented colonial singer to achieve success on the international stage would have been thought preposterous at an earlier time. However, with significant talent, determination and financial support (in Melba's case, from her father), the 1880s was a time when women could strike out. The "Tasmanian Nightingale", Amy Sherwin (1855–1935), is credited as the first Australian woman singer to become successful abroad, singing in America in 1879 and in Europe from 1882.[66] She toured Australia in 1887–1888, a year after Melba had left for Europe, and Melba was following on her success.[67]

In 1884–1886, based on a statistical analysis of the 1881 census data, the *Pall Mall Gazette* ran a series of articles, "Women Who Work". While noting marriage as "the great female profession", actresses slightly outnumbered actors (2,368 as against 2,197 men), and in music teaching, the numbers of women also approached that of men (11,376 as against 14,170 men). There were 11,526 nurses; 123,955 female teachers (as against 47,836 men). The compensation of female performers varied. Whilst in the theatre employment might be inconstant, a modest actress could expect £5–£12 a week; a leading actress £15–£50; if an actress at a good London theatre drew her own audiences, entitling her to a share of profits, she could expect £100–£200 a week (30% less in the provinces). By way of comparison, nurses' *annual* pay was reported as £35–£50 plus uniform, board and lodging. There was no figure given for teachers.[68]

Prima donnas would of course, receive considerably more than average earnings. In 1893 *The Musical Times* suggested that "an income of £2,000 a year is proof positive that an operatic singer is in the front rank of his or her profession". Operatic artist fees per season in England were higher than in France, Germany, or Italy, "because of the comparative shortness of the season and the absence of stock companies".[69] However, as Covent Garden Theatre Manager Augustus Harris noted, care needs to be taken in accepting at face value publicly stated fees. In negotiations,

> Some artists hold out for a certain sum, but if the manager is willing to insert their price in the contract, he may get a mutual arrangement by which twenty or twenty-five per cent. of the amount shall not be paid, on condition always that it is kept a secret, and that nobody shall know anything at all about it.[70]

There was clearly a symbolic status attached to a star's demand for high fees, whether or not these may be delivered in practice. Melba was famous for claiming a higher fee than her peers, including Caruso and Tomagno. The "Troubadour of Empire"[71] Peter Dawson reported that she insisted on a contractual clause that no artiste would receive a higher payment than herself; however while Melba was led to believe she was paid more than Caruso, he then received additional fees by way of "expenses".[72] Surviving early Melba contracts have no such provisions, so what is interesting here is the belief that such a negotiation would be entertained.

Leaving Australia in 1886, Melba sought voice training with Madame Marchesi in Paris, debuting in Brussels in 1887. Her French debut was in Paris in 1889, where some concern was expressed about her accent and, "Although Melba is called Australian in most reviews, there is a general confusion about what an Australian actually was and it is not uncommon for critics, for instance, to call her an American from Melbourne".[73] She adopted the stage name "Melba" through the suggestion of Madame Marchesi.[74] It was fashionable at the time for opera singers to adopt quasi-Italian names that pointed to an appropriate place of birth or residence,[75] and no doubt helped signal the worldliness of a "high-class" Continental entertainer. It also internationalised and blurred a déclassé colonial identity.[76]

By 1900 Melba was an internationally famous and talented prima donna starring in the grand opera seasons at Covent Garden, London, the Metropolitan Opera House, New York and at the major opera houses on the Continent. She had close connections to high society, in particular as a friend to Lady de Grey. Lady de Grey's influence had benefitted Melba early in her career as her word was "law" at the Royal Opera House, Covent Garden. Melba's account was that Lady de Grey told her, "You will be under my care and I shall see that you do not lack either friends or hospitality".[77] The social set in which Lady de Grey moved was also highly newsworthy. Her friends and acquaintances were described as the "smartest and richest people in the Great world of London",[78] including British and European royalty. Melba was adorned in expensive jewellery and stylish clothes that showed the world "Australians can dress as well as sing". She rode a bicycle "to keep down fat", was an early adopter of the motor car, and on occasion drove herself. She stayed at the most fashionable addresses and opened her elegant homes to reporters who, describing her selection of lavish furnishings advised readers that, "Household decorations are one of her hobbies".[79] Many aspects of her life were dutifully reported in the society pages in London, Paris and New York, with the stories republished in the colonies.

Melba was especially interested in the technique of singing, publishing several articles on voice training.[80] She was also involved in actions designed to improve orchestral performance across the "civilised" world, advocating the internationalisation of performing pitch through the adoption "French pitch" as a standard.[81] It is likely that while sharing the prejudices of her time, she was also curious about the new recording technologies. There are some references to recordings of Melba being recorded at the Metropolitan Opera House in New York in 1901.[82]

Melba served as a role model for establishment values, personifying commercial endeavour and its reward. As the most famous Australian abroad of her time, she also portrayed the achievements of Empire. Readers were told, "It was by persistent pluck, said Madame Melba, that she made her way to the front, and one of her greatest disadvantages was her Australian origin".[83] She was an exceptional representation of a modern woman of Empire in the late Victorian and Edwardian age. An association with her would provide the Company with a valuable means of communicating the artistic merit of the sound technology to an international market from a London base, and help promote the sale of a beautifully presented technological artefact to decorate the parlour (see Figure 6.3).

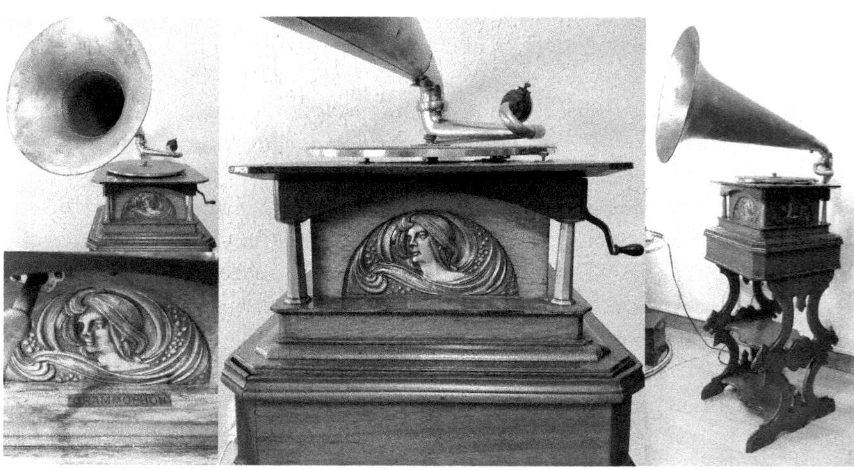

Figure 6.3 The "Melba" Gramophone, Gramophone & Typewriter Ltd (c. 1904)

Credit: Albert Garriga

"Her Friends Have Persuaded Her"

In 1903 Sydney Dixon put in place a scheme to "get Melba". A year later she wrote to the Board of the Company,

> I may perhaps now confess that; having heard the Gramophone under unfavourable conditions, and it having been frequently referred to in my presence in disparaging terms, I was until the last few weeks very inclined to an artistic prejudice against it, and had almost registered a vow that I would never sing to it, Mr. Dixon, however exercising so much patience, skill, courtesy and unfailing tact in representing its true value to me – both existing and potential – that my prejudices were finally swept away.[84]

Dixon's strategy involved more than thickly laying on his charm and attention. An advertisement that accompanied release of her records in 1904 which carried the heading "Her Friends Have Persuaded Her",[85] is very close to the truth (see Figure 6.4).

Dixon began by inviting her to come to the premises to hear the best recordings the company had made and for her to view the laboratory where she was photographed. There was no mention of her recording for them. She was then given a pedestal machine and "a mass of records" to take home. At the same time she placed an order for a machine of her own and for records to be sent as a surprise to her niece, Miss Nellie Patterson in Melbourne. The Sydney-based branch manager, Peter Bohanna, was tasked with ensuring the machine and records were correctly demonstrated in a manner that would impress so that Melba's sister, Belle, might write favourably back to her about the recordings and of her treatment by the company. Further Bohanna was to supply any further records that the family desired at no charge. He ended up sending a pedestal gramophone, two sound boxes or reproducers to which the stylus or needle is attached, 54 records including a mix of operas and popular titles and a current catalogue to Melbourne by steamer. It was then mooted that Melba might be interested in making a private record for her niece, and if so, "This may be the thin edge of the wedge to get her to sing for us".[86] However there is nothing to suggest that she obliged. The Company then provided Melba's former maid, Caroline Peeters, with a gramophone and records. Her father was also given a gift of an abundant supply of needles after she informed the Company that he was finding it difficult to obtain them. Bohanna considered these as significant expenses that would affect the profitability of his small office, so it was understood that these gifts were expenses London needed to bear.[87]

Melba's importance to the Company was such that in discussing her value Dixon suggested that they should, if necessary, offer her more than one half of the profits because "if we secure Melba we shall have done something far beyond what we have up to now achieved".[88] While Owen had been reluctant to pay any artists high fees, he left the firm in 1903. Nonetheless, Dixon's suggestion of better than half profits is rather extraordinary. It also reveals how

Figure 6.4 Gramophone & Typewriter Ltd advertisement

Source: *Illustrated London News*, 25 June 1904

quickly attitudes and decision-making in the Company over future prospects of the market for the technology had changed.

Melba was in New York in December 1903, coming to London to prepare for the Monte Carlo season, and appeared at a charity event in Monte Carlo on 18 February 1904. The first recording most likely took place at some time in between those dates. The recording was made at her own home in London with an orchestra of 50, rather than at the company premises, which Gaisberg noted posed considerable technical challenges. A number of tracks were recorded but their eventual fate remained in doubt. With the Company's assistance, she played the transcription of Traviata's 'Ah! Fors e lui' at a party in Monte Carlo where it was well received. After this, she further agreed to send it to her father but not to its commercial release. Her reservations imperilled the plan to co-ordinate the release with the opening of the Grand Opera season in London May 1904, supported by advertising planned in home journals in the US, ahead of the later New York opera season. Ultimately, however, she agreed under pressure from another direction.

At this time, Melba's lover was Haddon Chambers (1860–1921).[89] Chambers was a successful Australian playwright in London. His biggest break came after he had accosted actor-manager Herbert Beerbohm Tree in the Leicester Square Turkish Baths so he could read him his play, *Captain Swift* (1888), a drama about an Australian bushranger who retires to London, only to be pursued by the Queensland police. Tree consented to performing in it at Haymarket Theatre, and he went on to tour it in New York.[90] Though he never became as famous as Melba, Chambers liked to amuse the public by telling the story of his big break. The encounter with Tree, along with his home address and a list of his private club memberships in London and Paris, is mentioned in *Australasians Who Count in London* (1913).[91]

Chambers had met Melba at a dinner party in 1896 hosted by the conductor Landon Ronald's brother, Henry Russell, who soon after began to provide services to her as a drama coach.[92] In some correspondence Haddon is described as Melba's "press agent". It appears Dixon made an approach to obtain Chambers's assistance in pressuring Melba to record. He later noted that, "[I]t is practically due to his good offices that the deal was concluded. His services, however, were not offered to us gratuitously".[93]

For his assistance with getting Melba to record and agree to commercially release recordings, a contract was entered into whereby Chambers was entitled to a fee calculated at one-fifth of royalties paid on all Melba recordings. The "commission note" with Chambers is dated 24 February 1904. Her letter approving the commercial project arrived 11 days later, 6 March. The matter was specifically excluded from official correspondence because,

> Were Mme Melba aware that Mr. Haddon Chambers had exerted his influence for a material consideration and had benefitted financially from her singing, the knowledge of the transaction would unquestionably lead to a serious rupture, which might involve the Gramophone Company. . . . I shall

> be glad that after you have shown this letter to Mr Johnson you will treat it as a private communication and destroy it.[94]

The paper trail is only apparent today because while many originals may have been destroyed as requested, some original carbon copies of correspondence remain on file.

Detail of the agreement was further elaborated in a dispute between the Company and its American partner, Victor, in 1907. The correspondence shows how there are different cultural understandings of "deal-making", with the Americans adopting a far more hard-nosed view than their British-based counterparts. Following Melba's season at the Manhattan Opera House in New York the idea was that Victor should arrange for US recordings that might be more appealing to American audiences.[95] Johnson disputed that the US firm should have to pay or make any contribution toward a payment to Chambers. However, the UK executives considered their exclusive deal with Melba required all contracts, including ones entered into in the US, to be subject to the terms they had originally agreed to with all parties, including Chambers. By this agreement they reckoned that Chambers was entitled to 10 cents royalty on each US recording sold. The legal advice obtained by the Company suggested the commission agreement was "an exceedingly strong one, and one to which we are bound faithfully to adhere".[96]

Johnson correctly pointed out the legal distinction between the two firms and thus accordingly, they had different legal obligations,

> Whatever obligations you are under to Mr. Chambers cannot extend to us under the circumstances. If he thinks so, you may refer him to us; we will, of course, refer him to Madame Melba, which, I think, would end the matter of reference.[97]

Chambers ended up meeting with executives on both sides of the Atlantic to press his case. The Company ended up providing a firm of London solicitors with an undated cheque in favour of Chambers, with instructions to meet with him and fill in the date when Chambers agreed to discharge all future liabilities and hand back his copy of the original agreement.[98] He accepted a cheque for £3,750 on 26 June 1907 and this terminated any claim he had on Melba's future earnings.

Did Chambers and the Company act illegally?

British law creates clear legal obligations upon those involved in making a contract,

> CORRUPT AGREEMENTS: WHERE the person with whom an agent is negotiating on the part of his principal gives, or agrees to give, the agent a secret gratuity or commission, with the view of inducing the agent to act

> otherwise than with loyalty and fidelity to the principal, the agreement is a corrupt one, and is not enforceable at law.[99]

Secret commissions were a subject of public concern in the late Victorian era. In a lecture on the subject at the request of the Council of Legal Education the renowned barrister and Liberal Party politician Augustine Birrell (1850–1933) noted that there was no rule more deeply rooted in our English system of jurisprudence than that the trustee (or agent),

> is not to make one penny-piece of profit . . . unless he be a professional man specially authorized . . . to do so. . . .
>
> Nor is the present time one when either Parliament or judges are likely to relax the pressure of the rule in any single respect. The habit of secret commissions *given and taken every day* (so at least it is confidentially asserted) by person in good positions, who account themselves, and are accounted, honest men, is one to be scouted by courts of law.[100]

Birrell argued that "prosperity [from] commercial greatness and well-established success" is *only compatible* with businessmen acting with "absolute integrity".

If the Company's description of Chambers as an "agent" is true, he was legally obliged to provide Melba with a true account of his dealings on her behalf, and this clearly did not take place. Further, the Company can be characterised as having induced Chambers to enter into this corrupt agreement. The desire to maintain secrecy and instruction to destroy relevant communications shows that they were well aware that they had acted unethically and perhaps also, illegally. If Chambers was not actually Melba's agent, but simply enriching himself in exchange for exerting influence over her, this is very unattractive behaviour, but there would not be a breach of the law.

Gender affects how the deal is transacted here, from identification of Chambers as a potential ally, to how the parties conducted the negotiation, to the rationales given for covering up the illegality. Birrell's explanation that secret commissions were *being given and taken every day* also points to an awareness of the social and legal problems created by the grasping, competitive social order then emerging. He linked this to the rise of the middle class and the elevation of "the *natural man* whose instinct it always is to make a little money if he can".[101]

The "underside" of deal-making reveals the increasing fluidity between public and private lives in modernity. Here, Melba's personal and family connections were seen by the Company as a useful resource. There were no qualms about exploiting her family connections when, in ingratiating themselves, they could build sufficient goodwill that might make her more receptive to their overtures. Melba, her friends and family also benefitted from the arrangement. Subsequently, advertisements misrepresented the story of how Melba and the Company came to be connected. The full page advertisement published in the *London Illustrated News* timed to accompany the first releases naturally omitted reference to the Company's machinations behind the scenes. Instead what is highlighted is a fantasy – the idea that she approached them, with virtuous motivations in mind, wanting a recording to be made,

> IN APRIL LAST MADAME MELBA approached The Gramophone and Typewriter Ltd., with a view to obtaining a series of Records of her repertoire, in order that she might send these to her father in Australia.[102]

Women could be successful professionally without necessarily losing social position, but it was still more acceptable to explain to the public that she recorded her singing to please her father, rather than to further ensure her fame and to continue to be financially comfortable.

When it suited them, however, the Company could make conceptual distinctions between business and Melba's private life. Theodore Birnbaum, who served as Managing Director 1903–1909, sought to justify the company's role in royalty payments to Chambers by making a self-serving reference to a separation between business relations and private affairs,

> We of course as a Trading Company have nothing to do with the personal relations of Mr. Chambers and Mme Melba. We accepted Mr. Chambers co-operation as we should accept the aid of any other agent performing valuable service for a consideration.[103]

But what services were these? There is only one reference to him on file about these. In consideration for his commission, Chambers undertook to assist in obtaining articles and press notices for the Melba records. It is dated the same day as the agreement with him was entered into. However, there is nothing to suggest that he served in this role and plenty, as we will soon see, that demonstrates Dixon took pride in handling such matters himself. The instruction to remove from Company records any documentary trace of the "agency" arrangement is, in the circumstances, all too telling. The transaction is far more egregious than the leveraging of Melba's family ties. As well as being illegal, it was far more personally intrusive and exploitative. Whether Melba ever knew of the commission remains unclear.

Melba abruptly dropped contact with Chambers in 1904: "he suddenly ceased to be persona grata to her".[104] Neill muses that this might be a consequence of her discovering the agreement. If so, she kept it all to herself, as it is clear that in 1907 the Company had no suspicion of her knowing. Had she learnt of it, Melba would have faced a difficult dilemma. Whilst it had been common knowledge within their social set that she and Chambers were in a relationship, to complain openly about the secret commission could have drawn unwelcome scrutiny. Melba was certainly within her rights to sue over the private arrangement. However, her reputation previously had survived her divorce, and she may not have wished to test the public's acceptance again.

Other singers were on the rise. Unlike the "florid" and "earthy" Tetrazzini,[105] Melba had cultivated a controlled image, on and off stage. News of a scandalous sexual liaison with a colonial cad would have been a difficult for the prima donna to withstand, especially given the use of her name to promote decorative arts for the genteel British home.

Melba's terms

Her first contract was dated 11 May 1904. Melba agreed to make voice recordings exclusively for the company with the records to be sold at the price of 21 shillings each, of which she was to receive 5 shillings royalty. Another clause permitted the company to supply the Victor Talking Machine Company of Philadelphia who could sell the records in the US market for US$5, for which a royalty of 4 shillings was to be credited to her. Any alteration in price, leading to a pro-rata alteration in royalties, required her approval. Melba's advance on royalties was £1,000.[106]

The clause relating to record pricing was soon invoked. For one thing, the practice of fixing record prices at the time of contracting (for example, so that Melba's recordings cost a shilling more than Caruso's) would prove problematic for both the Company and retailers. It is worth noting that there is a mysterious undated scrawl on the back of the contract, "D [Dixon?] say that if she sings for these others (Columbia etc) we will not pay her any more royalties. Can we then in this same case make records whatever price we like". Melba herself soon received complaints from "home" about the excessive prices charged for her recordings, leading her to ask for a price reduction.[107]

Other understandings between Melba and the Company were not formally recorded in the agreement. She was to have some involvement in how her records were marketed, selecting a label design in mauve, and "carefully correct" the label content.[108] Most importantly, she negotiated a right of approval for each and every recording. Unsatisfactory master recordings were to be returned to her to be physically destroyed. Indeed, it appears she may have only signed the contract *after* she had reviewed and destroyed some of her initial recordings.

Before the establishment of a manufacturing plant in London in 1907, for which Melba laid the foundation stone, Company recordings were pressed in Hannover by Emile Berliner's brother, Joseph. The plant was apparently located in Germany due to Berliner's fear of British trade unionism.[109] Berliner was responsible both for preventing the unauthorised leaking of "samples" from the factory and for insuring that there was no inadvertent delivery to Johnson in Philadelphia of recordings Melba had not approved. Melba did reject a small number of the first Company recordings due to scratching, including an aria from "Boheme" which she thought was otherwise "a splendid record . . . that she is very anxious should be put on the market when she finally decides to have her Records sold".[110] Beyond this, there is some confusion amongst biographers as to exactly which recordings she approved and when. Partly this flows from comments in her autobiography,

> My first experiments in this direction were disastrous. . . . "Never again", I said to myself, as I listened to the scratching, screeching result. "Don't tell me I sing like that, or I shall go away and live on a desert island, out of sheer pity for the unfortunate people who have to listen to me." The records were therefore destroyed.[111]
>
> This comment has led some writers to suggest she is referring to recordings made prior to 1904, perhaps for another company.[112]

In any event, in 1907 Melba did sign a new recording contract with the Victor Talking Machine Company.[113] This contract formalised her right of approval:

> 3 That no record is to be considered as complete and perfect until approved by the said Madam Melba and a representative of the Victor Talking Machine Company, and if either party finds a record imperfect in any way it is to be remade until a satisfactory and perfect record for both parties has been produced.

In her dealings with the companies, Melba leveraged her bargaining position to establish the functional equivalent of what copyright scholars now call a moral right of integrity, that is, the right to object to any distortion, mutilation or other modification of the work which would be prejudicial to her honour or reputation.[114] This general concept does not enter international law until the 1928 Rome revision of the Berne Convention, and was not recognised in Britain until the 1980s; even today, moral rights generally are reserved for "authors" rather than mere performers. Yet at the beginning of the 20th century, Melba had achieved a very similar (and then quite novel) right by means of contract, so as to protect her reputational interests in the face of new technology.

Melba's "cleverness" at business perplexed Company officials who, later in her career, summed her up their experience of her this way,

> Melba is an institution. You can't get away from it . . . from Petrograd to Cape Town, from London to Vladivostock, she is what Jenny Lind and Adelina Patti were before her. This woman, who is essentially a business woman, is clever. . . . She is a snob. . . . A letter or bit of attention from the head of a concern is more to her than money. She has taken thirty years steadily increasing popularity to reach the top of the ladder. She is clever enough to hold the position.[115]

To the Company her personal involvement and the level of detail with which she oversaw her negotiations were unusual. A woman taking direct control of her career and destiny further confounded them. However, it was probably precisely because she was a female performer, a colonial, a divorcee and a snob that she felt the need to micro-manage her image, lest it be tarnished through public misunderstanding of her motivations. Melba was astute enough to recognise how closely her social position, professional standing and business prospects were intertwined. Or to put it another way, she never had the luxury of ignoring the centrality of gender as it framed her artistic and business opportunities, public reception and intimate relations.

"My Melba boom"

Dixon outlined his London marketing strategy in a candid letter to Alfred Clark, who headed the Parisian office,

> I hope you wont (sic) think it presumption on my part if I give you a sketch of the scheme with which I have worked my Melba boom here in England. . . . We have sold up-to-date 1,070 of these Records although we have not yet put in a single advertisement. . . .
>
> I commenced with an interview in the "Daily Express", which I wrote myself and worked through the editor. I followed this with the June number of our "Gramophone News" shewing Madame Melba singing in our Laboratory. . . .
>
> I then worked the demonstration with Lord de Grey before the King and Queen, and managed to get the "St. James Gazette" to put in a notice saying that the Records had been played. I sent this to the trade. Then, by a bit of luck, the King presented Madame Melba with a decoration for Art, Science and Music, which was quoted in the "Daily Mail". I sent this in turn to my trade. Finally following it up with the enclosed three-page circular, a post card shewing the papers we would advertise in, the facsimile testimonial from Madame Melba, the Melba book; and this morning an interview in the "Morning Post".[116]

As illustrated in Figure 6.4 from June 1904, Company advertisements routinely include the prominent personal endorsement:

> *HER FRIENDS HAVE PERSUADED HER*
>
> to allow these records to be published by the Gramophone & Typewriter Limited for the benefit of the whole world and for all future generations. Madame Melba, after the records were delivered to her, wrote the following entirely unsolicited testimonial:
>
> ***"Dear Sir,***
>
> ***I have tried the recordings and I find them really wonderful reproductions of my singing. I felt that in them, all the care and trouble to which your***

> ***experts went last month have found great reward. My friends who have heard them are simply delighted with them.***
>
> **Yours faithfully,**
>
> **NELLIE MELBA**

Privately the Company's officials remained very insecure with respect to their relationship with Melba. The extent of this is most apparent from a series of peculiar telegraphic exchanges between Company executives that occurred after Melba was involved in a car accident.[117] The emotional turmoil revealed in the correspondence sits oddly with the fictional constructs of confident masculinity presented in conventional business histories.

On 11 September 1904 Melba's car, in which she was travelling with her two nieces, struck and killed an unnamed elderly Parisian man. Although Australian reports, republishing cables from London, suggest Melba was driving, her English chauffeur was charged with manslaughter.[118] Dixon sent a wire to the Ritz hotel in Paris expressing his sympathies. He noted to Parisian office manager, Arthur Clark, that she replied "on her private paper" that she is "overcome with grief". Indeed, newspapers reported that Melba cancelled October performances due to "nervous prostration". Clark was then tasked with sending her favourite flowers, which they determined were red carnations. There was a minor delay as the carnations found at the market were not up to standard. Fresh carnations were duly dispatched the next day. Dixon and Clark then became concerned as nothing was heard back from Melba. Someone then was sent to quiz hotel staff as to the arrival of flowers. A week then passed, and consternation continued to grow,

> Madame Melba has, so far, not honoured me by acknowledging in any way receipt of the flowers which we sent her. . . .
>
> We sent a polite note from the Company (not written on the typewriter) expressing our regret at the unfortunate accident, and asking her to accept the flowers with our best wishes.

Dixon replied to Clark that perhaps she did not appreciate the flowers as coming from them as "gramophone may not be understood as referring exclusively to them". He then phoned her London home to try and resolve the mystery. Melba's butler told him she had left Paris for Monte Carlo.

Dixon still believed she might think the flowers had come from another source, noting that Pathé Feres, Bettini and another unknown person in "the Talking Machine World" had made approaches to her:

> our only desire was that she should know that the note came from a real Gramophone Company, and not from one of the many people who are after her for the purpose of getting her to make records for them.

The matter was not resolved until Melba lunched with Dixon in London at the end of the month. She asked him to pass on her thanks to all and explained that she thought she need not write as she would see him soon. Dixon told Clark that she was terribly distressed and it will take a long while for her to get over it. Indeed, etiquette books of this time noted,

> As regards presents in general it should be understood that a present demands a note of thanks in all cases when the thanks cannot be verbally expressed. . . . This applies equally to presents of game, poultry, fruit, or flowers. Some few people entertain the erroneous idea that presents of this nature do not require thanks. This is not only ungracious but raises a doubt in the mind of the giver as to whether the present sent has been duly received.[119]

In light of the importance of etiquette to those of Melba's social milieu, her silence in acknowledging the flowers was thought to be pregnant with meaning. Through the exchange of wires just described, the Company revealed a number of insecurities. Despite Melba signing an open-ended recording agreement that tied her exclusively to them, they remained concerned as to her loyalties. Given their own conduct in obtaining her consent to the contract this is unsurprising. Also, they thought the key to keeping in with her lay in having her appreciate that they represented a better class of gramophone company than their rivals. This anxiety may have derived in part from a problem with their image in the marketplace. The homely, sentimental connotations of the "Angel" and "His Master's Voice" marks might have reassured the public about the technology, but secondary branding could might allay the confusion in the marketplace created by adopting such a bland, generic company name.

The right to Melba's name

A concern that the Company be differentiated from other traders in the marketplace through an association with higher quality products soon led to an effort to prevent competitors from making references to Melba that could indirectly affect her, and the Company's, reputation.

Authorised dealers were informed in trade literature that only their "Exhibition Sound Box" (the part that holds the stylus or needle at the end of the arm), should be used in relation to their advertising and playing of her recordings. Competitors' attempts to associate the playing of Melba records with "unauthorised" devices, however, was a more obdurate problem. In late 1904 the Company sued to prevent the sale of a "Melba sound-box", referred to in an advertisement in the *Talking Machine News*.

The emergence of new music-box players in the market was always watched as, from 1902–1907, increasing numbers of often poorly capitalised ventures entered the trade.[120] Even small concerns were seen as a threat because the gramophone trade was still trying to break into a market dominated by cylinder recording technology. In 1905 Dixon told the Board, "In Great Britain the phonograph [cylinder] trade is gigantic and the disc trade is very small".[121] And, of course, the Company was seeking to redress public concerns about the quality of mechanically reproduced music in general. From the Company's standpoint the risk that their signature recordings might be heard on poorer quality equipment would have been especially concerning.

The advertisement that was the cause for concern inferred that Melba had consented to the playing of her records with a device sold by Messrs Howell Brothers and Mr Almscliffe.[122] When legal papers were served it transpired that the company, "appears to be a lady, Mrs Howell, who admitted to our clerk that there was no Cyril Almscliffe and that she was the Proprietor of the Business".[123] When the case came to hearing *The Times* report notes that evidence for the defence was given by Mr Charles William Howell, presumably her husband or brother.

Dixon tendered evidence which included Melba's recording agreement and also a new agreement to affix her name to a new sound-box under development. He told the court "they had a large sale of Melba records and spent £4000 in advertising them in three months". His claimed advertising spend does not square with his recent boasting to Clark that in the first two months sales were achieved without advertising, nor with his report to the Board dated less than two months later which refers to an advertising appropriation of £900, and an actual spend of £734.15. However, the legal question to be proved was not about what the Company had spent on getting Melba's endorsement, on advertising or whether Melba had or had not approved the rival device. The legal issue was simply whether in calling their product the "Melba" sound box Howell was making a fraudulent misrepresentation. Howell's defence was that

> Melba is not the name of a person carrying on business. . . . No one would think a "Melba" sound-box was the production of Madame Melba. The name was used as one might use the name of "Shakespeare" or "Dickens". They might have called this sound-box the "Nightingale".[124]

Although judgement was reserved, the Howells' defence most likely would eventually have succeeded. Section 5(3) of the *Merchandise Marks Act* 1887 (UK) made it an offence to apply any false trade description to goods, but it also required that the prosecutor prove a criminal intention on part of the person charged. This was generally considered as a significant evidential challenge. A common line of defence was that the "pretended use" of the name was merely descriptive rather than being fraudulently deceptive. But it was all too much for the small family firm, and the parties soon came to terms privately.[125] A settlement, rather than a judgement, suited the Company well. There was considerable concern about the case generating publicity and causing the terms of the royalty arrangement with Melba to reach the public. If so, she would not have been happy – to say nothing, presumably, of other less well-compensated celebrity. The term agreed to was that the Howells would physically remove Melba's name from any stock. After doing so the firm would be allowed to sell it and then wind up.[126]

Not all competition could be so easily overcome. The company had to tolerate competition from subsidiary businesses producing substitute and interoperable product that merely made playful references to their trademarks. An innovative example can be seen at Figure 6.5. The "Dog and Angel" design alludes to the company's two most recognisable marks, yet makes no appropriation of either.

As a consequence of the litigation with the Howells the company became aware of a significant legal oversight. They realised that they had no legal basis to support their claim to an exclusive right to the Melba name or to sue in her name to protect their interests. Accordingly, immediately after the conclusion of the litigation an indenture was affixed to the 1904 recording contract entitling the Company to commence proceedings to protect their "exclusive enjoyment of the word 'Melba'". She was indemnified against incurring any costs in such proceedings.[127]

It is interesting to note that, as a matter of business practice, the legal right to use the diva's name, unaddressed in the original recording contract, was attended to only after the Company had made a significant investment in production, advertising and distribution of the "Melba" product range. The Company was working out how to use the law to support the commodification of celebrity

Figure 6.5 "Dog and Angel" needle box. Origin unknown

Credit: Nederlandse Pianola Sociëteit

on the fly. In so doing they also learnt that current laws would not necessarily support their business strategies. Special labelling arrangements, such as Melba's mauve label were phased out, with red labels used for recordings of all celebrity artists, that were sold at a higher fee from 1907, and after August 1910, the "His Master's Voice" trademark appeared prominently on all discs.

Against this backdrop, the Company became far more proactive in supporting the cause of stronger intellectual property protection, even where this affected their profit margins in the shorter term.

The value of Melba's celebrity to copyright law reform

As discussed, the Company was not legally required to pay royalties to copyright owners of musical compositions in order to use these on recordings.[128] At this time recorded music commonly comprised a mix of opera, operettas, popular and traditional songs, many new enough to be potentially subject to protection. In copyright terms there were two potentially relevant rights: the composer's right to the musical work and the lyricist's or librettist's right to the related literary work (the lyrics or libretto). To understand what was financially at stake for all concerned, it is worth considering the copyright status of 30 musical and literary works recorded by Melba in London, 1904–1905. Traditional songs recorded by Melba, such as *God Save the King* and *Auld Lang Syne* had no known authors. These works were already in the public domain and thus no licence was required. Copyright is limited in time. Copyright had already expired in both the words and music for *Lucia Di Lammermoor*, *The Marriage of Figaro*, *Il Pensieroso* (Sweet Bird), *Home Sweet Home* and *Old Folks at Home* (Swanee River). In total, at the time of the making of the recording 9 of the 30 of the songs she recorded (both the underlying musical and literary works) were in the public domain; the other 21 (or 70%) remained with at least one or both works in copyright.[129] Copyright payments to librettists and composers, or their assignees, would potentially mean significant costs for the new sound recording trade.

The Gorell Committee (1909) was established to consider British law reform. The Company's British co-founder, the lawyer Trevor Williams was a member. Given the new industry's generally parsimonious attitude toward payment of recording artists and already existing concerns about the profitability of celebrity titles, one might have expected that the Company would have actively lobbied against copyright reform that would lead to them needing to pay additional copyright licence fees to music publishers (represented on the Committee by William Boosey), and composer/songwriters. However, as discussed, the Company's stance on intellectual property was more nuanced.

What is not especially noticed in the conventional histories is that the Company did not take such a hard line. Williams acknowledged at the outset,

> I am entirely in accord with the Committee "that the authors of musical works should have protection against the adaptation of their works

> to instruments which can produce them mechanically". [However] An immense industry has been built up under the immunity of the existing law, and consequently this new right should only be conferred subject to complete protection of the industry and to the preservation of vested interests.[130]

The Company not only conceded the need for reform to protect composers. Rather astonishingly after originally opposing any retrospective rights being conferred, they later agreed to retrospective payments of 2.5% of retail price on all existing recordings. Interesting, the latter proposal did not come to pass, being objected to by the Orchestrelle Company; Steinway and Sons; Sir Herbert Marshall and Sons, Limited; the Perforated Music Company; and other large firms invested in other mechanical forms of music reproduction.[131]

In addition to their general supportive stance of intellectual property, there are additional considerations that help contextualise the Company's negotiating logic.

First, there was a diplomatic lesson in the 1908 Berlin Revision of the Berne Convention, which introduced new provisions favouring "owners" devised in a forum where "technology companies" – film and sound firms – were not represented. The Company may have perceived an advantage in being actively engaged in the reform process at the national level. Also, the Company already had close connections with jurisdictions where royalties applied to mechanical reproduction. The industry's general international prospects as well as the Company's position as "speaking for" the entire UK and Continental trade, would be impacted by how Williams behaved on the Gorell Committee.

Second, licensing the works would facilitate the inclusion of printed words of songs with recordings, which would offer considerable advantages to users of the gramophone.[132] Though the input costs would rise, growth was dependent upon generating larger sales.

Third, the music publishers had argued that copyright was an author's right and that as the recording company merely provided a mechanical input the entire industry was parasitic on the artistry of the composer and lyricist. Without accepting this characterisation, the Company strategically endorsed music copyright owners' entitlement to compensation for mechanical reproductions, and relying upon the cultural status accorded to their artists they seeded the idea that they also made contributions that deserved copyright recognition. Gramophone records now mattered internationally to the public as well as the legislature, and alongside this, it was possible to make cultural claims about the essence of a sound recording that blurred a distinction between the contributions of the technology company and the artiste.

Promoting the celebrity performer

When Melba's recordings were first released, gramophone "concerts" also eventuated. For example, the largest Melbourne music store, Allan & Co staged a "by invitation" private demonstration of Melba's records on 16 September 1904. Soon after, a public concert was held at the packed Melbourne Town Hall. Visual interest and a sense of Melba's presence were provided by the projection of a newsreel of the diva in London, in itself a highly novel experience for audiences of that time.[133] The program involved the playing of Caruso, Francesco and Tomagno recordings as warm-up acts to 12 by Melba. These early public performances served as advertising spectacles for gramophone makers and artists, as well as providing a new source of income to the music retailer and to the promoters, the Tait brothers, who arranged the concerts.[134] In the public imagination, gramophone recordings and concerts were a means of connecting with internationally acclaimed artists, transcending geographical barriers. One result was that interest in the gramophone became so intense that Allan & Co soon rented an entirely new building to function as a showroom and listening space; by 1907 it took up five floors.[135] Together, these developments laid the foundation for a broader reconsideration of the contribution of the sound recording industry to society.

The Company could appeal to the power of the emotional connections between artists and their fans when they advocated that,

> the phonogram represents the personal creation of the artiste whose rendering gives life to the composer's thought. We claim that every phonographic manufacturer should be entitled to give his individual interpretation to the work.[136]
>
> The person who purchases the sheet of music buys it for the author's composition solely: the person who purchases the phonogram buys it also for the voice and the interpretation of the performer.
>
> In other words, the saleability of the phonogram depends almost exclusively on the reputation of the artiste who *created* the record, and on its setting and quality.[137]

Thus, celebrities whose artistry was beyond doubt became a politically useful tool in this copyright debate. There was little discussion by the Company of their entire catalogue. Rather, discussion centred on their (possibly loss-leading) celebrity label. It was claimed that the company paid "large, often extravagant, royalties" and, in the case of celebrity artists, it was the performer who initially selected the works they wish to record. Further, the music heard in the recording was distinguished by reference to the art of the recordist.[138] Thus, it was argued, whilst a phonograph was a reproductive technology, recordings were also artistic "creations" and not merely mechanical "copies" of musical works. As the skill of the gramophone maker, including that of the recording technician, involved creative labour, the technology involved far more than the application of science potentially deserving of a patent. The technological artefacts produced – the sound recording players and records – were individualised by the mark of their particular makers. It was also argued that the composer benefitted from the recording through the greater popularity of the song, leading to an enhanced reputation and increased sheet music sales. Numerous letters written by composers and music dealers in support of this view were submitted to the Committee by the company as additional evidence.[139]

Lastly, the Company reminded the Committee that concerns over anti-competitive conduct were as real in Britain as overseas. Evidence was given that by virtue of a contract with sheet music publishers, a "single firm" on the Continent might claim an exclusive right to record the large number of works controlled by those publishing houses.[140] If this arrangement was legal, the Company could be left without access to the most valuable repertoires of contemporary music and, accordingly, few artists would seek their recording services. The public would thus be denied access to the best recorded music by the best artists. It was argued that just

> because a publisher has acquired rights of publication in the sense of the law of 1842, it does not necessarily follow that he is the person who has the right to publish by an entirely different process, which was unknown at the time.[141]

A Gramophone Company Executive, John Drummond Robertson, not only gave evidence. He also advocated for a sound recording copyright in the press. In a letter published in *The Times* he told the public,

> A phonographic record is not a mere copy of the author's work, like a sheet of music, but it is the result of the labours of at least three separate personalities – (1) the composer who writes the work; (2) the artist who performs it for the purpose of recording the sound waves of his voice; and (3) the inventor and mechanician to whom is due the possibility of registering and subsequently producing in commercial form a means by which those sound waves, the artist's voice, may be reproduced.[142]

The latter contribution was, he argued, as indispensable as that of the other two creators. In this advocacy the Company leans heavily on the contributions of their female performers, helping further blur the distinction between a technology company and a creative endeavour. The accounting of the collaboration with the performer elides the reality that the performer was not entitled to a copyright over her performances. Whatever control (however great or small) she had and the fee for services was left entirely governed by a private negotiation in the recording contract. But an association with artistes is highly influential in reconceiving the technology company's inventorship into a contribution equivalent to authorship.

The ensuing reform to British copyright law shows how much the Company had achieved in a very short time frame. By the end of the first decade of the 20th century it is possible to refer to the recording industry, and in particular the Gramophone Company as its key representative, as a "vested interest", alongside the large music publishers.[143] This position was achieved through the

Company's successful management of international business relations and their understanding of new commodity markets and negotiation of cultural politics. They forged new connections between science, art and the law against a gendered reading of the art of the deal, while benefitting from a stripped down, highly selective and gendered reading of how business relations are constituted within the framework of copyright. However, without it having first established mutually beneficial relationships with celebrity artistes such as Melba, it is doubtful that the industry or the Company would have achieved this result.

Melba's legacy

Throughout the 20th century Melba's name remained familiar to most Australians. She was remembered for her talent, for being so celebrated abroad, for representing old-fashioned ideas of Empire and of the cultural supremacy of European high culture. Yet a greater legacy that resonates into the 21st century remains largely unknown. The untold story is of how Melba created a business opportunity for the Company. She mobilised her artistic accomplishments and helped them to transform the cultural and legal landscape, eventually producing the leviathan music industry that provides the sound track to our lives today. As a celebrity artiste she exercised agency navigating a very complex terrain of competing, complicated demands, expectations and opportunities. But while she was able to take care of her own financial interests, she was also taken advantage of. Her gender was both a benefit and a liability.

Melba sought to connect with her fans by claiming her "ordinariness". In a contribution she penned for Australian women's magazine, entitled 'The Magic of Home', Melba wrote,

> I should like to contradict a legend about myself. . . . An English paper which has been very kind to me has said, "Of course, women like Dame Nellie Melba, who are citizens of the world, cannot attach the same importance to home as the ordinary woman". . . .
>
> How very little the writer of that paragraph knew about me! The very fact of my being a citizen of the world is a reason to clinging with all one's heart and soul to that little corner of the world which one has made one's own.
>
> I say to myself – "Yes – there is a silver magic on the roofs of Venetian palaces, but it has for me nothing of the radiance of the moon as it shines through the windows of my Australian home. . . . And I would sacrifice every Roman hyacinth that ever grew for one spray of yellow wattle".
>
> . . . though I am a citizen of the world I do not wish to be confused with her. I have always believed that one of the finest qualities of this Australia I hold so dear, is that its women reverence their homes more than any women whom I have met in any part of the world.[144]

It appears that Melba not only understood why her gendered image promoted by the Company resonated with the public; in fact, she identified with it.

This meant she too suppressed the reality that she was simultaneously star, performer, consumer, business woman, lover, mother and a self-styled Australian citizen of the world. And as the complexity of her life and roles remained hidden, a different kind of successful public life for professional women in the industry remains invisible.

Contemporary power asymmetries in the recording industry

Today, there is significant research interest in questioning the role of gender in the sound recording industry. Recent studies of women's inclusion in the industry is demoralising reading for women considering music as a career. The US-based Annenberg Inclusion Initiative study involved analysis of Billboard charts which are produced by Nielsen Broadcast Data Systems and derived from a compilation of retail and digital sales and streaming activity data. The analysis was of 1,239 artists attached to the 600 top Billboard songs from 2012–2017.[145] The Billboard statistics collectively reflect the deals made within the recording industry in the US, including consideration of copyright payments, take down notices and distributions of advertising revenue linked through digital information tracked by industry-supported data management systems.[146] While today the US share of trade is completely dominated by digital sales, the US easily remains the largest world market (including physical, digital, performance and synchronisation rights combined), followed by Japan, UK, Germany and France.[147] In 2012, with the demise of the EMI Group (the firm historically associated with the original Gramophone Company), the Big Three record labels have been dominant. Sony BMG, Universal Music Group and Warner Music Group, combined, currently are estimated to control 60–80% of the global trade.[148]

The key US findings for *performing artists* were:

- 83.2% of artists were men and only 16.8% were women. This calculates into a gender ratio of 4.9 male artists to every 1 female artist. 2017 was a six-year low for female artists (16.8%) in popular content where the top two genres were pop and hip hop/rap.
- Roughly a third (32.5%) of all individual artist credits were to women, with 2017 a six-year low (25.6%).
- Very few women were credited as band members (8.7% female, as against 91.3% male) and even smaller percentages were featured in duos (5.1% female, 94.9% male).
- Of the 44 unique bands appearing in the sample one or more times, 31 or 70.5% featured all men, 11 or 25% were comprised of men and women, and only 2 or 4.5% were made up entirely of women. The most frequently appearing bands in the sample were all male.
- 42% of artists were from underrepresented racial/ethnic groups. This statistic is slightly above US Census, which is 38.7%. But of the diverse artists, 413 (79.4%) were male and 107 (20.6%) were female.

When it comes to *songwriters*, a similar pattern emerges:

- 87.7% were male and 12.3% were female. This calculates into a gender ratio of 7.1 male songwriters to every 1 female songwriter. This ratio was stable from 2012–2017.
- The most frequently working male songwriter had a total of 36 credits across the sample, while the top female had 15. All but 1 of the top females in the sample were singer-songwriters, whereas only 1 of the males was also credited as an artist.
- The top nine male songwriters were responsible for almost one-fifth (19.2%) of the songs in the six-year sample. Thus, these individuals are driving the work product and content of popular music and setting an agenda for the entire music industry.
- Analysis also suggests that when a female artist is present, a female songwriter is more likely to be involved in the writing process than when only male artists are in the recording studio.

Producers is the category where women are least represented across a sample of 300 songs and 651 producers over three years:

- 98% were male and only 2% were female. The gender ratio of male producers to female producers is 49.1 to 1.
- 95.7% of recordings did not feature a single female producer.

Indicators of *industry esteem* are also strongly gendered. Analysis of a total of 899 individuals nominated for a Grammy Award between 2013 and 2018 showed:

- 90.7% were male and 9.3% were female.
- Females were most likely to appear in the Best New Artist category, followed by Song of the Year.
- In contrast, fewer than 10% of the nominees for Record or Album of the Year were female. Over the last six years, no women have been nominated as Producer of the Year.

The results were very similar in the UK. Of 219 artists signed to UK music labels, 80.31% were men; 19.69% women. Of 106 writers signed to UK music publishers 85.82% were men; 14.18% women. Of those working for US music publishers 63.33% were men; 36.67% women, but 82% of CEOs were male.[149]

The hundred years or so since Melba's passing has been characterised by a new feminist politics, different from that of the Victorian and Edwardian eras, which included the suffrage movement. We have seen significant change in women's gender roles in society. Women are employed as executive deal-makers in the music industry and credited as social "influencers" and "taste-makers".[150] There are obviously more sexualised and more varied genders performed and expressed, on and off stage. But despite the opening up of gender politics on the surface of the music world and very regular appearances of girl power, androgyne identity, gender fluidity and affirming dispatches from the Beyhive, the statistics make it hard to be confident about there being much significant improvement in the position of women in the industry. 2017 was reported as a peak year in music consumption, with overall consumption growing by 12.5%, with a 59% increase in on-demand audio streams offsetting declines in track and album sales.[151] The Annenberg Inclusion report shows, however, it was also the year of a six-year low for representation of female artists. Rather than gender equality improving with the shift to online consumption, the "new technologies" may be reinforcing or accelerating existing dynamics.

A lack of control over their lives, creative outputs and image routinely features in contractual disputes between performers and labels. This can also include claims of sexual abuse.[152] As part of her legal attempt to free herself from her recording contract with Dr Luke whom she claimed was an abusive partner, Kesha told the court in her countersuit,

> You can get a divorce from an abusive spouse. . . . You can dissolve a partnership if the relationship becomes irreconcilable. The same opportunity – to be liberated from the physical, emotional, and financial bondage of a destructive relationship – should be available to a recording artist.[153]

Claims of failure to account and pay for royalties, breach of the covenant of good faith and fair dealing, and a declaration of the impossibility of upholding the agreement without court supervision or Sony's assistance because of the abuse and acrimonious relationship, were rejected. Grounds in support of dismissing the counter-claim included the unsettling finding that as Kesha had admitted that Gottwald's abusive behaviour had started at the outset of their relationship in 2005, allegedly abusive behaviour was foreseeable.[154]

How do we begin to explain this situation?

Misunderstanding what the recording industry transacts

This chapter has argued that there is a fundamental misunderstanding of what the recording industry is, what it transacts and the role of intellectual property rights within it.[155] The fixation on the deal as the heart of the business – the contractual negotiations and the protection of defined intellectual property rights attached – comes from a gendered understanding of law and business. It allows gendered ideas about technology and economics to be reproduced through their interactions with the domains of intellectual property and contract, and helps protect the institution of law from broader critique about the constitution of legal power through the social reproduction. In typical industry critiques, sexism and misogyny are presented as personal problems that afflict bad apples who perform their masculinity without fairness, sensitivity and ethical regard for the autonomy and well-being of their victims. Criminal and personal injury law, perhaps anti-discrimination law (in some jurisdictions) or even affirmative action targets, pose as the solution. There is no recognition of the institutional and broader communicative function of law that sustains the gender privileges of the status quo.

From its earliest days, what has been transacted in the recording industry is not patent or copyright rights. What has been transacted and disseminated alongside the music has been a gendered construction of image, name and persona that influences our understanding of the cultural value of creativity and individual contributions to it. To address the current constraints faced by women and significantly change the culture of the industry we need to stop pretending that the current situation is simply the result of accumulated individual decisions made by men over time. Addressing institutional discrimination is not about changing attitudes alone, but more critically considering the history of the legal objects and subjects of the trade. One place to start is to ask ourselves why there has been so little change from the basic terms and conditions of Melba's early 1900 contracts to those of the present day.

Notes

1 Mark Savage, 'From Prince to Megan Thee Stallion: When Music Contracts Go Wrong' *BBC News* 2 Mar 2020 <www.bbc.com/news/entertainment-arts-51704533>

2 Joe Coscarelli, 'Kesha Again Blocked from Breaking Contracts with Dr Luke' *New York Times*, 29 May 2019

3 Kevin Cornell, 'Taylor Swift and Big Machine: Contract Lessons for Independent Artists' *TuneCore Blog* 25 Nov 2019. www.tunecore.com/blog/2019/11/taylor-swift-and-big-machine-contract-lessons-for-independent-artists.html

4 The original name established in 1897 was 'The British Gramophone Company'. The name changed to the 'Gramophone and Typewriter Ltd' in 1900 after entering into an arrangement to distribute the new Lambert typewriter, an additional product line in case the gramophone market failed. After 1907 it is known as 'The Gramophone Co'. Hereafter it will be referred to as the 'Company'

5 Thanks to Hyo Kang for this phrasing

6 Joanne Conaghan quoted in Margaret Davies, 'Law's Truths and Truth about Law. Interdisciplinary Refractions' in Vanessa Munro and Margaret Davies (eds), *The Ashgate Research Companion to Feminist Legal Theory* (Ashgate 2013) 73

7 For an overview of feminist legal scholarship, see ibid

8 The focus of this chapter is primarily on the history of the British industry and the Gramophone Company in particular. Works considered include Geoffrey Jones, 'The Gramophone Company: An Anglo-American Multinational, 1898–1931' (1985) 59(1) The Business History Review 76; Peter Martland, *Recording History. The British Record Industry 1888–1931* (Scarecrow Press 2013) 76–100; William Boosey, *Fifty Years of Music* (Ernest Benn Ltd 1931); Johnson Okpaluba, 'The Phonogram: A Tale of Vested Interests and Seized Opportunities' in Brad Sherman and Leanne Wiseman (eds), *Copyright and the Challenge of the New* (Wolters Kluwer 2012)

9 For works that address the gendered construction of invention more generally see Deborah J Merritt, 'Hypatia in the Patent Office: Women Inventors and the Law, 1865–1900' (1991) 35(3) Am J Legal Hist 235–306; Cressida Limon and Sara Ramshaw, 'Surprise of Invention: Making Fun of the Statutory' (2012) 37 AFLJ 3; Kara Swanson, '"Great Men" Law, and the Social Construction of Technology' (2017) 43(3) Law & Soc Inquiry 1093

10 Richard A Posner, *The Law & Economics of Intellectual Property* (Daedalus Spring 2002) 6
11 Ibid 12
12 For example, Charles F James, *The Story of the Performing Rights Society* (Performing Rights Society 1951); Cyril Ehrlich, *Harmonious Alliance: A History of the Performing Rights Society* (OUP 1989)
13 Martland (n 8) 48–49, 53–54
14 Arthur Clark, who had co-invented a gramophone sound box with Eldridge Johnson in 1896, filed five sole inventor patent applications in the US between 1896 and 1902. He ran the Parisian affiliate Compagnie française de Gramophone, succeeding another American, Theodore Birnbaum, who had significant import/export expertise in relation to moving product between Britain and America. Birnbaum was a Managing Director of the Gramophone Company from 1909. He was awarded five patents in the US and eight in the UK between 1901–1909. Johnson held 54 US patents between 1897–1910. Allen Koenigsberg, *The Patent History of the Phonograph 1877–1912* (APM Press 1990)
15 Martland (n 8) 48–49, 53–54
16 Jones (n 8) 77
17 The US and UK Parliaments permitted foreign patent applicants to apply for a patent in each other's jurisdiction within seven months of the original filing (later extended to twelve months), with the patent taking effect at the date of the first filing. Patent duration was limited to the term of the inventor's shortest running foreign counterpart. The patent term was 14 years in the UK, 17 in the US. See s 103, *The Patents, Designs, and Trade Marks Act*, 1883 (46–47 Vict c 57); Revised Statutes of the United States, Section 4487
18 Koenigsberg (n 14)
19 Raymond Wile, 'The Seventeen-Year Itch: The Phonograph and the Patent System' in Allen Koenigsberg (ed), *The Patent History of the Phonograph 1877–1912* (APM Press 1990)
20 The Berliner patents were: Invention: Gramophone (lateral cut cylinder phonautograph), US Patent No. 372,786, Filed 4 May 1887. UK Patent No. 15,232; Invention: Process of Producing Records of Sound [Etching], US Patent No. 382,790, Filed 17 Mar. 1888. UK Patent No. 7204/88; Invention: Gramophone [Groove-driven reproducer; basic], US Patent No. 534,543. Filed 30 Mar. 1892. No UK Patent Filed; Invention: Sound-Record & Method of Making Same [Zinc/Copper], US Patent No. 548,623, Filed 18 Mar. 1893. No UK Patent Filed; Invention: Gramophone [Photo-engrave reciprocating glass disc], US Patent No. 564,586, Filed: 7 Nov. 1895. No UK Patent Filed. The American Gramophone Co patents were: Inventor: Joseph W Jones (½ assignment to JA Vincent). Invention: Production of Sound Records. US Patent No. 688,739, Filed 19 Nov. 1897. UK Patent No. GB189805710 (A); Inventor: Thomas H Macdonald (AGC/Pathé License). Invention: Recording & Reproducing Sounds [5inc Grand/Concert], US Patent No 714,651, Filed 5 Dec. 1898. UK Patent No. GB190123678 (A). Ibid
21 Martland (n 8) 126
22 The emergence of the modern conceptual distinction between copyright and patent outlined by Sherman and Bently – the idea that copyright subject matter is created, whereas patent subject matter is discovered – may have supported the growth of professionals skilled in drafting required patent specifications, but the impact of this jurisprudential development on business culture and practice is far less clear. Brad Sherman and Lionel Bently, *The Making of Modern Intellectual Property Law* (CUP 1999) 154–155
23 The idea of capitalism as performative and processual is now common with respect to the "new economy" and often linked to the development of global advertising. E.g. Anne M Cronin, 'Gender in the Making of Commercial Worlds' (2008) 9(3) Feminist Theory 293. However, Bellido's work suggests a need to reconsider the history

of intellectual property in the early 20th century and in advertising. See Jose Bellido, 'Toward a History of Trade Mark Watching' (2015) 2 Intellectual Property Quarterly 130

24 *Boosey v Whight* [1899] 1 Ch 836. Affirmed [1900] 1 Ch 122

25 *Revised Berne Convention* for the Protection of Literary and Artistic Works of November 13, Berlin, 1908. Article 13 pertains to mechanical reproductions of musical works

26 See generally, Craig H Roell, *The Piano in America, 1890–1940* (U of North Carolina P 1991) 59–63

27 Germany suggested compulsory licensing modelled on the patent system at the outset of the Berlin Conference, including that once a composer had agreed to one mechanical recording, other companies could record the same subject to a compulsory fee. See 'Mechanical Musical Instruments Article 13. Paragraph 1' International Union for the Protection of literary and artistic works, Records of the Diplomatic Conference: Convened in Berlin, Oct 14 to Nov 14, 1908

28 Mr Cassell, *House of Commons Debates, 17 August 1911, Vol 29 cc.* 2159–2163

29 S19 *Copyright Act* 1911, 1–2 Geo. 5. CH. 46

30 Okpaluba (n 8) 114

31 Boosey (n 8) 147

32 Ibid 148–149

33 Ibid

34 As Kimmel observes,

> [t]he very processes that confer privilege to one group and not to another are often invisible to those upon whom that privilege is conferred . . . men have come to think of themselves as genderless, in part because they can afford the luxury of ignoring the centrality of gender. . . . And the invisibility of gender to those privileged by it reproduces the inequalities that are circumscribed by gender.

Cited in Christine Beasley, 'Rethinking Hegemonic Masculinity in a Globalised World' (2008) 11(1) Men and Masculinities 86–87

35 There is enormous literature discussing the author-function as first elaborated by French literary theorists, Roland Barthes, 'The Death of the Author' (1967) and Michel Foucault, 'What Is an Author?' (1969). See Chapter 2

36 The importance of understanding cross-industry dynamics is also discussed in Chapter 4

37 TM number UK219,499. Image Mark: "Angel" Filed 15 Nov 1895; Registered Class 8 Instruments included in class 8 for reproducing sound

38 Francis Barraud, '"His Master's Voice": How Nipper Became World-Famous' (1916) 52 *The Strand Magazine* 150, 151

39 Leonard Petts, 'The Story of "Nipper" and the "His Master's Voice" Picture Painted by Francis Barraud' in *The Talking Machine Review International* (E Bayly 1973) 12–13. TM number UK235,053. Image mark: "His Master's Voice" Filed 22 Dec 1900. Registered Class 8: Gramophones and other sound recording and reproducing instruments; TM number UK 325592; filed 21 July 1910. Registered Class 9: Talking machines, talking machine needles, talking machine records and fittings for talking machines

40 Barraud notes that copies of his painting were also hung in every branch of the corporation. His contribution to the corporation's success was recognised with the award of a £250 annuity in 1921. 'His Master's Voice Artist Rewarded' *Evening Telegraph* (London) 18 Mar 1921, 3

41 Martland (n 8) 132

42 Jones (n 8) 88

43 Ibid 93

44 Martland (n 8) 124

45 Ibid 160–161

46 Roell (n 26) 46

47 Ibid 54
48 Ibid 17
49 Ibid 57–59
50 Marsha Siefert, 'Aesthetics, Technology, and the Capitalization of Culture: How the Talking Machine Became a Musical Instrument' (1995) 8 Science in Context 417, 431–432
51 Jerrold Northrop Moore, *A Voice in Time: The Gramophone of Fred Gaisberg 1873–1951* (Hamish Hamilton 1976) 69–71
52 Green notes that Haweis's 1871 book, *Music and Morals* went through ten editions in 12 years, making him the most popular Victorian author on the subject of music. Edward Green, 'Music and the Victorian Mind: The Musical Aesthetics of the Rev HR Haweis' (2008) 39 *International Review of the Aesthetics and Sociology of Music* 239, 242
53 Roell (n 26) 13–14 (note omitted)
54 Ibid 22–24, 32
55 Paula Gillett, *Musical Women in England, 1870–1914: "Encroaching on All Man's Privileges"* (St Martin's Press 2000) 6
56 Suzanne Aspden, '"An Infinity of Factions": Opera in Eighteenth Century Britain and the Undoing of Society' (1997) 1(9) *Cambridge Opera Journal* 1
57 Green (n 52) 239–256; Derek B Scott, 'The Sexual Politics of Victorian Musical Aesthetics' (1994) 119(1) Journal of the Royal Musical Association 91
58 Hilary Poriss quoting Anne Schreffler in her 'Divas and Divos' in Helen M Greenwald (ed), *The Oxford Handbook of Opera* (OUP 2014) 379
59 Roberta Montemorra Marvin, 'Idealizing the Prima Donna in Mid-Victorian London' in Rachel Cowgill and Hilary Poriss (eds), *The Arts of the Prima Donna in the Long Nineteenth Century* (OUP 2012); Kerry Powell, 'Gendering Victorian Theatre' in Joseph Donoghue (ed) *The Cambridge History of British Theatre Volume 2: 1660 to 1895* (CUP 2004) 352–368
60 Montemorra Marvin, ibid 22
61 Joel H Kaplan 'Musical Iconography in "The Illustrated London News": An Introduction' (1982) 29(4) Fontes Artis Musicae 161
62 Montemorra Marvin (n 59) 28
63 Ibid
64 The proprietor, George Allan, was well known to Melba's father, David Mitchell. Both were unsuccessful gold prospectors who transitioned into highly successful Melbourne businessmen. Together they helped establish the Melbourne Philharmonic Society in 1853. Peter Game, *The Music Sellers* (Hawthorn Press 1973) 18
65 Nellie Mitchell to Signor Cecchi (undated), JR McEwen, Papers 1845–1870, SLV: MS 9016
66 Deirdre Morris, 'Sherwin, Francis Amy Lillian (1855–1935)' in *Australian Dictionary of Biography* (Australian National UP 1976)
67 Melba complained to a friend about the fuss made over Sherwin in Australia, given she only sings at second- and third-rate concerts in London and has never sung on the Continent, cited in Alison Gyger, *Opera for the Antipodes, 1881–1939* (Currency Press, Pellinor 1990) 58
68 'Women Who Work. No. XVI. Their Numbers and Employments' *The Pall Mall Gazette* (London) 3 Oct 1884; 'Women Who Work. No. XXXII. Ladies of the Stage' *The Pall Mall Gazette* 17 Dec 1885; 'Women Who Work. No. XX. Nurses of the Sick Poor' *The Pall Mall Gazette* 14 Nov 1884
69 'Stars and Salaries' (1893) 34(600) *The Musical Times and Singing Class Circular* 79
70 'Sir Augustus Harris on the Opera' (1893) 34(608) *The Musical Times and Singing Class Circular* 585
71 The Australian born singer also recorded for the Company under many names: Peter Dawson (Art songs, Operatic, Choral, Ballads), Hector Grant (Scottish songs), Frank Danby (light popular songs) and Will Strong (Music Hall hits) and lists nine more names

he used to set songs. He was "able to be simultaneously Australian, Scottish and British and to express these identities both separately and within the overall context of a truly imperial patriotism through the medium of song". Jeffrey Richards, 'The Troubadour of Empire: Peter Dawson' in *His Imperialism and Music: Britain 1876–1953* (Manchester UP 2001) 469–524

72 Peter Dawson, *Fifty Years of Song* (Hutchinson & Co 1951) 21

73 Kerry Murphy, 'Melba's French Debut: Another White Voice?' (2011) 33(1) Musicology Australia 3

74 Anne Blainey, *I Am Melba: A Biography* (Black Inc 2009) 62–63

75 'Musician's Names' *The Musical Times* (London) 1 July 1898, 448

76 Following Melba's lead other Australian singers also debuted with foreign-sounding names: Madame Benda in 1903 (Kate Samuels of Bendigo, Victoria); Madame Ballara in 1907 (Florence Fawez of Ballarat, Victoria); Elsa Stralia in 1914 (Elsa Fischer of Adelaide). Angela Woollacott, *To Try Her Fortune in London: Australian Women, Colonialism and Modernity* (OUP 2001) 161

77 Nellie Melba, *Melodies and Memories* (AMS Press 1971) 37. See also Mr Neill Forsyth, (Royal Opera House, Syndicate Secretary) cited in Henry Saxe Wyndham, *The Annals of Covent Garden Theatre: From 1792 to 1897. Vol 2* (Chatto and Windus 1906) 284–285

78 Wyndham, ibid 282–283

79 The short quotes are all taken from the gossip magazine, *Table Talk* (Melbourne) 1885–1939

80 A collection of six articles authored by Melba are reproduced as 'Melba's Advice on the Art of Singing', in William R Moran (ed), *Nellie Melba: A Contemporary Review* (Greenwood Press 1985) 365

81 Simon Purtell, '"A Souvenir of My Deep Interest in Your Future Achievements": The "Melba Gift" and Issues of Performing Pitch in Early 20th Century Melbourne' (2011) 1 Grainger Studies: An Interdisciplinary Journal 75–95

82 New York resident Gianni Bettini filed sound recording patents in the US from 1889. US Patent 409,005. Recording by mechanical cutting, deforming or pressing, e.g. of grooves or pits; reproducing by mechanical sensing; record carriers therefor. He was credited as recording Melba by Moran (n 80) 426–427, 447–448

83 Melanie Fashington, 'Strictly Confidential. A Causerie for Women Only' *Table Talk* (Melbourne) 12 July 1895, 16

84 Nellie Melba to Chairman, Gramophone and Typewriter Ltd, Correspondence, 6 Mar 1904, EMI: Melba Artist File

85 'Melba Has Made Gramophone Records' *Illustrated London News* 25 June 1904

86 Mr SW Dixon to Mr PH Bohanna, Correspondence, 4 Dec 1903. EMI: Melba Artist File

87 Mr SW Dixon to Mr TB Birnbaum, Correspondence, 2 Sep 1903; Mr SW Dixon to Mr PH Bohanna, Correspondence, 3 Sep 1903; Mr SW Dixon to Mr P Bohanna, Correspondence, 4 Sep 1903; Gramophone & Typewriter Ltd to Mr Fassett Esq, Messr S Hoffnung & Co, Correspondence, 2 Mar 1906. EMI: Melba Artist File

88 Deutsche Grammophon-Aktiengesellscahft to Mr Dixon, Monte Carlo, Correspondence, 15 Feb 1904. EMI: Melba Artist File

89 BG Andrews, 'Chambers, Charles Haddon Spurgeon (1860–1921)' *National Centre of Biography, Australian Dictionary of Biography* (Australian National UP). http://adb.anu.edu.au/biography/chambers-charles-haddon-spurgeon-5547/text9455, published first in hardcopy 1979. For a discussion of his plays see Elizabeth Schaffer, 'A Tale of Two Australians: Haddon Chambers, Gilbert Murray and the Imperial London Stage' in Elizabeth Schafer and Susan Bradley Smith (eds), *Playing Australia: Australian Theatre and the International Stage* (Rodolphi 2003)

90 See Roger Neill, 'Haddon Chambers and the Long Arm of Neglect' (July–August 2008) Quadrant 78ff

91 Mrs Leonard W Matters, *Australasians Who Count in London and Who Counts in Western Australia* (JA Truscott & Sons 1913) 22
92 Blainey (n 74) 162–163
93 Mr TB Birnbaum to Mr Calvin Child, Correspondence, 28 Feb 1907; 6 Mar 1907. EMI: Melba Artist File
94 Ibid
95 Johnson later noted that he was disappointed in her American recordings. Further given improvements in the technology he would like to have her record the entire catalogue again. However, as she would not return to the US for some time he mused about trying to record her in Australia, assuming they could find appropriate orchestration. Mr ER Johnson to Mr SW Dixon, Correspondence, 11 Jan 1909. EMI: Melba Artist File
96 Mr TB Birnbaum to Mr Calvin Child (Victor Recording Manager) Correspondence, 28 Fe. 1907, 6 Mar 1907. EMI: Melba Artist File
97 Mr ER Johnson to Mr TB Birnbaum, Correspondence, 14 June 1907. EMI: Melba Artist File
98 Broad & Co Solicitors to the Managing Director, Gramophone and Typewriter Ltd, Correspondence, 6 June 1907. EMI: Melba Artist File
99 William Evans, *The Law Relating to the Remuneration of Commission Agents* (2nd ed, W de Bracy Herbert 1900) 151. Thanks to Emeritus Professor Mark Aronson for this point
100 Augustine Birrell, *The Duties and Liabilities of Trustees: Six Lectures Delivered in the Inner Temple during the Hilary Sittings, 1896* (Palgrave Macmillan 1896) 66–67
101 Ibid 66 (my emphasis)
102 'Melba Has Made Gramophone Records' *Illustrated London News* 25 June 1904
103 Mr TB Birnbaum to Mr Calvin Child, Correspondence, 28 Feb 1907; 6 Mar 1907. EMI: Melba Artist File
104 Henry Russell cited in Neill (n 90) 75, 83
105 Nicholas E Limansky, 'Luisa Tetrazzina. Colatura Secrets' (2004) 20(4) The Opera Quarterly 540, 566
106 'Agreement between The Gramophone and Typewriter Limited . . . and Helen Melba of Great Cumberland Place London' 11 May 1904. EMI: Melba Artist File. Chambers consent was also required for any changes in pricing of Melba records
107 With recurring droughts depressing the local economy, disposable incomes in Australia were far less than those in Britain. From July 1907 all the celebrity recordings were released as "Red Label" records priced at 20 shillings. Pricing of other records was 12 shillings sixpence. Gramophone and Typewriter Ltd to Hoffnung & Co, Correspondence, 31 May 1906. EMI: Melba Artist File
108 The Gramophone and Typewriter Ltd to Mr A Clark Esq., Correspondence, 3 May 1904. EMI: Melba Artist File
109 Moore (n 51) 28
110 The Gramophone and Typewriter Ltd to Joseph Berliner Esq, Deutsche Gramophon Actiengesellschaft, Correspondence, c24 Apr 1904; 28 Apr 1904. EMI: Melba Artist File
111 Melba (n 77) 251
112 Roger Neill, 'Nellie Melba's First Recordings' *Historic Masters* (2012). Neill also claims that Melba attended Bohanna's Sydney offices to hear the recordings and arrange a gift for her niece; however it is clear that Dixon wrote to Bohanna, rather than the reverse. In October 1903 Bohanna notes he was travelling in September and would attend to Dixon's request and forward the gift to Miss Patterson promptly
113 Agreement between the Victor Talking Machine Company of Camden New Jersey and Madam Melba now residing in the city of New York and a member of the Manhattan Opera Company, dated 7 Mar 1907, EMI: Melba Artist File

114 Art 6bis provides: (1) Independently of the author's copyright, and even after transfer of the said copyright, the author shall have the right to claim authorship of the work, as well as the right to object to any distortion, mutilation or other modification of the said work which would be prejudicial to his honour or reputation. See generally Elizabeth Adeney, *The Moral Rights of Authors and Performers: An International and Comparative Analysis* (OUP 2006)
115 It is not until 1919 that there appears to be a concerted attempt at closer co-operation between the companies in dealing with artist negotiations, with Johnson's admission that "the most important purpose of our agreement . . . is that we should co-operate fully in controlling the said artistes". Mr A Clark, Memorandum to ER Johnson: Artistes. Co-operation with the Victor Company 22 Oct 1919. EMI: Melba Artist File
116 Correspondence, Mr Sydney Dixon to Mr Alfred C Clark, 21 June 1904. EMI: Melba Artist File
117 The exchange is between Mr Dixon (London) to Mr Alfred Clark Esq (Paris) dated 14–30 Sep 1904. EMI: Melba Artist File
118 'Killed by a Motor Car: Driven by Madame Melba' *The Daily News* (Perth, WA) 13 Sep 1904, 7. All charges were later dropped
119 'A Member of the Aristocracy', *Manners and Rules of Good Society or Solecisms to Be Avoided* (38th ed, Frederick Warne & Co 1916) 259. See also Andrew Maunder, '"Alone into the Wide, Wide World": Trollope's Miss Mackenzie and the Mid-Victorian Etiquette Manual' (2000) 26(2) Vic Rev 48
120 Martland (n 8) 76, 98–100
121 Cited in Peter Martland, *Since Records Began. EMI: The First Hundred Years* (EMI Group 1997) 64
122 Mr Dixon to J Broad Esq, Correspondence, 4 Nov 1904. EMI: Melba Artist File
123 Cheston and Sons Solicitors to Mr Dixon, Correspondence, 27 Oct 1904. EMI: Melba Artist File
124 'The Police Courts. Clerkenwell' *The Times* (London) 10 Dec 1904, 4
125 DM Kerly and FG Underhay, *The Law on Trade Marks and Trade Names* (3rd ed, Sweet and Maxwell 1908) 18
126 Cheston and Sons Solicitors to Mr Dixon, Correspondence, 1 Dec 1904, Melba Artist File, EMI Archives
127 Indenture dated 19 Dec 1904, affixed to 'Agreement between The Gramophone and Typewriter Limited . . . and Helen Melba of Great Cumberland Place London' dated 11 May 1904. EMI: Melba Artist File
128 *Boosey v Whight* [1899] 1 Ch 836. Affirmed [1900] 1 Ch 122
129 Calculations were made using the catalogue information provided on *Melba, Nellie. London Recordings* (1904) Naxos Historical, released 2002, and private research. The 1842 copyright term was for the author's life plus seven years or 42 years from first publication. This was extended in the *Copyright Act* 1911 to the life of the author plus 50 years. Applying the term 1911 extension to the same works, only one work recorded by Melba moves from public domain to being in copyright
130 Report of the Committee on the Law of Copyright, Cd. 4976, HMSO, 1910, 35
131 'Copyright Bill. CLAUSE 19. (Provisions as to Mechanical Instruments.)' House of Commons Debates, 17 Aug 1911, Vol 29, cc2154–2157
132 Gramophone and Typewriter Ltd to S Hoffnung & Co London, Correspondence, 19 Dec 1905. EMI: Melba Artist File
133 T O'Brien, *The Greater Union Story 1910–1985* (Greater Union Organisation 1985) 16
134 Copyright payments for the public performance of the music was required under the *Copyright Act* 1912 (Cth), although there is no mention of fees being paid
135 This includes instrument sales. Game (n 64) 146–147
136 Evidence of Mr John Drummond Robertson on behalf of the Gramophone Co Ltd *Law of Copyright Committee 1909, Minutes of Evidence,* HMSO, 1910 (hereafter Gorell Committee Evidence) 230

137 Ibid
138 He was questioned further about this. See Evidence of Mr John Drummond Robertson, Gorell Committee Evidence, Para 1268–1275, 54
139 Evidence of Mr John Drummond Robertson (recalled) Gorell Committee Evidence, Paras 3248–3275, 147–148; Further Statement Gorell Committee Evidence, 250–255
140 Evidence of Mr John Drummond Robertson on behalf of the Gramophone Co Ltd, Gorell Committee Evidence, 227
141 Evidence of Mr John Drummond, Gorell Committee Evidence, Para 1000, 44
142 J Drummond Robertson, 'Copyright Bill' *The Times* (London) 9 May 1911, 4
143 Okpaluba (n 8) 114
144 Dame Nellie Melba, 'The Magic of Home' *The Home* 1 Mar 1924, 17, 73
145 Dr Stacy L Smith, Marc Choueiti and Dr Katherine Pieper, *Inclusion in the Recording Studio? Gender and Race/Ethnicity of Artists, Songwriters & Producers across 600 Popular Songs from 2012–2017* (USC Annenberg School for Communication and Journalism, Jan 2018); Tracy Bain, *Counting the Music Industry: The Gender Gap 2019 Report.* https://countingmusic.co.uk/
146 The best known of these is ContentID. See Evanto Market, *Buyers Guide to YouTube Content & Copyright Notices.* https://help.market.envato.com/hc/en-us/articles/204484680-Buyers-Guide-to-YouTube-Content-ID-Copyright-Notices; Nicholas Thomas DeLisa, 'You(Tube), Me, and Content ID: Paving the Way for Compulsory Synchronization' (2016) 81 Brook L Rev
147 IFPI, Global Music Report, 2019, 13
148 'The Big Three: How the Internet Disrupts Record Label Revenue' 14 Dec 2016. www.nasdaq.com/article/the-big-three-how-the-internet-disrupts-record-label-revenue-cm721240; Worldwide Independent Market Report, The Global Economic & Cultural Contribution of Independent Music (2015). http://winformusic.org/.files/WINTEL%202015.pdf
149 Bain (n 145)
150 'Women in Music 2017: The Most Powerful Executives in the Industry' *Billboard* 30 Nov 2017
151 Neilsen 2017 US Music Year-End Report. www.nielsen.com/us/en/insights/reports/2018/2017-music-us-year-end-report.html
152 The experiences of Taylor Swift, Erin Andrews and Kesha and a feminist reading of contract law are explored in Nikki R Breeland, '"All the Truth I Could Tell": A Discussion of Title VII's Potential Impact on Systemic Entertainment Industry Victimization' 25 UCLAWLJ 135
153 Eriq Gardner, 'Kesha's Amended Lawsuit against Dr Luke Rejected by Judge' *Hollywood Reporter*, 21 Mar 2017
154 Gottwald v Sebert 2017 WL 1062924 (N.Y.Sup.), 2017 NY Slip Op 30521
155 For a different view see Andreas Rahmatian, 'Music and Creativity as Perceived by Copyright Law' (2005) 3 Intellectual Property Quarterly 267

7 Why Margaret Atwood, Radiohead and Banksy are not anti-copyright

This book has sought to explain how relations between authors and producers came to be defined by distinctive commercial infrastructures that were assembled in the late 19th and early 20th centuries to exploit what became the ubiquitous cultural commodities – books, magazines, films, performances and sound recordings. Chapters have shown how the agency of creators was impacted by this development, tracing shifts in the ability of different kinds of creators in different parts of the world to define their own market opportunities. There is a common theme that arises from looking at commercial histories of creators whose names have endured: it was the creators who connected with and generated new audiences in new territories who could call themselves professionals, having secured some kind of personal financial security.

Contrary to popular anti-establishment sentiment that blames multi-nationals for the rise of corporate control at the expense of creators, collaborations between multi-national companies within industries and across industries were not designed to suppress authors and artists. But they were designed to grow company profits first and foremost. The most commercially successful creators discussed in this book – Conan Doyle, Hall Caine and Nellie Melba – actively participated in developing the new commodity forms and markets in ways that were mutually beneficial to the growth of international cultural markets and the corporations they transacted with. Artistic reputations and authority in managing business affairs grew alongside profits. But alongside enjoying success, many creators, in particular, Hume, Doyle and Melba, also felt caught between competing expectations – to satisfy fans by repeating their signature formulas for success and producing something that was artistically satisfying and fresh. It is important to note than none of the creators who were financially successful took their audiences' affections and their ongoing ability to make profit for granted. They worked hard to maintain profiles, curate images and maintain authority as spokespeople for their craft. In performing the role of celebrity, personal factors, such as nationality, gender and class, were relevant – not simply for creating degrees of privilege or being taken for granted. These factors were also engaged as ways of individualising a public identity in a mass market. Melba is particularly interesting in this regard. Some of her decision-making was very risky. As a commercial actor she was experimental and non-conformist, alongside operating within extremely conservative cultural strictures that she navigated and played with, depending on context and participants.

Intellectual property rights, and copyright in particular, were reformed in the modern era to facilitate the growth of international cultural trade and underpin the cultural industries, but the technical detail of rights has never mattered as much as the socio-legal context of the transactions between players. Law reform enabled protection of new kinds of technological artefacts such as films and sound recordings, and encouraged international collaboration between industries. This enabled the establishment of control over the free movement of cultural goods and the international distribution of commercial opportunities for creators that was key to the emergence of media empires. However, this transformation was only possible due to popular reception of the idea of authorship and inventorship across the globe that could be relied upon to justify the rearrangement of commercial interests. Accordingly, in the early 20th century the idea of authorship was transformed by its incorporation into industry dynamics. Romantic-era formulations of authorial property had been genre-specific and informed by suspicion of commodity relations. Such limitations were overwritten by a far more generous and indiscriminate modern formulation that collapsed respect for the artistic work with the celebrity of the author.

Nonetheless, critiques of copyright have remained commonplace. Indeed, they are now mainstream, and this current dynamic requires further explanation in light of the history disclosed in this book. What does authorship mean in the age of streaming and outlaw art? This concluding chapter historicises this recent development. It explores the relevance of copyright history to contemporary commercial dynamics, reflecting upon critiques of the cultural industries that have widely circulated across the globe, by three well-established celebrity authors and artists, Margaret Atwood, Radiohead and Banksy.

Canadian poet and author Margaret Atwood has a long and distinguished career that includes self-publishing, editions with small presses and republication by a feminist press, Virago, alongside mainstream publishing. The diversity of her publishing practice over many years grounds her authority to speak about the life of the professional author and the creative and commercial choices to be made. Recently, Atwood has expressed concern about the rise of platform culture and free culture. Her 'Introduction' to Lewis Hyde's *The Gift. How the Creative Spirit Transforms the World*[1] explores the ongoing importance of copyright to authors today linking this to the centuries' old concern about how artists can be paid for their work. She has frequently promoted *The Gift* at author festivals around the globe, highly recommending it to creative artists and writers. In it she notes the ongoing importance of copyright to artists, in the face of commodity culture.

There are some similarities in this position with that of British recording artists Radiohead, who, in 2007, at the height of hysteria about online music piracy and predictions of the death of multi-national recording companies, broke with the successor to the Gramophone Company, EMI, and released their album, *In Rainbows*, from their website, where fans could pay what they wished for the download. At the time, this action was much commented on as an anti-copyright, anti-establishment position; however, in reality, the artists' position was much more nuanced and, like their music, experimental. Discussion of the controversy is contextualised with reference to artist advocacy during the early 21st-century "copyright wars". It is argued that in the recording industry today, copyright no longer commands the central authority it once did. Labels have also pulled back on publicly promoting copyright as a universal property right that artists need to survive because this only exacerbates tensions with artists over unfair contracts in the industry. As discussed in Chapter 6, this tension is not showing any signs of abating. Further, today multi-nationals can commercialise their existing and substantial copyright portfolios through negotiations with online platforms on terms that are invisible to the public and hard for artists to penetrate. At the same time, an artist's copyright position has begun to function more as a brand. A copyright position communicates something distinctive about the artist-producer's image and their desired relationship with fans-consumers. The content is fixed by the terms set by the artists on the sites where their music and merchandise is available. Correspondingly, authorship is also starting to be described as a creation without any fixed content, merely a branding choice that assembles fans for particular commercial purposes.

Pseudonymous street artist Banksy presents a greater challenge to the idea of authorial property, indeed to private property altogether than Radiohead. Yet his infamous practice of "Brandalism", a collision of vandalism and brand management pulls in contradictory directions. His book *Wall and Piece* was published by multi-national Penguin Random House including the inscription, "Copyright is for losers©™" alongside an assertion of his moral rights and a publisher disclaimer about not encouraging or inducing graffiti.[2] Banksy's creative play with site-specific art and ephemeral works, and his ambivalence about authorial attribution and control, have crossed over into the mainstream with the invention of the new genre of street art, and auction sales managed by multi-national art-houses such as Christies and Sotheby's. Banksy's establishment of his own art authentication agency, Pest Control Office Limited, and branded sales through Gross Domestic Product™ (GDP), further plays with the idea of incorporation and raises the question whether it is possible to resist commodity relations. All three contemporary critics are discussed in relation to this dilemma.

Margaret Atwood – moving inside and outside the mainstream

Atwood's early publications

Unpublished authors learn about publishing opportunities from speaking to other writers, discussions in literary magazines, media coverage of cultural debates, as well as formal literary education and writing courses. What is conveyed by these contacts is not only practical information and advice, but also political opinions about the current state of the publishing industry. Along the way, these conversations also convey an understanding of the status quo. And as discussed in several chapters of this book, laws, cultural investments in particular ideologies, collaborations between commercial enterprises, institutional practices help reinforce existing privileges and affect distribution of business opportunities. In addition, there are preferred genres, styles of writing and existing cultural networks that advantage some writers over others. The publishing market differs depending upon where one resides. However, the status quo does not reproduce itself. Reproduction of historic privilege is also resisted and the status quo is challenged by broader social factors and new ideas circulating within artist communities and beyond.

Margaret Atwood's early forays into publishing were informed by an understanding of Canadian publishing history. The longer-term impact of Hall Caine's Canadian tour, discussed in Chapter 4, had been felt in later decades, with the results apparent from the publishing landscape that emerged in Canada.

> The majority of early twentieth century publishing houses were branch plants of foreign publishers whose headquarters were primarily in Great Britain and in the United States, or, like Ryerston Press, were institutionally connected. Their primary objective was to sell books, and to do so reflecting the colonial tradition, they imported employees from their home country. In this way they avoided integrating Canadians into their hierarchies who might otherwise have promoted their own culture and literature (although, it must be said in all fairness, that Canadians were not all that well-versed in their own literary history at this time).[3]

By the 1950s and '60s only proven local writers were published by major presses. This situation was exacerbated by the Canadian Author's Association that advanced a narrow conception of literature, promoting conservative poets steeped in British Romantic and Victorian traditions.[4] Canadian literature was not taught in schools or universities.[5] Even a 1960s poetry boom was serviced by commercially driven, depersonalised publishers that had dominated the market since the 1920s. However, post-WWII Canadians witnessed the rise of international human rights discourse and resistance to the continuation of colonial dynamics. This broader politics impacted the international publishing scene dominated by the multi-national corporations. The stifling of independent Canadian publishing houses generated counter-cultural movements, with a presence within universities where Atwood studied and taught.[6] Acting upon the idea that Canada should not remain a place of "invisible literature" where original writing by Canadian authors could not be found would change the local publishing landscape.

Atwood's first publication, *Double Persephone* (1961) was a 16-page chapbook. It was self-published. The pages were assembled by the author herself, producing around 220 copies. Her second publication, *The Circle Game* (1964), was a book of poetry, illustrated in collaboration with lithographer Charles Pachter.[7] Only 15 hand-made copies were produced. Small-scale, hand-crafted productions are not the last resort for new and original voices – works to be later set aside and treated as minor or immature offerings by writers whom, at that time, lacked the standing or merit to attract a major publisher. Rather, cottage and small press productions have their own independent histories and significance, reaching across centuries to connect contemporary readers with the Romantic concern for maintaining a space for art and poetry separate from commodity culture, as was discussed in Chapter 2. Such productions by Atwood and others speak to an enduring interest in making art for its own sake, to be appreciated by small numbers of fellow travellers.

In post-WWII Canadian society, local literary experimentation was accompanied by the development of new small independent presses. One such venture established in 1952 was Contact Press. This was "a non-profit organisation . . . formed to take the place now largely abandoned by the larger commercial book houses – the publication and encouragement of poetry in Canada".[8] Contact Press editors were established modernist poets. They financed company productions. Where possible, determining whether or not a manuscript was accepted relied upon consensus decision-making that referenced the press's foundational principles,

> First, . . . a self-conscious response to the popularization of commercial media; second, it strove to remain faithful to literary and artistic traditions; and third it was inspired by the new and creative which is both universal and implicit in the spirit of modernism.[9]

Anti-commercialism was expressed in a commitment that the author retain full control over the presentation of the work to the public. Like cottage productions, the format and design was left in the author's hands to prevent the "interference" of other production values mediating the crafting of the work for anticipated readers.[10] Atwood's *The Circle Game* was not accepted at first blush, but Contact Press agreed to publish it in 1966. It then won the Governor-General's Literary Award for Poetry or Drama in 1967. There were not enough copies available to meet demand. Though Contact Press soon wound down as the founders became engaged in other activities, the book was reprinted by another independent, Anasi Press, in 1967.

While continuing to work as a university lecturer, Atwood also published essays, including a provocation about the state of Canadian literary culture. *Survival: A Thematic Guide to Canadian Literature*[11] was positioned as a teacher's guide, interrogating the Canadian-ness of the nation's poetry and prose. It was highly controversial for its use of four victim tropes and unflattering portrayals to classify creative endeavours by well-respected authors. The essay invigorated discussion about the state of Canadian literature and literary education.[12] After

1969 Atwood's poetry was published by Oxford University Press (UK) and Atlantic Little Brown (US), reflecting her standing as a rising talent, as well as her desire to reach a much wider international audience.

Atwood's first novel, *Up in the Air So Blue* (1964) was not accepted for publication by established Canadian publisher, McClelland and Stewart. Her second, *The Edible Woman* (1965) was accepted after winning the Governor-General's prize, though the manuscript had not been read at the time.[13] The publisher had shown initial interest but had lost it.[14] Publication of many more novels, short fiction, children's books, essays, poetry, sound recordings and television scripts followed, with works published by mainstream and small presses.[15]

Formal recognition came in the form of many literary prizes, writers-in-residency appointments and interest in the author as a celebrity. However, Atwood remained both insider and outsider, a participant in and critic of the mainstream literary culture and its values,

> When women are judged to have written well, Atwood argues, it is because they have written in a 'masculine' way or, conversely, when a man writes in a 'feminine', it is to be applauded: 'when a man writes about things like doing the dishes, it's realism; when a woman does, it's an unfortunate feminine genetic limitation'. She also finds that women writers themselves are derogated through being sexualized, thus trivializing their work: 'the ploy diverts attention from the woman's achievement as a writer – the area where the man feels threatened – to her sexuality, where either way [through insult or compliment] he can score a verbal point'.[16]

The Edible Woman was reprinted by feminist press, Virago, as a Modern Classic paperback in 1980. The emergence of Virago press stemmed from another concern for the world's invisible publications – the neglect of the works of women writers,

> The series emerged from an earlier initiative, the Virago Reprint Library, begun in 1977, which was in part inspired by Sheila Rowbotham's Hidden from History, and her problematization of the ways in which women's cultural, economic and social status had been concealed throughout history. Virago's Reprint Library was its first attempt to uncover this history, a task that was continued and expanded with the Modern Classics.[17]

The decision to republish Atwood's book was a feminist act and a response to second-wave feminism. It reflected ambivalence about the relevance of law reform designed to advance gender equality, when these efforts were not supported by strategies to effect cultural change. For equality to advance there was a need to address the socio-legal context in which the law operated. This included challenging roles and stereotypes that reinforced gender values in daily lives,

> women were denied parity of pay even when they were carrying out work of equal value to their male colleagues, as Anna Coote (a member of Virago's Advisory Group) and Tess Gill pointed out: 'Women's average earnings are still little more than half those of men. Many employees have been able to avoid the impact of the Equal Pay Act by keeping women in low-paid grades of work or transferring them to "women's jobs" where they have no chance of comparing their pay and conditions with male workers'. It was noted that the assumption that women would also be caregivers – in ways not assumed of men, even if they too were parents – contributed to the discriminatory attitudes that structured the working day. 'Not only are there few women managers, employers and supervisors, but most women are employed in low-wage and low-status jobs, have little opportunity for training and promotion and are forced to work hours adapted to their other job as housewives and mothers'.[18]

The Edible Woman challenged gender stereotypes, and problematised the role of housewife. Other writers published in the series included Angela Carter and Zoe Fairbairns.

Virago's cultural and commercial agenda was different to that of small presses. Hegemonic change required reaching the widest possible audience with gender critiques and empowering messages. This was a political ambition that coalesced with an emerging international demand for feminist literature. Riley notes, "In the Classics series, then, business acumen collided with feminist principle".[19] The editors had experience working at mainstream houses such as Penguin and Frank Cass, where obscure and out-of-print texts had also found revival markets. In its first decade Virago published 136 classics, alongside 24 new works of fiction. Market success led to a situation where the new trade press was able to bid for the most esteemed contemporary writers, as well as consider expanding the operation.[20]

Chapter 3 explained why the value of copyright to publishers is not simply counted in royalties that evidence the demand for a particular text by a recognised author. How a work is presented to the public, and how interest is refreshed over time, matters. In publishing with Virago the value of the copyright in *The Edible Woman* was not only invigorated by making the story available to new generations of feminist readers. A bookshop shelf presence, situated amongst other feminist writers, with the volumes sharing readily identifiable green covers, white text on the spine, modern art covers and sharing the company Apple trademark (a reference to forbidden fruit), assisted readers to locate other works that belonged to the new genre, improving the ability to place all feminist fiction with booksellers and for these works to find readers. In a similar manner to the way Conan Doyle's publishing innovations in the new crime genre enhanced the value of Sherlock Holmes's publisher, George

Newnes Ltd, Virago itself became a desirable investment opportunity. At the same time, the huge demand for Virago productions became too much for their independent book distributor, Wildwood House, to service. Wildwood House only had five UK representatives to manage all their export orders.[21] The financial options for expansion considered by Virago were to borrow large sums, sell parts of the company to outsiders, or sell to interested mainstream buyers. In 1982 Virago was sold to Chatto, Bodley Head and Cape (CBC) who increased an initial offer of £150,000 to £244,000 becoming 'Chatto, Virago, Bodley Head and Jonathan Cape' (CVBC). This connection vastly improved warehousing, sales and distribution services.[22] The transition of the old Virago into the conglomerate increased year-on-year profitability, as well as a growing and diverse list of lauded names. But Virago was incorporated into established business and legal infrastructures. There was no reinvention of the vessels that carried feminist content to readers across generations. Virago's books were now simply global commodities, albeit with feminist themes.

Copyright: a commodity and gift?

In her brief introduction to a new edition of Lewis Hyde's, *The Gift*, Atwood describes the book as an "essential work" about gift-giving and its relation to art, and "a book about the core nature of what it is that artists do".[23] She reflects on a change that occurred with the cover design between the original Vintage edition of 1983 and the 2011 one. The original paperback bore a Shaker painting on the cover of a basket of apples. The apples were golden, "glowing with energy"; each apple, probably representing a single Shaker, "warmed and glimmering with an inner gift, but not thereby standing out in the community, for all the apples are the same size". They are held together in a transparent basket that may have meant "Divine Grace".[24] In explaining the selection of the image, Hyde had included a note that informed readers,

> The Shakers believed that they received their art as gifts from the spiritual world. . . . Shaker artists were known as "instruments"; we know only a few of their names, for in general it was forbidden that they be known to any but the church elders.[25]

Atwood observes,

> This note is followed by a copyright line that, in view of the origins of *Basket of Apples*, reads ironically: "Basket of Apples is reprinted through the courtesy of The Shaker Community Inc". So the community of gift-givers has now become incorporated, and its gifts have been transformed to property by the commodity market that now surrounds us on all sides.[26]

She goes on to note that copyright functions as the body of law that straddles the realms of art and commodity. And, in this instance, despite the dominance of commodity markets, the term "courtesy of" indicates the survival of non-commercial gift exchange and property relations guided by shared communal ethics.

But this is not just a Shaker ethic. It is the main theme of Hyde's book: "Is a work of art a commodity with a money value, to be bought and sold like a potato, or is it a gift on which no real price can be placed, to be freely exchanged?".[27] Atwood believes contemporary e-audiences need to more thoughtfully engage with the reciprocal nature of the gifts that artists bring, because, "if works of art are gifts and nothing but, how are their creators to live in the physical world, in which food will sooner or later be needed by them?".[28]

In raising the profile of copyright as the body of law that regulates the terms of ethical exchange, she reminds readers that individuals and communities can determine how to share their copyright. Like the Shakers, the publishers Arrowsmith and Jarrold & Sons also practiced generosity as discussed in Chapter 3. They shared copyright royalties with authors Conway and Hume, not due to any formal legal obligation but because it was felt the right thing to do. However, this occurred at an earlier time in the development of publishing markets. Atwood's wry observation about Shaker copyright hints at the larger problem described in this book: commodity markets do now surround us on all sides. Acknowledgements of copyright ownership and of permissions are featured in the front-matter of all books, alongside, but separate to the publisher's details and global distribution affiliations. These compact property notifications obscure far more complex legal and business connections, including the chains that connect individual copyrights to charters of incorporation and shareholding. Atwood passes over that fact that there are legal demands that sit alongside Hyde's inclusion of this copyright notice. It may also have been intended as ironic and a home-spun equivalent to the American conception of a trade courtesy, but these kinds of notices are a standard requirement of publishing agreements. Publishing contracts task the author with arranging permission and paying for such inclusions so that quotations may be reproduced in copies of the book, whether or not copyright law itself requires these licenses. This practice is not just a matter of ethics, commercial efficiency and convenience. The ubiquity of the © notice helps nourish the fiction that copyright remains a simple matter of the circulation of original works with the permission of the original artist, helping us to enter the text and find our connection with its author, leaving to one side what we know about the complex commodity relations that regulate access to works on an industrial scale.

This is a theme explored in all the chapters of this book. Further, in analysing the process of commodification, the history has stressed the importance of attentiveness to matters of genre, creative medium and distribution mechanisms regulated by contracts. Following from this, it might be thought that because books, sound recordings and films are now digitally distributed, much of the critique and underlying nuances are no longer relevant. However, in terms of multi-national behaviour, digital disruption in the publishing industry has primarily impacted on booksellers. It has not led to the collapse of the Big Five. Amazon Publishing, founded in 2009, has also become a major house separate to the Big Five, and in the US alone sold more than 68 million copies, mostly as e-books, in 2016. Although, "the Amazon Publishing business model is remarkably similar to the Big Five business model", taking into account the presence of imprints, parent companies, and the focus on bestselling genres,[29] smaller presses are experimenting with new models. This includes moving into multi-platform publishing to build new audiences with story-bombing, podcasting and storyphones.[30] However, because of the strength of the historical connection between authors and the Big Five publishers and the terms of past publishing contracts that have assigned control over existing works to traditional firms, these kinds of experiments remain small scale. This is why research into the study of author contracts and the limited availability of published works, and campaigns in support of reversion rights, are so important at this point in time.[31] One of the reasons there has also been less investment in new distribution platforms in publishing than in the sound recording industry relates to the way authors let go of their "back catalogues" without the same degree of consideration of the implications for their later career as has preoccupied recording artists. Why this occurred in the recording industry, and what it means for 21st-century copyright, is explored next.

Radiohead's *In Rainbows* experiment (2007)

The face of digital music

Radiohead's release of *In Rainbows* "for tips" via the band website in October 2007 raised enormous popular interest and discussion about the future of the music industry and the industry's loss of control over music culture. A huge band bypassing the traditional role of an industry label by cutting out the middleman was, to many, highly significant. But this move was also, in many ways, treated as unsurprising. In legal journals the event has mainly been recorded in passing as a side note that marks the winding down of industry campaigns about online music piracy featuring popular artists.[32]

In the previous decade there had been significant law reform and litigation to shore up the industry's existing distribution models to offer greater protection to digital copies of music and to delay the development of legal and illicit digital downloads.[33] However, authorised download platforms were very slow to develop, and the mainstream download services that did emerge, such as the iTunes and MSN Music store, had quite limited, predictable ranges of songs largely covering the mainstream genres that were already readily available in other formats, and the file formats were proprietary. The copies included copyright protection measures that impeded the ability to use files downloaded for fees, at a time when the world-wide-web had created the illusion of immediacy of connection and free information flows. In e-commerce terms, international banking payment systems were clumsy, insecure and slow for consumer transactions, but there remained a perception that there was one-big world-wide digital market. This view was promoted by the mammoth technology purveyors such as Apple, feeding a naïve, egalitarian expectation that the same cultural works would be available to all and experienced on the same liberating terms, regardless of location.[34] The challenge that faced the labels was not just that pirate sites offered sound recordings for free. Pirate sites provided a potentially unbounded range of music (and films) for free, where the technology worked more efficiently and files downloaded could be readily transported across devices and shared further afield. Traditional market demarcations – genre categories, distinctive packaging, timed-releases, limited local distributions – had little relevance on pirate sites. And there was no shortage of new pirate sites replacing those that were successfully shut down through litigation. Further, outside of the US, music industry attempts to assert territorial copyrights only exposed them to complaints about a history of price discrimination and drew further attention to the inferior selections of music available in many parts of the globe – a reality of these cultural markets produced by copyright's 20th-century design.[35] By the middle of the noughties all the major legal commentators were predicting further troubles for the industry ahead.[36] Radiohead's release of *In Rainbows* needs to be understood against this backdrop.

Copyright as an investment opportunity in the 21st century

Radiohead's decision to release the album without the approval or support of their former label for the past six albums, EMI, has been attributed as one of the reasons leading to the demise of that corporation.[37] However, it was also well recognised in the industry that EMI, then the fourth largest recording company and largest music publisher, had been struggling for some time. As discussed in Chapter 5 in relation to the film industry at various times from the early 1900s to the 1930s, major technological change leads to new alliances, buy-outs and consolidations. One of the factors that contributed to EMI's vulnerability was its initial decision in 1996 to split from the electrical engineering company, Thorn, to focus on music, whereas competitors like Sony and Universal remained supported by industrial combines. Radiohead's management company was of the view, "The day that EMI demerged from Thorn and became a standalone shareholding music company . . . was the beginning of the end".[38]

As a publicly listed stand-alone company, EMI was vulnerable to take-over bids. The constraint of regular profit reporting in a time of reducing revenue limited management's capacity to independently control the direction taken. Merging or acquisition by another label was the most attractive option by 2000. However, competition law had developed considerably since the situation described in Chapter 5. Given the existing market concentration in the music industry in 1999[39] any further take-overs were likely to be subject to European and US regulatory approval. This was not impossible to achieve, as became evident by the EU approval of Universal Music Group's purchase of Sony BMG for £1.1 billion in 2006, but the process took eight months and had conditions attached.[40] Acquisition of EMI by Warner Music was under discussion throughout 2006, when a new private equity investment firm, controlled by Guy Hands, emerged. As an entirely new player in the industry, there would be no competition law complications.

Terra Firma's purchase of EMI for £4.2 billion in May 2007 was financed by Citibank, with security provided by EMI's copyright portfolio. Terra Firma's research indicated that 90% of signed acts were losing money.[41] However, EMI remained "an asset rich business with market-leading publishing and recorded music catalogues. . . . We felt that the business needed to switch from being primarily focussed on 'music hits' to a business more broadly focussed on rights management services".[42] It was anticipated that physical sales would continue to decline, and correspondingly, by controlling back catalogues, profits would increasingly be tied to copyright licensing on digital platforms. This was not an unreasonable assumption. It echoes the film industry strategy of collaborating with book publishers in the early 1900s to control film adaptation rights to the most popular stories. However, apart from obstacles that arose due to the financing of the investment opportunity and the global financial crisis,[43] Terra Firma did not appreciate the cultural specificities of copyright, and especially so in the context of digital music markets. Indeed, as an investment opportunity, Terra Firma had a very limited understanding of cultural commodification. Hands believed that creation was separate from distribution,

> "If you are a small technology company making a bio-technology drug, you make that by yourself and then you get a major drug company to distribute", he explains, "Very few of the major drug companies today are developed all the way through by the drug companies. They will tend to buy them later. To some extent with music, what was happening was that EMI and the other labels – were spending an absolute fortune on trying to find the hits, rather than using their strengths to basically distribute and market the hits. They were literally just throwing money against the wall.[44]

There was little appreciation that the value of a copyright portfolio as an asset is parasitic upon the standing of the recording artists whose works are accumulated within it. This value is created by more than merely marketing music product. Across the chapters of this book we have seen how various industries have drawn upon the idea of a personal connection between a creator and the creative product associated with their name, to distinguish the commodity in the marketplace as it is being mass reproduced and distributed across the globe. The value of these aggregations of rights is not static, but linked to the ongoing capacity of the artists behind the works to continue to connect with audiences and their capacity to produce future interest, not just in past works, but also in new ones, or upgraded versions of old ones. Terra Firma's investment strategy was backwards looking, based upon a misunderstanding of the importance of "hits" and fashions, especially in the most popular genres. Further, different music genres had their own unique features. And due to the changes in the way music was searched for and consumed online, the distinction between a unified mass market product and a niche one had less importance. Not only were niche markets not insignificant when understood as global ones serviced from the one storefront, the very idea of a mass market continued to splinter, segment and grow into new categories, including as identified by new online audiences. The growing segments of the market such as rap, hip hop, folk and alternative, are particularly prone to these dynamics.

Radiohead, for instance, was branded as an "alternative rock" band, with post-punk roots and a strong interest in experimental electronic music. Lyrically, band frontman Thom Yorke described it as a time when,

> there was a sense that saying political stuff in lyrics or talking about it in magazines had some significance. . . . Good music has always been a form of rebellion, whether it's the Beatles or Public Enemy. All good artists have that element. In order to change things, or in order to form any resistance, people need a language in which to express it, and that can be music, art, literature, journalism.[45]

Fans had an established expectation of some ongoing faithfulness to this positioning. A private equity-fund's control over the copyright in the Radiohead back catalogue was not just personally upsetting to members of the band,[46] it undermined the very idea of what Radiohead stood for. Another comparison might be apt here. In producing more Sherlock stories Conan Doyle may have suffered the discomfort of feeling like an old dog returning to his vomit,[47] but hiding his discomfort from his audiences was important to the value of his past and future copyright. With Radiohead, their positioning in the market and expectations of fans would not be that they would obediently acquiesce to a "sell-out" to anonymous bankers in suits. In the fallout and ensuing PR war with Terra Firma, in a blog on the band website, Thom Yorke told fans, "What we wanted was some control over our work and how it was used in the future by them".[48] This position, of course, aligned with traditional messaging about why copyright was important.

Fans and the simply curious could download from the band's online site and pay what they liked, or make a donation to an approved charity. Files were not encumbered with any digital rights management. It is estimated that there were 1.2 million downloads, with estimates of payments between two-thirds of downloaders paying between US $5 and $15, and roughly a third electing to download for free, or less optimistically, 38% paid on average $6 per album, equating to $2.26 per album factoring in free uses. After nearly three months, Radiohead disabled the download portal and released the versions of the album in the traditional manner, including premium editions.[49]

Copyright advocacy by recording artists

Diverse positions of recording artists within the copyright wars were very apparent well before 2007. Recruiting successful artists to propel anti-piracy messages had a long legacy. Nineteenth-century lobbies fronted by authors were successful, but at this time it was possible to exercise some control over messaging through the selection of spokespersons and because of the established links between business and political channels, and newspaper reporting. However, the media landscape of the 21st century was vastly different. Industry co-ordination of what artists might say was difficult, if not impossible, to achieve. Hetcher[50] highlights three distinct phases amongst the "anti-piracy norm entrepreneurs" where there were attempts to co-ordinate messaging to the public about copyright.

The first phase, April 2000–February 2001 saw Dr Dre and Metallica front public relations efforts, with the emergence of a new lobby group, Artists Against Piracy (AAP), in July 2000, underwritten by the Recording Industry Association of America (RIAA). AAP promoted a very traditional copyright message released alongside litigation against the most popular music file-sharing service, Napster. Copying without permission violated the act of creativity – the gift of the artist, as well as involving theft of their private property. However, in raising the profile of authorial property, a second phase in the messaging unfolded, centred upon decades of complaints by artists about unfair industry contracts and clauses that stifled both creative freedom and the ability to share from profits. AAP folded by April 2001 which Hetcher attributes to its close industry ties. At the same time, a new organisation, the Recording Artists Coalition (RAC) emerged. This marked a third phase in anti-piracy norm advocacy in this era. The RAC encouraged "top-down regulatory or legal action to address recording industry contract practices, . . . [and took] its campaign to the public, using the clout of its artists to fundraise and increase awareness of the issue".[51] It was not in the industry's interest to open up this line of inquiry, but hosing it down was also difficult, given that celebrities and bands had an independent online presence, with many sites run by artists' management and by fans. Further, "artists, led by the Recording Artists Coalition, determined that resolving the issue of contracts had to precede any joint efforts between artists and the music industry to curb illicit digital copying". During the third phase, the RIAA continued promoting the message that "artists are victims" despite the lack of support from artists.[52] However, alongside this, artists messaging about the ethics of online file-sharing also changed. Some artists "began viewing online distribution as a means of breaking a recording industry monopoly to empower themselves". Alanis Morrisette stated in 2002, "This new technology is threatening the bottleneck monopoly of record companies. I just bless the Internet for coming onto the scene and shining all this light on analog-era recording contracts".[53] In 2009 a new artist's coalition, the Featured Artist's Coalition, emerged, to "promote and protect the artist community", promote "transparency and fairness" within the industry and support music entrepreneurs. Original supporters included Robbie Williams and Radiohead. Advocacy included promoting licensing of copyright for fixed terms, rather than outright assignment; a "use it or lose it" approach; the right of artists to negotiate the terms on which their works are presented and monetised in interactive formats; and raising performers' right to an equivalence to copyright.[54]

The artists' new copyright stance has centuries-old roots. In practice, however, taking back control over the means of distribution was complicated by late recognition by the labels of the significance of the shift to online search engines and platform culture for online music consumption. Fighting about copyright policy in public with artists or with fans was no longer a desirable strategy. Further, through using digital identifiers and agreements with video platforms such as YouTube and online music streaming services such as Spotify, labels – the original content/copyright aggregators – could receive micro-transactions for online use of their catalogues, including fair uses, where, as a matter of US law, fees should not apply.[55] Licensing agreements with the big platforms and services maintained, if not increased, the future value of old and new copyrights. It also freed labels from some of the cost burden of scouting and building an artist's profile (artists and repertoire or A & R costs), and of promoting the distinctive works by particular artists. Radiohead producer, Neil Godrich explains,

> The way that Spotify works is that the money is divided up by percentage of total streams. Big labels have massive back catalogues so their 40 year old record by a dead artist earns them the same slice of the pie as a brand new track by a new artist. The big labels did secret deals with Spotify and the like in return for favourable royalty rates. The massive amount of catalogue being streamed guarantees that they get the big massive slice of the pie (that $500 million) and the smaller producers and labels get pittance for their comparatively few streams. This is what's wrong.[56]

Individual returns to artists on these deals are notoriously low and there is no agreed method of accounting for them.[57]

Copyright becomes a branding technique

These developments in the music industry are leading to promotion of new career models for artists. Individuals and bands need not be tied to a label. Artists may prefer to be proactively entrepreneurial using professional managerial services to develop their careers or go it alone. Whatever the model, it is openly acknowledged that the commercial value of the artist is co-dependent upon multiple channels of communication and intermediaries over their career span to build the artist's profile.[58] The development and maintenance of a brand identity, that is, a commercial profile attached to the product linked to an artist's personal image and reputation, has always been a part of the music industry. It has been the case from the beginnings of the recording industry when EMI's forerunner, the Gramophone Company, first pursued Melba. Then the "technology company" needed the assistance of the diva to position itself in the market and promote sound recordings as a new way of enjoying music. Melba was curious to explore the benefits of an affiliation with the new technology and it provided as an innovative way for her to connect with and grow an internationally dispersed fan base. In terms of branding, Melba's linking up with the Gramophone Company occurred at a time when she did not know whether or not the venture would thrive or fall over. This is little different to contemporary artists circa 2007, choosing to affiliate with what was then a new German-based online music distribution platform, Sound Cloud, or the new American-based Bandcamp in circumstances where both the artists' and platforms' reputations hoped to grow through the association. Social positioning has always been the heart of the commercial transaction with sound recordings. It has mattered to music consumers in a far more public way than with book publishing, where tastes have remained more private and hidden.

However, in Melba's day, copyright was promoted as having a universal meaning – primarily signalling the intimate relationship between an artist and their work. Today, copyright has lost a fixed frame of reference and, at one and the same time, it has become part of the artist's brand. There are a number of factors that have contributed to this situation. First, today fans are far more highly visible in asserting their connections with recording artists to promote their own self-images. In the music industry today a fan community is a collection of individuals who share and communicate identity positions through advertising their emotional connection to selected artists and performers. And, as is discussed in regard to Radiohead earlier, to some fans the copyright position of the artist matters to their own image. Second, the default position, the universal idea is outmoded not just due to the piracy wars but because choices have to be made by stakeholders about the model of music distribution that is going to be utilised, at a time when these are shifting and morphing. Without doing more, a copyright identity will be communicated by the choices that are made about how the recording will be made available to the public. Third, it remains useful for an artist to explicitly project some kind of copyright position to fans because these terms regulate a very important part of the relationship between the artist-producer and fan-consumer. Licensing choices set the terms on which the fan can engage with the recording and this affects how relationships flow within the fan community. Fourth, because copyright is now recognised as socially embedded and an integral part of artistic and commercial choices made by the creator, what copyright position is taken can vary from artist to artist, track to track, between releases and across distribution platforms and products.

As a consequence of the interaction of all these factors, the significance of owning a sound recording copyright is far more fluid and overtly context-dependent than it was in the previous century. Copyright has become a sign that functions in a similar way to a conventional trademark. It operates to communicate something distinctive about the sound recording product's origin, quality and characteristics, where its precise meaning depends upon the specifics of its use and circulation. Alternative copyright branding remains co-dependent upon the traditional idea of authorship, the core reference from which difference can be mapped. Accordingly, the traditional idea of authorship still has reach and continues to be reproduced in the echoes of the brand positions that revolve around an artist's copyright practice. However, the social reproduction of the idea of copyright as a universal natural right lacks the structural stability and certainty it had in the previous century. Indeed, today it may be a DJ or remixer that brings an "original" artist to notice of fans.

This transformation has impacted upon the present idea of authorship. Authorship is also starting to be described by industry commentators as a creation without any fixed content, merely a branding choice that assembles fans for particular commercial purposes,

> By creating a distinct brand, artists clarify their authorship, situating themselves in relation to a particular genre and practice (self-social authorship), while declaring their position with respect to existing institutions and broader social influences such as fans, labels, and promoters (sociocultural authorship). While many other forms of authorship exist, branding provides a useful lens to explore artists' authorial process.[59]

Bandcamp is a good practical example to explore this development. The storefront banner positions the service as being a place to "Discover amazing new music and *directly support* the artist". This links a new service with a traditional idea of copyright. The artist's self-social authorship includes signalling themselves as up and coming, rather than as established, but, as with artists of old, as creators who want to be "in control", supported by their connection with a fan community. This fan "community" may exist outside the site, or only be a virtual community, or both.

The artist's image, their self-social authorship, is also portrayed through the design choices, music selections and other merchandise available: "Bundle your digital music with your vinyl, posters, tickets, t-shirts" and administer and track orders using a "streamlined fulfillment interface". Control is, in reality, technologically determined by the Bandcamp platform, but communicated to fans in terms of sociocultural authorship, most emphatically in relation to the artist's copyright licensing position: fans can pay what they want, a fixed price or give music away for free in exchange for an email address (tagged "Copyright-free"). Bandcamp is one of many new interesting services stepping into the breach to assist leagues of new artists seeking to find a way to survive and prosper. They are not replacing the traditional label, nor necessarily a stepping stone to the older kind of recording deal. Rather, this kind of development is testament to the reality that while large multi-national labels have survived, now integrated into platform capitalism, copyright has ceased to play the traditional role that has been promoted throughout copyright's history.

The traditional idea of copyright is not entirely spent. However, what has opened up as a consequence of the disruption to traditional approaches to commodification is a growth in popular understanding that the audience is the foundation of any commercial and cultural relationship. That the audience is the primary commodity created by the artist, where custom might follow an artist across all mediums of communication is not a new idea,[60] but unlike in the mass media analogue landscape of the 20th century, copyright exclusivity is no longer thought as essential to the terms of cultural and economic exchange. This positioning is troubling to many, who struggle to accept the displacement of the visibility of copyright within international cultural trade. Nowhere is this more apparent than in discussion of Banksy, his copyright and his brand.

"The revolution is for display purposes only" – Banksy[61]

Banksy's law

As a person of legal interest Banksy is invariably analysed in terms of his "fit" within existing legal categories – criminal law,[62] property and contract law,[63] cultural heritage and cultural property,[64] and, especially, copyright.[65] This is odd, given Banksy's self-proclaimed status as a guerrilla artist, an art revolutionary. Fitting within the existing legal order is hardly his ambition. Evading police, playing with the authority of the law and disrupting the facilitation of commodity relations by producing unsigned ephemeral works, as well as claiming others, is integral to his artistic practice. This practice entails a radical critique of law and society, destabilising the meaning of concepts whose authority and relevance is often taken for granted in the legal domain.[66] Banksy is both artist and prankster, but legal analysis has primarily only taken seriously the former pursuit, decoupled from the jokes on law and legal institutions, and a far more scathing critique of law and capitalism inherent in his artistic practice. Concepts and important legal distinctions vandalised by Banksy include many of the constructs central to the traditional idea of copyright discussed across chapters of this book. This includes:

original/copy
object/performance
fixation/ephemera
right/permission
creative expression/play
art/commerce
corporation/agency
audience/constituency
profession/the creative life
copyright/brand

Banksy problematises and destabilises the reproduction of the behavioural norms inherent in these binaries. His art generates discussion about whether it is possible to sustain a contrary position in a world where, as Atwood puts it, "the commodity market surrounds us on all sides".[67]

Banksy commodities

While it is by no means clear that Banksy has been inspired by Marxist thought, the difficulty inherent in standing outside of commodity relations was described by Marx when he noted the "metamorphosis of commodities",

> the exchange of commodities implies contradictory and mutually exclusive conditions. The further development of the commodity does not abolish these contradictions, but rather provides the form within which they have room to move. This is, in general, the way in which real contradictions are resolved. For instance, it is a contradiction to depict one body as constantly falling towards another and at the same time constantly flying away from it. The ellipse is a form of motion within which this contradiction is both realized and resolved.
>
> In so far as the process of exchange transfers commodities from hands in which they are non-use values to hands in which they are use-values, it is a process of social metabolism. The product of one kind of useful labor replaces that of another. Once a commodity has arrived at a situation in which it can serve as a use-value, it falls out of the sphere of exchange into that of consumption.[68]

Despite crafting statements that are political and incorporate jokes, Banksy's labour is continually appropriated and, through unwanted attributions of authorship, drawn into commodity relations. His guerrilla art is reconstructed as a new genre, "street art", the new classification signifying a significant cultural and economic transformation from an origin as a communicative action, a humorous, political address to those who share the physical space in which the message is situated, into an immaterial art object and property. "Street art" denotes a collective assembly of mass audiences with shared visual tastes. Banksy remains pestilent, reimaging ways to contest his incorporation within the art industry and the associated legal norms, but as an artist he has struggled to manage attribution of an absent presence. In an image-saturated world, the uncertain nature of Banksy's identity generates hype that adds an additional signifier of prestige to the visual image, feeding a new investment opportunity that circulates around the premium of his mysterious authorship. The political and jurisprudential tension that ensues is well illustrated by, on the one hand, Banksy saying he is "kind of glad" that his Valentine's Day Bristol mural of a young girl firing a slingshot at a bunch of flowers was shortly thereafter defaced with spray paint,[69] and on the other, the police providing an escort to a removal of piece of wall bearing an illegal Banksy image about urban pollution, *Season's Greetings*, reputably bought for a six figure sum, to "save it" from vandalism and display it in a new Street Art museum.[70]

In the film he directed, *Exit through the Gift Shop* (2010),[71] Banksy described his original artistic motivations as entirely non-commercial, motivated by an interest in disrupting the normative arrangement of the visual landscape,[72] and talking back to the visual assault caused by corporate advertising in our communities,

> The people who run our cities don't understand graffiti because they think nothing has the right to exist unless it makes a profit, which makes their opinion worthless. . . .
>
> The people who truly deface our neighbourhoods are the companies that scrawl giant slogans across buildings and buses trying to make us feel inadequate unless we buy their stuff. They expect to be able to shout their message in your face from every available surface but you're never allowed to answer back. Well, they started the fight and the wall is the weapon of choice to hit them back.[73]

There was not originally any ambition to document these artistic interventions. Defacement and likely erasure was not considered surprising or problematic. However, images began to circulate online. The internet created the possibility of site-specific art, messages designed to be responsive to the landscape in which they sat, being brought from the underground to the surface, reaching a larger constituency. Commodification was not inherent in the original act of creation, nor necessarily in posting the images for others to see. Although the images were being reproduced by the artist using a hand-crafted technique of reproduction using stencils, this technology was attractive because it provided a practical advantage in producing the works quickly, in situations where the risk of detection and interruption was high. It also communicated a critique of what fellow artist, Shepard Fairey, describes as the "received power" generated by repetition, circulation and notoriety in contemporary art and culture.[74] Banksy's appropriation of public and private space, and choice not to individualise his image through attaching his signature or certifying works as "original Banksy", was an attempt to denounce private property relations and disavow ownership of the product of his labour. However, through the labour of others using a camera and the internet, a far broader circulation of imagery, art abstracted from place, and commodification, was facilitated. While preservation and documentation expanded the potential constituency for the political message of outsider art, it also changed the essence of the "work" and its legal referent through the new manner of its circulation.

In situ, the work was socially designated as a product of illegality and vandalism, and sitting outside of commodity relations, even though, as Alison Young observes, it may have been legal, depending upon where it is placed.[75] Through the intervention of mass reproduction technologies by unknown actors and the imposition of copyright norms, Banksy's outsider art becomes a reproducible image with entirely different properties. Copyright law creates layers of rights to the abstract image itself: intangible property "owned" by the original artist and the photographer who reproduces it. Banksy's disinterest in claiming the status of an original author is irrelevant to this process of commodification. Given this development, Banksy changed tack. The commercial and legal significance of acts of attribution are sought to be undermined by commercial releases by the artist, producing authenticated prints and commodities retailed at prices that seek to disrupt investment values, including sales through an online and occasional "pop-up" store, Gross Domestic Product™, launched on Instagram with the slogan, "It sells art, homewares, and disappointment".[76]

Banksy has also spoken about unintended problems that have occurred due to his pseudo-anonymity. The public are exposed to a number of vulnerabilities and unexpected complications, including deceit by entrepreneurs who trade on the ambiguity of the attribution and misrecognition of Banksy product. An hilarious example of misrecognition was the creation of wads of art currency, £10 notes bearing the image of Princess Diana. In distributing these at a music venue, Banksy noted that, knowingly or otherwise, recipients started to trade the artworks for drinks as counterfeit money. With late recognition of the potential legal implications, the remaining copies were not further circulated.[77] Banksy has however recycled them. His "handling service", Pest Control Office Limited, established in 2009, issues authenticity certificates that repurpose the old stock, with half a "Di faced tenner" stapled to authenticity certificates. The tenner has a handwritten ID number on it which can be matched to the number on the other half of the note held by Pest Control, providing a bespoke security measure. Banksy has also registered trademarks. For example, the word "Banksy" is registered in the UK in 18 classes of goods and services.[78] A Gangsta rat image is registered in five classes.[79] The classes of registration cover many of the extended merchandising ventures conventionally used in popular culture, in particular the music industry. It has been proposed that the ambition is to try to use these marks to enforce copyright and shut down unauthorised merchandising, without having to disclose who the author is. This unconventional use of trademark registration perplexes legal professionals, obsessed with reading the performance as a conventional act of rights enforcement, and ignoring the social messaging inherent in these interventions. Through engaging in trademark enforcement activity, many Banksy fans will appreciate his identification of transgression of community norms, unconcerned whether or not the litigation falls over.[80]

Banksy and his management team participate inside and outside the art market, sell works "too cheaply", make works for sale that are considered deliberately unmarketable, authenticate some works commonly traded online on eBay and other art sites but not others, and perform trademark activity. This plays with the inherent tension surrounding the connection between the original author and the law – private property rights and the mass reproduction of commodities. In displaying the characteristics of an artistic oeuvre, this activity has led some commentators to argue that Banksy has become a performance artist, where his inaccessibility and manufacturing of confusion creates affective reverberations that increase his cultural capital as artist-celebrity. Banksy's brand is subsequently defined as an art performance of verification, repetition and circulation of an unstable, impermanent process, where value is extracted by his "seemingly always-disappearing process",[81]

> the apparently immaterial nature of performance work has also capitulated to an expanding notion of capital no longer restricted to objects but wilfully embracing service, process, and performance. Understood in this way, Banksy's apparently flagrant disavowal of market forces may in fact be nothing of the sort. His staged sale of massively underpriced canvases and his careful advertising of that now inaccessible event may not be quite the affront to the capitalist market that it at first appears. It might instead be a canny manipulation of just such a market, a product primed to sell in the "affect factory".[82]

The spectacle of the Sotheby's 2018 auction of the self-destructing artwork for US$1.4 million is most easily identifiable as a performance work. The image shredded after the final bid for *Girl Releasing a Balloon* was accepted. The image is one of the most repeated motifs attributed to Banksy commonly displayed on t-shirts, calendars, posters and sold on canvas. In response to the work's public destruction, some in the art world claimed that Banksy was having his cake and eating it too,

> New York magazine critic Jerry Saltz praised the artist for "prank[ing] the insidious auction world, disrupt[ing] the flow of capital – if only for a minute"; another writer described Banksy's shredded piece as "a rebuke of empty consumerism from a master". Contrasting these celebratory views, Huffington Post's Priscilla Frank pointed out that the impromptu performance immediately caused the work to at least double in value, and argued that rather than critiquing capitalism, Banksy was taking part in it. Perhaps, indeed, as filmmaker Kaveh Abbasian stated (on Twitter), he was doing so in the most deceptive manner, that is, "while selling itself as anti-capitalism".[83]

The "is he or isn't he" a sell-out to capitalism debate projects the possibility that there is a space for art that exists outside of market dynamics – where private property rights and the disciplinary and normative power of law do not form part of the cultural and economic frame of reference for artistic expressions. This fantasy is particularly odd given that Banksy's practice is productive precisely because it generates tensions through his jokes about art, law and society,

> A rebel persona works both through and against a neoliberal branding logic. For instance, as much as Banksy critiques corporate brands (like Disney) and neoliberal ownership within the art market, he is a brand in and of himself gaining success precisely through his 'signature look'.[84]

However, there is a key difference between Banksy's performance of brand and the copyright as brand position identified in the contemporary music industry discussed earlier. Banksy exercises a high degree of control over the terms of his work's original display – over the means of production. Further, as his labour is appropriated and reappropriated by others he periodically intervenes and inserts himself back into the terms of exchange to disrupt the orderly reproduction of commodity relations and the predictability of commercial calculations underlying transactions. This is a political act – not merely a branding technique. However, as Marx observed, capitalism carries within it the capacity to absorb contradictions and tensions. The game will go on.

Historical answers to contemporary questions about corporate control

Margaret Atwood, Radiohead and Banksy are, in their own ways, transgressive but they are not anti-copyright. Their opinions and practices draw upon decades of knowledge and experience in making decisions about the reproduction and global circulation of creative endeavours. Traditional ideas of copyright are refracted in this decision-making, even while the artist explores different possibilities.

This is not to underplay the significance of the shift from analogue to digital cultural markets. For many, but not all, authors and artists, their commercial practice has had to realign to new arrangements of space and time, shifting the constitution of what is transacted and of labour markets across the digital landscape.[85] Platform capitalism has also empowered the mega technology firms such as Apple, Google, Amazon, Facebook and Microsoft, alongside Chinese firms Tencent and Alibaba, who produce the online ecosystem, in particular, through ever-increasingly complex artificial intelligence programs and data management. However, creators do not have the same legal and business relationships with big platforms to that which developed with Big Media, because platform capitalism propagates different cultural values in order to produce ongoing interest in engaging with the content that drives us to use their technologies.

Due to the vast array of cultural experiences and commodities on offer (with choices instantly refreshed), audiences are in some ways far less predictable in their consumption behaviour than with traditional media. Analysis of huge aggregations of personal data based upon invasions of user privacy attempts to manage this problem. However, the cultural marketplace currently requires more differentiation than that currently made visible through selections generated by data drawn from established services like Google, Facebook, YouTube, Spotify, taste predictability scores linked to streaming patterns (co-dependent upon old Media genre delineations), and illusions of connection and variety in life produced from viewing user-generated and AI-generated content. Regardless of the sophistication of the algorithms that offer users endless consumption choices, the articulation of distinctive authorial identities is still relied upon to help users navigate the cultural landscape by clarifying the character, properties and value of the content available.

This "new" cultural ordering does not require fidelity to any particular copyright position beyond that which is necessary to produce the author as brand. But the relationship between creator, platform and user also still draws upon a historical dimension of the socio-legal construction of authorship. Platform capitalism reinforces the belief that artists *should have* the capacity to make choices about the terms of distribution of their art and through these choices determine the emotional, educational and commercial connections they would like to make with readers, listeners and viewers. Given the social complexity inherent in the nature of the cultural exchanges between creators and consumers today, an artist's potential constituency and audience is more mobile and fluid than in the 20th century. But the distribution choices available to artists also permit far quicker, more reflexive decision-making in building, refreshing and renewing these relationships – if the artist has retained control of their copyright.

This history has shown how the cultural hegemony of Big Media was constituted through connections forged in the late 19th and early 20th century that linked philosophy, law, business structures and political ambition. It has explained how and why some creators thrived as this developed, but also why the possibility of an author or artist thriving, or even surviving, has been influenced by factors beyond their control. It should also now be clear to readers why relying upon the management skills and commercialisation expertise developed for a different historical period is no longer sensible, given the maturation of platform capitalism. Authors and artists today need to make important decisions about the production and distribution of cultural content, their audiences, brand and licensing terms, rather than relying upon others. This is a good thing. As this book has argued, all creators have travelled more comfortably, commercially, and in artistic terms, where they have exercised a higher degree of agency and considered the terms of the incorporation of their authorship into commodity relations.

Notes

1 Lewis Hyde, *The Gift: How the Creative Spirit Transforms the World* (Canongate 2006)
2 Banksy, *Wall and Piece* (Random House 2006)
3 Collett Tracey, *The Little Presses That Did: A History of a First Statement Press, Contact Press and Delta Canada and an Assessment of Their Contribution to the Development of Modernist Poetry in Canada during the Middle Part of the Twentieth Century* PhD Thesis, Universite de Montreal 2001 4–5
4 Ibid 3
5 Ibid 8; Catherine Riley, *The Virago Story* (Berghanh Press 2018) 21
6 Education: Victoria College, University of Toronto, BA 1961; Radcliffe College, Cambridge, Mass, 1962; Harvard University, Cambridge, MA, 1962–63; 1965–1967. Employment: Lecturer in English, University of British Columbia, Vancouver, 1964–1965; Instructor in English, Sir George Williams University, Montreal 1967–1968; University of Alberta, 1969–1970; Assistant Professor of English, York University, Toronto,

1971–1972. Atwood has also had appointments as writer-in-residence and many awards. See margaretatwood.ca/biography

7 Riley (n 5) 40 (notes omitted)

8 Tracey (n 3) 20

9 Ibid

10 Ibid 33

11 Margaret Atwood, *Survival: A Thematic Guide to Canadian Literature* (Anasi 1972)

12 J Lee Thompson, 'Can Canada Survive Survival? An Article on Survival: A Thematic a Guide to Canadian Literature' (1973) 3(2) American Review of Canadian Studies 101

13 Margaret Atwood, *The Edible Woman* (McClelland and Stewart 1969)

14 Helmut Reichenbacker, 'Challenging the Reader: An Analysis of Margaret Atwood's Creative Technique in Her First Published Novel' in Reingard M Nischik (ed), *Margaret Atwood. Works and Impact* (Camden House 2000) 265

15 Margaret Atwood, 'Full bibliography'. http://margaretatwood.ca/full-bibliography-2/

16 Riley (n 5) 40 (notes omitted)

17 Ibid 21

18 Ibid 13

19 Ibid 44

20 Ibid 26

21 Lennie Goodings, *A Bite of the Apple: Behind the Scenes at Virago Press* (OUP 2020) 41

22 Riley (n 5) 26–27

23 Margaret Atwood, 'Introduction' in Lewis Hyde (ed), *The Gift: How the Creative Spirit Transforms the World* (Canongate Books 2012) vii

24 Ibid ix

25 Ibid viii

26 Ibid

27 Ibid ix

28 Ibid

29 Per Henningsgaard, 'Types of Publishing Houses' in Alison Baverstock, Richard Bradford and Madelena Gonzalez (eds), *Contemporary Publishing and the Culture of Books* (Routledge 2020) 55

30 See for example, Australian publisher of short fiction, Spineless Wonders. https://shortaustralianstories.com.au/

31 See Rebecca Giblin, *The Author's Interest*. https://authorsinterest.org/author/authorsinterest/

32 This conclusion is drawn from a study of two legal journal databases using the search term "Radiohead". The Hein Online Law Journal Library generated a list of 207 responses. Results were then ordered with reference to the "Number of Times Cited by Articles" function, with texts reviewed to locate context. A Westlaw UK search (to partially correct for North American bias) generated only a handful of further responses, none of which were included in the Hein Online dataset. Searches were conducted 3 Apr 2020

33 Significant clarifications surrounding the legality of peer-to-peer technology, the liability of intermediaries whose actions assisted online music piracy and the private sharing of music came about across the globe, with activity increasing significantly following the passage of the *Digital Millennium Copyright Act* 1998 (DMCA) (US)

34 See Kathy Bowrey, 'Telling Tales: Digital Piracy and the Law' in *Law and Internet Cultures* (CUP 2006) 137–169

35 This is discussed in Chapter 4

36 Seminal socio-legal literature from this period includes: William W Fisher, *Promises to Keep: Technology, Law, and the Future of Entertainment* (Stanford UP 2004); Lawrence Lessig, *Free Culture: How Big Media Uses Technology and the Law to Lock Down Culture and Control Creativity* (Penguin 2004); Siva Vaidhyanathan, *The Anarchist in the Library: How the Clash between Freedom and Control Is Hacking the Real World and Crashing the System* (Basic Books 2005); Yochai Benkler, *The Wealth of Networks: How Social Production Transforms Markets and Freedom* (Yale UP 2006)

37 Radiohead had signed with Parlophone, a division of EMI in 1991. Eamon Forde, *The Final Days of EMI* (Omnibus Press 2019) 89
38 Ibid 2
39 By share of record sales in 1999, IFPI reported percentages of market share by record company as: BMG (10.10%), Warner (11.4%), EMI (11.8%). Sony (17%), Universal (21.7%), and Independents (28%), ibid 5
40 Ibid 49
41 Ibid 49, 95
42 Terra Firma, *The EMI Investment: An Analysis* www.terrafirma.com/portfolio/current-investments/investment/emi-case-study.html
43 Ibid
44 Forde (n 37) 44
45 David Marchese, 'Talk: Thom Yorke' *The New York Times Magazine* 28 Oct 2019, 14
46 Retaliation in the form of releasing a "Best-Of" compilation without consulting the band "out of spite" in December 2007 only further exacerbated tensions. Forde (n 37) 101–102
47 See Chapter 3, 80
48 Forde (n 37) 101
49 Leah Belsky, Byron Kahr, Max Berkelhammer, and Yochai Benkler, 'Everything in Its Right Place: Social Cooperation and Artist Compensation' (2010) 17 Mich Telecomm Tech L Rev 1, 7
50 Steven Hetcher, 'The Music Industry's Failed Attempt to Influence File Sharing Norms' (2004) 7 V and J Ent L & Prac 10
51 Ibid 30
52 Ibid 24
53 Ibid 32
54 Emma Way and Richard Taylor, 'Featured Artists' Coalition – a Strong Voice in Shaping the Music Industry of the Future' (2009) Ent L R 149
55 See for example, Lauren D Shinn, 'Youtube's Content ID as a Case Study of Private Copyright Enforcement Systems' (2015) 43 AIPLA Q J 359; Nicholas DeLisa, 'You(Tube), Me, and Content ID: Paving the Way for Compulsory Synchronization Licensing on User-Generated Content Platforms' (2016) 81 Brook L Rev 1275
56 Quoted in Dianne Hughes, Mark Evans, Guy Morrow and Sarah Keith, *The New Music Industries: Disruption and Discovery* (Palgrave Macmillan 2016) 4
57 Tim Ingham, 'Should Spotify Change the Way It Pays Artists?' *Rolling Stone* 7 Dec 2018
58 Ibid 17–35
59 Ibid 67
60 This is discussed in Chapter 3
61 Banksy (n 2) 47
62 Ian Edwards, 'Ian Banksy's Graffiti: A Not-so-Simple Case of Criminal Damage' (2009) 73(4) *Journal of Criminal Law* 345; Jani McCutcheon and Jordan Leahy, 'Illegal Copyright Works and the Remedial Discretion of the Court' (2019) 9 Queen Mary J Intell Prop 326
63 Dan Karmel, 'Off the Wall: Abandonment and the First Sale Doctrine' (2011–12) 45 Colum J L & Soc Probs 353; Peter Salib, 'The Law of Banksy: Who Owns Street Art' (2015) 82 U Chi L Rev 2293
64 Susan Bird, 'Aesthetics, Authority and the Outlaw of the Street' (2009) 3 Public Space: Journal of Law and Justice 1; Charlotte Woodhead, 'Art, Culture and Heritage: Law in Context' (2013) 18 Art, Antiquity & Law 1, 5; Griffin Barnett, 'Recognized Stature: Protecting Street Art as Cultural Property' (2013) 12 Chi-Kent J Intell Prop 204
65 Jennifer Kwong, 'Moral Rights in the Ballpark: Banksy and the Right to Integrity of Authorship' (2015) 20(1) MALR 46; Enrico Bonadio, 'Street Art, Graffiti and Copyright' in Enrico Bonadio and Nicola Lucchi (eds), *Non-Conventional Copyright: Do New and Atypical Works Deserve Protection?* (Edward Elgar 2018) 43

66 Some socio-legal aspects of this are explored in Alison Young, *Street Art World* (Reaktion Books 2016)
67 Atwood (n 23) viii
68 Karl Marx, *Capital* Volume 1, 2(a) 198. Thanks for Henrique Carvalho for this reminder
69 'Banksy Reveals Why He's "Kind of Glad" His Latest Mural Was Vandalised' *Huffington Post* 22 Feb 2020
70 Simon Worrall, 'How to Get a Banksy off the Wall' *New Stateman* 7–13 June 2019, 18
71 Dir. Banksy Pro Jamie Dicruz, *Exit through the Gift Shop* (Paranoid Pictures, 2010)
72 The disruption to the normative arrangement of space is a recurring theme. See Anjali Nath, 'Seeing Guantánamo, Blown Up: Banksy's Installation in Disneyland' (2013) 65(1) American Quarterly 185
73 Banksy (n 2) 8
74 Dicruz (n 65)
75 Alison Young, *Street Art. Public City: Law, Crime and the Urban Imagination* (Routledge 2014) 4
76 Banksy on Instagram, 16 Oct 2019
77 Dicruz (n 65)
78 TM number UK2457210. Word Mark: Banksy; Owner: Pest Control Office Limited. Registered 1 June 2007
79 TM number UK3354581. Figurative Mark: Gangsta Rat; Owner: Pest Control Office Limited. Registered 19 Nov 2018
80 '"A Frankly Pointless Step" – Why Banksy Pop-Up Shop Could Hinder Trademark Case' *World Trademark Review* 2 Oct 2019
81 Isabel Stowell-Kaplan, 'Selling Himself in Central Park: Banksy Does New York' (2015) 162 Canadian Theatre Review 18, 20
82 Ibid 21
83 Pedro Erber, 'Beautiful Money; or, What Can Contemporary Art Teach Us about the Neoliberal Economy' (2019) 72(2) Revista Hispánica Moderna 149–150. Citations omitted
84 Nath (n 72) 191
85 Martin Kenney and John Zysman, 'The Platform Economy: Restructuring the Space of Capital Accumulation' (2020) Cambridge Journal of Regions, Economy and Society. https://doi.org/10.1093/cjres/rsaa001

Index

For Product Safety Concerns and Information please contact our EU
representative GPSR@taylorandfrancis.com
Taylor & Francis Verlag GmbH, Kaufingerstraße 24, 80331 München, Germany

www.ingramcontent.com/pod-product-compliance
Ingram Content Group UK Ltd.
Pitfield, Milton Keynes, MK11 3LW, UK
UKHW022130190926
475702UK00013B/1733